Best Practices for the Learner-Centered Classroom

A Collection of Articles
by Robin Fogarty

IRI/Skylight Training and Publishing, Inc.
Arlington Heights, Illinois

Grateful acknowledgement is made to the following publishers for permission to reprint copyrighted material.

Association of Supervision and Curriculum Development for "Ten Ways to Integrate Curriculum" by Robin Fogarty. From *Educational Leadership*, October 1991, pp. 61–65. © 1991 by ASCD.

The Ohio State University, College of Education for "Educating Teachers for Higher Order Thinking" by Robin Fogarty and Jay McTighe. From *Theory Into Practice*, Summer 1993, pp. 161–169. © 1993 by The Ohio State University, College of Education.

Teachers College Press for "The New School 'Lecture': Cooperative Interactions That Engage Student Thinking" by Robin Fogarty and James Bellanca. In *Enhancing Thinking Through Cooperative Learning*, edited by Neil Davidson and Toni Worsham. © 1992 by Teachers College, Columbia University.

Best Practices for the Learner-Centered Classroom
A Collection of Articles by Robin Fogarty
Second Printing

Published by IRI/Skylight Training and Publishing, Inc.
2626 S. Clearbrook Dr.
Arlington Heights, IL 60005
Phone 800-348-4474 or 847-290-6600
FAX 847-290-6609
irisky@xnet.com
http://www.business1.com/iri_sky/

Creative Director: Robin Fogarty
Managing Editor: Julia Noblitt
Editor: Amy Wolgemuth
Type Compositor: Donna Ramirez
Formatters: Donna Ramirez, Heidi Ray
Cover and Illustration Designer: David Stockman
Book Designers: Michael Melasi, Bruce Leckie
Production Coordinator: Maggie Trinkle

LCCCN 95-75387
ISBN 0-932935-93-1

1495B-4-96V
Item number 1334

For Betsy Kuzich

my principal
my mentor
my friend

Table of Contents

Introduction

Best Practices for the Learner-Centered Classroom

Educational change depends on what teachers do and think. It's as simple and as complex as that.—Sarason

What teachers do is what works. In fact, over time, they develop what are called "best practices." These innovations may come from books and workshops, classroom experiences, trial and error, sharing and mentoring, or pure teacher intuition. But the one thing that they all have in common, first and foremost, is a practical focus. Best practices help teachers do what teachers do best. Best practices help teachers teach; they help teachers teach kids; they help teachers teach kids well!

As innovations dot the educational scene, teachers are expected to embrace the newest notions, often funneled from the top down. Yet, history has shown that the educational innovations that survive, that truly become institutionalized in the schools and evolve as best practices, are the ones that work in the classroom.

Best practices are strategies embraced at the classroom level because they make sense. If an innovation is to happen, if it is to become part of the schooling process, it's because teachers are making it happen. Without the support of staff, change doesn't happen—at least not in any significant, long-term way.

Consider this anecdote as an illustration of Sarason's statement about teachers and change. In the early 1970s, metrics came down the educational pike and teachers were expected to teach the metric system as part of the new curriculum. There was the usual resistance to the innovation, as people tried to come to terms with this foreign way of measuring things. Teachers were uncomfortable with it. They did not understand it or internalize it in any meaningful way. Teachers used metrics as a comparative measurement rather than a functional measuring system. They never learned to think in metric.

Looking back on the metric movement, it seems obvious, in hindsight, what really occurred. A quiet revolution swept across the schools throughout the United States. Teachers paid homage to the two or three pages of metric measurement that gratuitously appeared in the textbooks, but they did not really teach metrics.

In fact, they still don't. In schools across the United States, the metric system still remains a skeleton in the schools' closets. Teachers stubbornly hang on to the traditional and familiar, their preferred measuring system. Only in the high school science classes, where metric measurements are relevant to scientific investigations, does the metric system reign supreme.

While this anecdote represents a minor educational innovation in context, it also tells the story of how change does or does not occur in schools. Knowing that change depends on what teachers do and think, the concept of best practices takes on an even more substantive meaning. For best practices imply that teachers must not only perform the practice, they must also think about it within the context of their own content and grade level. They must be reflective about tailoring it to their discipline.

In other words, best practices are grounded in the reflective practices of our nation's teachers. They carry the honored endorsement of seasoned staff. Best practices rank high on the list of teacher favorites.

With that perspective in mind, this collection presents a teacher-tested, tried-and-true "parade of practices." It consists of a decade of articles, essays, and chapters by Robin Fogarty that have been published or submitted for publication in other sources. Practical strategies from the staff room to the classroom make this an invaluable resource for any educator.

The strategies in *Best Practices for the Learner-Centered Classroom* fall into five educational arenas: integrated curricula, thoughtful instruction, active learning, reflective transfer, and authentic assessment.

Section one presents a panoramic view of natural, holistic, *integrated curricula* created through the use of ten different structures or frames. It includes a discussion of thematic instruction and the critical role of teacher teams. Ending with vignettes of three schools with an integrated curricula mission, the section offers practical insights and real-world examples.

Moving beyond the big picture of curriculum integration, section two focuses on the concept of *thoughtful instruction.* The first essay offers a rationale supported by the research espousing higher-order thinking, problem solving, and decision making. Other essays feature the three-story intellect and a survey on the multiple intelligences. Culminating with vignettes of five teachers who exhibit varying levels of the three-story intellect, this section offers best practices of rigor in thinking.

Inseparable from section two, the third section corrals the ideas, or best practices, that drive *active learning.* Undergirding the thinking in this section is an essay on the research behind cooperative learning, followed by a presentation of the Bellanca/Fogarty BUILD model of cooperative learning. Complementing this cognitive model, the next piece targets ways that high school and college teachers can make their lectures more interactive. Section three closes with three teaching scenarios that exemplify active learning classrooms.

Section four focuses on the ultimate goal of schooling—*reflective transfer* for lifelong use. This section profiles metacognitive approaches to learning, where the target is learning for a lifetime, not for a test. Articles include strategies for teaching for transfer and a six-level prototype for assessing student transfer. The section concludes with six short teacher profiles that illustrate the levels of reflective transfer.

The final section on *authentic assessment* discusses learning logs and portfolios, as well as ways to use Gardner's theory of multiple intelligences as expressive tools for assessing. A tri-assessment model completes the survey of assessment strategies with a triangulation approach to assessing human cognitive capacities. The section closes with a look at seven different learners and their multiple intelligences profiles.

The strategies in this collection are intended to merge into a finely focused image of the exemplary classroom and the best practices that create it. Best wishes as you make them your own!

Section 1

Integrated Curricula . . . Commonsense Connections

There are perhaps about one hundred billion neurons, or nerve cells, in the brain, and in a single human brain the number of possible interconnections between these cells is greater than the number of atoms in the universe.—Robert Ornstein and Richard F. Thompson

Just as the interconnections within the brain are innumerable, so too are the interconnections between disciplines. Best practices evidenced in the curricular arena encompass an array of designs that naturally connect the curricula in commonsense ways. Over the years, teachers have devised creative and innovative plans that sequence, combine, and thematically weave together different subject matter content. Examples familiar to all are integrated, holistic projects like publishing a school newspaper, producing the holiday musical, or instituting a student council as the governing body of the school.

Based on the impressive body of brain research (Caine & Caine, 1991) and knowing more about how the mind works (Gardner, 1983), the call for this kind of purposeful learning is widespread. To help teachers formalize their best practices in integrating the curricula, a number of articles and essays address this issue directly.

"Ten Ways to Integrate Curriculum," the granddaddy of them all, outlines, in text and graphics, a spectrum of models that foster curriculum connections. Among the ten options are ideas for fragmenting, connecting, nesting, sequencing, sharing, webbing, threading, integrating, immersing, and networking with typical school curricula. Each model has its signature qualities, yet combining several models is inherent in the process. For example, teachers often web content to an umbrella theme, and at the same time, they thread a thinking skill through the content.

To elaborate on thematic instruction, the second article, "Thinking About Themes: Hundreds of Themes," delineates a six-step procedure for developing themes that have vigor and rigor. The THEMES acronym guides a process that helps teachers explore how fertile candidate themes may be.

Since the key to curriculum integration is to begin conversations across the curricula, the formation of high functioning teacher teams is essential. The third article, "Developing Teacher Teams," addresses the concerns that accompany collaborations and teamwork.

"Vignettes: Integrating Curricula" completes the first section with a trio of vignettes. Each profiles an integrated curricular approach that is unique, exciting, and purposeful: one elementary school uses Gardner's seven intelligences as its integrative force, a high school threads life skills through the various disciplines, and a third school organizes their K–8 curriculum around the visual and performing arts. Each model offers plenty of food for thought in grappling with best practices for integrating curricula.

REFERENCES

Caine, R. N., & Caine, G. (1991). *Making connections: Teaching and the human brain.* Alexandria, VA: Association for Supervision and Curriculum Development.

Gardner, H. (1983). *Frames of mind.* New York: Basic Books.

Ornstein, R., & Thompson, R. F. (1984). *The amazing brain.* Boston: Houghton-Mifflin.

Ten Ways to Integrate Curriculum

by Robin Fogarty

To the young mind everything is individual, stands by itself. By and by, it finds how to join two things and see in them one nature; then three, then three thousand . . . discovering roots running underground whereby contrary and remote things cohere and flower out from one stem. . . . The astronomer discovers that geometry, a pure abstraction of the human mind, is the measure of planetary motion. The chemist finds proportions and intelligible method throughout matter; and science is nothing but the finding of analogy, identity, in the most remote parts.—Emerson

To help the young mind discover "roots running underground whereby contrary and remote things cohere and flower out from one stem" is the mission of both teachers and learners. Educators can achieve this mission, in part, by integrating the curriculum. The 10 models described here present ways along a continuum to accomplish this (Figure 1).

Beginning with an exploration *within single disciplines* (the fragmented, connected, and nested models), and continuing with models that integrate *across several disciplines* (the sequenced, shared, webbed, threaded, and integrated models), the continuum ends with models that operate *within* learners themselves (the immersed model) and finally *across* networks of learners (the networked model). Figure 2 briefly describes and provides an example of each of the 10 models that teachers can use to design integrated curriculums.

From *Educational Leadership*, October 1991, pp. 61–65.

Figure 1
How to Integrate the Curriculum

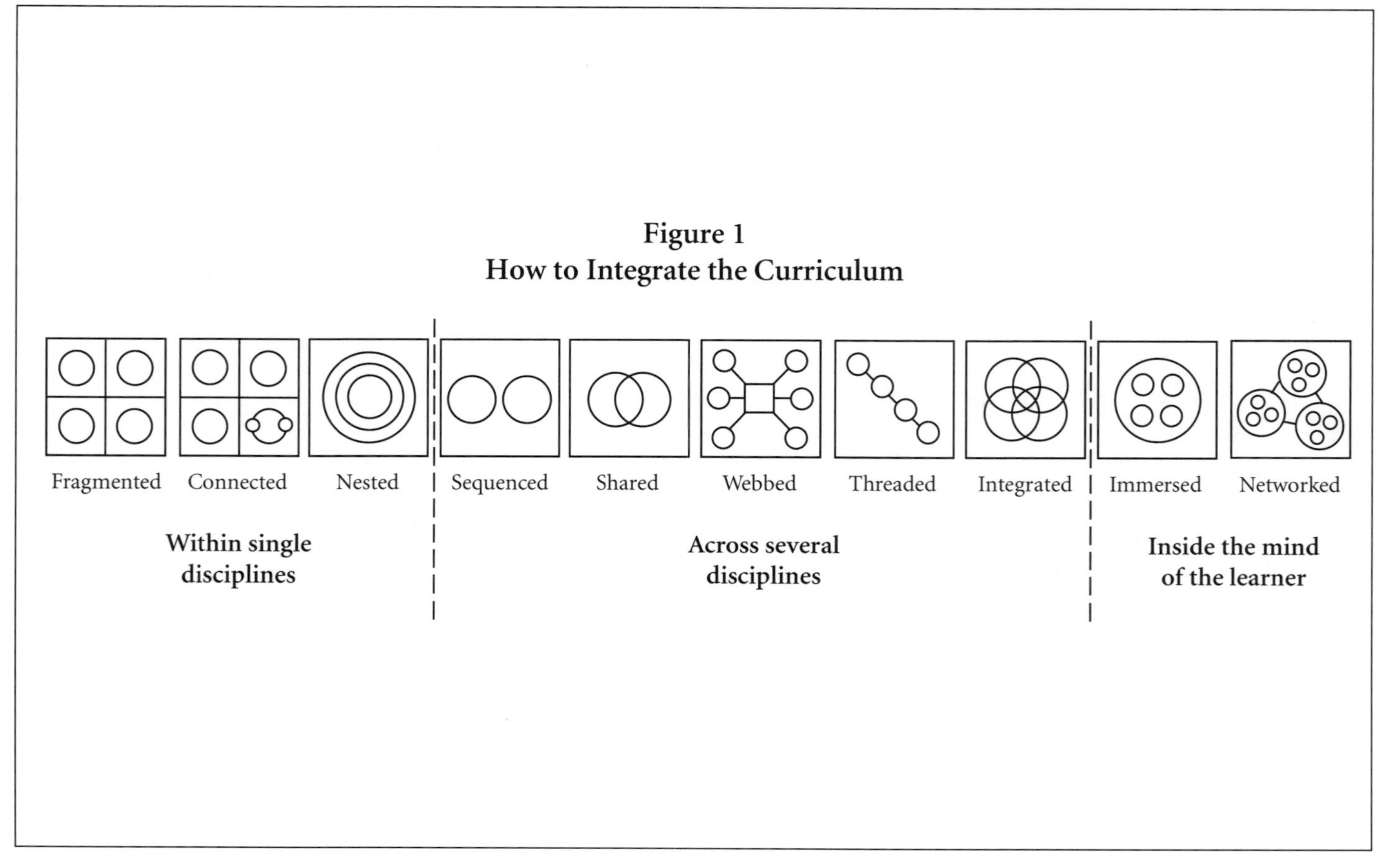

Figure 2
Ten Views for Integrating the Curriculum: How Do You See It?

1 

Fragmented
Periscope—one direction; one sighting; narrow focus on single discipline

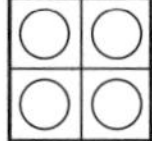

Description
The tradiional model of separate and distinct disciplines, which fragments the subject areas.

Example
Teacher applies this view in Math, Science, Social Studies, Language Arts OR Sciences, Humanities, Fine and Practical Arts.

2 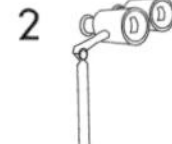

Connected
Opera glass—details of one discipline; focus on subtleties and interconnections

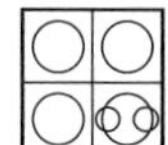

Description
Within each subject area, course content is connected topic to topic, concept to concept, one year's work to the next, and relates idea(s) explicitly.

Example
Teacher relates the concept of fractions to decimals, which in turn relates to money, grades, etc.

3 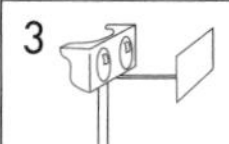

Nested
3-D glasses—multiple dimensions to one scene, topic, or unit

Description
Within each subject area, the teacher targets multiple skills: a social skill, a thinking skill, and a content-specific skill.

Example
Teacher designs the unit on photosynthesis to simultaneously target consensus seeking (social skill), sequencing (thinking skill), and plant life cycle (science content).

4 

Sequenced
Eyeglasses—varied internal content framed by broad, related concepts

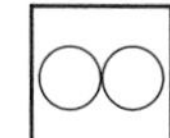

Description
Topics or units of study are rearranged and sequenced to coincide with one another. Similar ideas are taught in concert while remaining separate subjects.

Example
English teacher presents an historical novel depicting a particular period while the History teacher teaches that same historical period.

5 

Shared
Binoculars—two disciplines that share overlapping concepts and skills

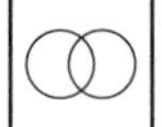

Description
Shared planning and teaching take place in two disciplines in which overlapping concepts or ideas emerge as organizing elements.

Example
Science and Math teachers use data collection, charting, and graphing as shared concepts that can be team-taught.

6 

Webbed
Telescope—broad view of an entire constellation as one theme, webbed to the various elements

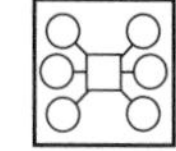
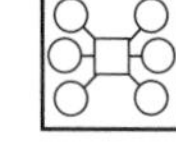

Description
A fertile theme is webbed to curriculum contents and disciplines; subjects use the theme to sift out appropriate concepts, topics, and ideas.

Example
Teacher presents a simple topical theme, such as the circus, and webs it to the subject areas. A conceptual theme, such as conflict, can be webbed for more depth in the theme approach.

7 

Threaded
Magnifying glass—big ideas that magnify all content through a metacurricular approach

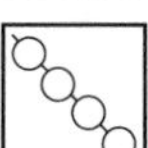

Description
The metacurricular approach threads thinking skills, social skills, multiple intelligences, technology, and study skills through the various disciplines.

Example
Teaching staff targets prediction in Reading, Math, and Science lab experiments while Social Studies teacher targets forecasting current events, and thus threads the skill (prediction) across disciplines.

8 

Integrated
Kaleidoscope—new patterns and designs that use the basic elements of each discipline

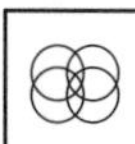

Description
This interdisciplinary approach matches subjects for overlaps in topics and concepts with some team teaching in an authentic integrated model.

Example
In Math, Science, Social Studies, Fine Arts, Language Arts, and Practical Arts, teachers look for patterning models and approach content through these patterns.

9 

Immersed
Microscope—intensely personal view that allows microscopic explanation as all content is filtered through lens of interest and expertise

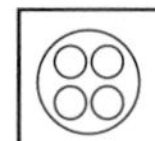

Description
The disciplines become part of the learner's lens of expertise; the learner filters all content through this lens and becomes immersed in his or her own experience.

Example
Student or doctoral candidate has an area of expert interest and sees all learning through that lens.

10 

Networked
Prism—a view that creates multiple dimensions and directions of focus

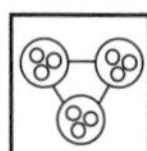

Description
Learner filters all learning through the expert's eye and makes internal connections that lead to external networks of experts in related fields.

Example
Architect, while adapting the CAD/CAM technology for design, networks with technical programmers and expands her knowledge base, just as she had traditionally done with interior designers.

*Extrapolated from "Design Options for an Integrated Curriculum" by Heidi Hayes Jacobs in *Interdisciplinary Curriculum*, ASCD, 1989.

THE FRAGMENTED MODEL

The *fragmented* model, the traditional design for organizing the curriculum, dictates separate and distinct disciplines. This model views the curriculum through a periscope, offering one sighting at a time: one directed focus on a single discipline. Typically, the major academic areas are math, science, language arts, and social studies. Each is seen as a pure entity in and of itself. Relationships between subject areas—physics and chemistry, for example—are only implicitly indicated.

The *fragmented* model . . . views the curriculum through a periscope, offering one sighting at a time: one directed focus on a single discipline.

In middle and secondary schools, the disciplines are taught by different teachers in different locations, with students moving from room to room. Each separate encounter has a distinct cellular organization, leaving students with a fragmented view of the curriculum. A less severe model of fragmentation prevails in elementary classrooms, where the teacher says, "Now, put away your math books, and take out your science packets." The daily schedule shows a distinct time slot for each subject, with topics from two areas only occasionally related intentionally.

A high school student explained the fragmented curriculum like this: "Math isn't science, science isn't English, English isn't history. A subject is something you take once and need never take again. It's like getting a vaccination; I've had my shot of algebra. I'm done with that."

Despite the drawbacks of this traditional model, teachers can use it, individually or with colleagues, by listing and ranking curricular topics, concepts, or skills. In this way, teachers or teacher teams can begin to sift out curricular priorities within their own content areas—a much-needed first step.

THE CONNECTED MODEL

The *connected* model of the integrated curriculum is the view through an opera glass, providing a close-up of the details, subtleties, and interconnections within one discipline. While the disciplines remain separate, this model focuses on making explicit connections within each subject area—connecting one topic, one skill, one concept to the next; connecting one day's work, or even one semester's ideas, to the next. The key to this model is the deliberate effort to relate ideas within the discipline, rather than assuming that students will automatically understand the connections.

In middle or secondary school, for example, the earth science teacher could relate the geology unit to the astronomy unit by emphasizing the evolutionary nature of each. This similarity between the two units then becomes an organizer for students as they work through both. Teachers help students make connections by explicitly making links between subject areas.

THE NESTED MODEL

The *nested* model of integration views the curriculum through three-dimensional glasses, targeting multiple dimensions of a lesson. Nested integration takes advantage of natural combinations. For example, an elementary lesson on the circulatory system could target the concept of systems, as well as facts and understandings about the circulatory system in particular. In addition to this conceptual target, teachers can target the thinking skill cause and effect as well.

Another example might be a lesson in a high school computer science class that targets the CAD/CAM (computer-assisted design/computer-assisted manufacturing) programs. As the students learn the workings of the program, the teacher can target the thinking skill of "envisioning" for explicit exploration and practice. In this nested approach, students in the computer class may also be instructed in ergonomics as they design furniture for schools of the future.

THE SEQUENCED MODEL

The *sequenced* model views the curriculum through eyeglasses: the lenses are separate but connected by a common frame. Although topics or units are taught separately, they are rearranged and sequenced to provide a broad framework for related concepts.

Teachers can arrange topics so that similar units coincide. In the self-contained classroom, for examples, *Charlotte's Web* can accompany the unit on spiders. *Johnny Tremain* can parallel the study of the Revolutionary War. The graphing unit can coincide with data collection in the weather unit. In secondary school, one might synchronize study of the stock market in math class with study of the Depression in history.

John Adams once said, "The textbook is not a moral contract that teachers are obliged to teach—teachers are obliged to teach children." Following the sequence of the textbook may work well in some cases, but it might make more sense to rearrange the sequence of units in other cases. The new sequence may be more logical if it parallels the presentation of other content *across* disciplines.

THE SHARED MODEL

The *shared* model views the curriculum through binoculars, bringing two distinct disciplines together into a single-focused image. Using overlapping concepts as organizing elements, this model involves shared planning or teaching in two disciplines.

The *shared* model views the curriculum through binoculars, bringing two distinct disciplines together into a single-focused image.

In middle and secondary schools, cross-departmental partners might plan a unit of study. The two members of the team approach the preliminary planning session with a notion of key concepts, skills, and attitudes traditionally taught in their single-subject approach. As the pair identify priorities, they look for overlaps in content. For example, the literature teacher might select the concept of The American Dream as an organizer for a collection of short stories by American authors. At the same time, the history teacher might note that his unit on American history could also use The American Dream as a unifying theme. In this way, the literature teacher and the history teacher team up to point out commonalities to students.

Elementary models of shared curriculums may embody standard planning models already in wide use. Typically, whole-language curriculums draw upon many curricular areas. The self-contained classroom teacher might plan a science unit (simple machines) and a social studies unit (the industrial revolution) around the concept of efficiency models. Teachers may ask themselves and each other: "What concepts do these units share?" "Are we teaching similar skills?"

THE WEBBED MODEL

The *webbed* model of integration views the curriculum through a telescope, capturing an entire constellation of disciplines at once. Webbed curriculums usually use a fertile theme to integrate subject matter, such as Inventions. Once a cross-departmental team has chosen a theme, the members use it as an overlay to the different subjects. Inventions, for example, leads to the study of simple machines in science, to reading and writing about inventors in language arts, to designing and building models in industrial arts, to drawing and studying Rube Goldberg contraptions in math, and to making flowcharts in computer technology classes.

In departmentalized situations, the webbed curricular approach to integration is often achieved through the use of a generic but fertile theme such as Patterns. This conceptual theme provides rich possibilities for the various disciplines.

While similar conceptual themes such as Patterns provide fertile ground for cross-disciplinary units of study, one can also use a book or a genre of books as the topic, to organize the curriculum thematically. For example, fairy tales or dog stories can become catalysts for curricular webbing. Figure 3 shows typical lists for theme development.

Figure 3
Theme Development Ideas for Curricular Webbing

CONCEPTS	TOPICS	CATEGORIES
freedom	the individual	animal stories
cooperation	society	biographies
challenge	community	adventure
conflict	relationships	science fiction
discovery	global concerns	the Renaissance
culture	war	Medieval times
change	the Pacific Rim	the impressionists
argument & evidence	partnerships	great books
perseverance		

THE THREADED MODEL

The *threaded* model of integration views the curriculum through a magnifying glass: the "big ideas" are enlarged throughout all content with a metacurricular approach. This model threads thinking skills, social skills, study skills, graphic organizers, technology, and a multiple intelligences approach to learning throughout all disciplines. The threaded model supersedes all subject matter content. For example, "prediction" is a skill used to estimate in mathematics, forecast in current events, anticipate in a novel, and hypothesize in the science lab. Consensus-seeking strategies are used in resolving conflicts in any problem-solving situation.

The *threaded* model . . . views the curriculum through a magnifying glass: the "big ideas" are enlarged throughout all content with a metacurricular approach.

Using the idea of a metacurriculum, grade-level or interdepartmental teams can target a set of thinking skills to infuse into existing content priorities. For example, using a thinking skills curriculum, the freshman team might choose to infuse the skill of analysis into each content area.

As thinking skills or social skills are threaded into the content, teachers ask students: "How did you think about that?" "What thinking skill did you find most helpful?" "How well did your group work today?" These processing questions contrast sharply with the usual cognitive questions such as, "What answer did you get?"

THE INTEGRATED MODEL

The *integrated* model views the curriculum through a kaleidoscope: interdisciplinary topics are rearranged around overlapping concepts and emergent patterns and designs. Using a cross-disciplinary approach, this model blends the four major disciplines by finding the overlapping skills, concepts, and attitudes in all four. As in the shared model, the integration is a result of sifting related ideas out of subject matter content. The integration sprouts from within the various disciplines, and teachers make matches among them as commonalities emerge.

At the middle or secondary school, an interdisciplinary team discovers they can apply the concept of argument and evidence in math, science, language arts, and social studies. In the elementary classroom, an integrated model that illustrates the critical elements of this approach is the whole language strategy, in which reading, writing, listening, and speaking skills spring from a holistic, literature-based program.

THE IMMERSED MODEL

The *immersed* model of integration views the curriculum through a microscope. In an intensely personal way, it filters all content through the lens of interest and expertise. In this model, integration takes place *within* learners, with little or no outside intervention.

Aficionados, graduate students, doctoral candidates, and post-doctoral fellows are totally immersed in a field of study. They integrate all data by funneling them through this area of intense interest. For example, a doctoral candidate may be a specialist in the chemical bonding of substances. Even though her field is chemistry, she devours the software programs in computer science classes so she can simulate lab experiments, saving days of tedious labwork. She learns patent law in order to protect the ideas for her company and to avoid liability cases.

Likewise, a 6-year-old writes incessantly about butterflies, spiders, insects, and creepy-crawlies of all sorts. Her artwork is modeled on the symmetrical design of ladybugs and the patterns of butterflies. She counts, mounts, and frames bugs; she even sings about them. Her interest in insect biology is already consuming her. The books she chooses reflect her internal integration of information around her pet subject.

An immersed learner might say, “It is a labor of love. It seems that everything I *choose* to pursue with any fervor is directly related to my field.” Just as writers record notes and artists make sketches, immersed learners are constantly making connections to their subjects.

THE NETWORKED MODEL

The *networked* model of integration views the curriculum through a prism, creating multiple dimensions and directions of focus. Like a three- or four-way conference call, it provides various avenues of exploration and explanation. In this model, learners direct the integration process. Only the learners themselves, knowing the intricacies and dimensions of their field, can target the necessary resources, as they reach out within and across their areas of specialization.

The networked model is seen to a limited extent in elementary schools. Imagine a 5th grader who has had a keen interest in native Americans since his toddler days of playing cowboys and Indians. His passion for Indian lore leads him into historical readings—both fictional and nonfictional. Aware of his interest, his family hears about an archeological dig that recruits youngsters as part of a summer program. As a result of this summer "camp," this learner meets people in a number of fields: an anthropologist, a geologist, an archeologist, and an illustrator. Already this learner's networks are taking shape.

USING THE MODELS

Whether you are working alone, with partners, or in teams, the 10 organizers presented here can function as useful prototypes. In fact, a faculty can easily work with them over time to develop an integrated curriculum throughout the school. Each staff member or team might choose one model to work with each semester. As teachers begin the conversation about integrating the curriculum, they can work with the models to explore the connections within and across disciplines and within and across learners.

These models are just beginnings. Teachers should go on to invent their own designs for integrating the curriculum. The process itself never ends. It's a cycle that offers renewed energy to each school year as teachers help the young mind discover "roots running underground whereby contrary and remote things cohere and flower out from one stem."

Thinking About Themes: Hundreds of Themes

by Robin Fogarty

Dinosaurs; The Future; Man vs. Nature; Whales; Myths; Robots; Time After Time; The Dawn of Civilization; Inventions; Friendship; Bears; The Environment; Up, Up, and Away; Old Favorites; America, the Beautiful; Our Canadian Neighbors; Across the Sea; Simple Machines; Shoes; Win or Lose?; Animals; Long Ago; Change; Patterns; Survival; Why Man Creates; Biases; The Media; Biography; The Renaissance; How Dry Is the Desert?; The Ice Age; The Solar System; Water; Friend or Foe?; Cultural Diversity; Sound; Light; Insects; The Cemetery Study; The Mind; Birds; Under the Sea; Around the World; The Pyramids; War; War and Peace; Native Americans; The Circus; Hats; Shapes; Statistics; The Shrinking Globe; Conflicts; Transportation; Argument and Evidence; Beginnings; Perseverance; Family Treasures; Pilots and Passengers; Connections; When Time Began; 2020; Profiles in Courage; Fear; Trade; Exploration; Discovery; Love; Citizenship; Food, Clothing, and Shelter; The Community; The Zoo; Nature's Fury; Dreams and Nightmares; Skyscrapers; Volcanoes; Earthquakes and Other Natural Disasters; The Weather; Heroes; Male vs. Female; Creatures; Craters; Submarines; Fish; Seashells; Colors; Rainbows; Reptiles; Technology; Television: Good or Evil?; Tragedy; Romance; Space; Spiders; Pioneers; Halloween; Holidays; The Wild West; Careers; Wisdom; Courage; Authority; Nutrition; Wellness and Fitness; Global Economy; Latin America; Natural Wonders; Death and Dying; Pets; Decisions; Mysteries; Magic; and Mammals.

These are real themes from real classrooms around the country. Themes are fun, inviting, and doable, and they make learning exciting for students and for teachers. Themes also organize content and create manageable chunks of connected ideas.

Figure 1
T-H-E-M-E-S

T	Think of themes
H	Hone the list
E	Extrapolate the criteria
M	Manipulate the theme
E	Expand into activities
S	Select goals and assessments

But, there are many questions about how we can make these themes work for us. How do we infuse integrity into our thematic units? How do we manipulate themes for real accountability? How do we align themes to our valued goals? How do we think about themes before plunging in? The answer to these questions is as simple as T-H-E-M-E-S (see Figure 1).

Think about themes by generating a lengthy list. As a faculty or team, brainstorm an initial list of twenty, thirty, or fifty ideas. Post the list on large paper in the teachers' lounge. Commit to doubling the list by the end of the week. Then start "stealing" ideas from everywhere. Gather ideas from books, journals, neighboring districts, other teachers, old units, and textbook concepts. Collect as many different ideas as possible. Think of the various disciplines and themes that are inherent in your studies. Create a list with students; assign another list for homework and get the parents involved. Do whatever it takes to compile a longer list of candidate themes than the one depicted at the beginning of this piece. Challenge yourselves; try to add to the list without duplicating any words already listed. Have fun!

Hone the list. Just because you've brainstormed, collected, gathered, and listed one hundred themes does not mean that all of them are great—or at least great for your purposes. So, start sorting out the ideas. Divide the list into three distinct sections: topics, concepts, and problems. Discuss or define: What is a concept? Which things are topics? Where are the problems? Or just start sorting out the words on the list and see what defining elements occur in your slotting process. Then, try to put defining words into the columns to delineate the differences among topics, concepts, and problems. Sift through the monstrous list and group the themes into three more manageable lots. Then, with your colleagues and/or teammates, select three champion themes, one from each of the three categories (e.g., a topical theme—dinosaurs; a conceptual theme—systems; and a problematic theme—How Does Man Survive?) Display the champion themes for all to see. Use whatever method is necessary to reach agreement on the three. Then, take a moment to reflect on how your team finally reached its decision.

Extrapolate criteria. Think about the tug of war discussions that result in champion themes. Recall the reasons, rationale, and persuasive arguments that convince everyone that a particular theme had merit or that one theme was better than another. Find the proof for selecting one theme as superior over another. Justify your choices and demand justification for others' choices. Know why one theme stands out above the rest. Dialogue with team members and uncover their reasons for choosing the champion themes. List the emergent criteria on large paper and post them next to the champion themes. Be clear about the criteria for selecting themes; these criteria are revisited each time a new theme is needed (see Figure 2). Then, select one of the three themes to work with further.

Manipulate the theme. Massage the theme. Reflect on possible questions that naturally occur. What do you want to know? What are the essential questions—the ones that pique interest and invite investigation? Capture the questions of the children. Pose questions of value and notice how the thematic focus is transformed and raised to higher levels. Search for the question that provokes the mind and incites the emotions. Think about the hows, whys, and wherefores. Transpose the theme into a question that evokes curiosity and intrigue—a question that drives the theme and brings all on board. Don't

Figure 2
Sample Criteria

1. Relevant
2. Intriguing
3. Resources

Figure 3
Sample Questions

Theme		Transformed Theme
Desert	→	How Dry Is the Desert?
Creativity	→	Why Does Man Create?
Citizenship	→	How am I a Good Citizen?
Technology	→	Technology: Problems and Solutions
The American Dream	→	The American Dream: Fantasy or Reality?
Environment	→	Feast or Famine?
Power	→	When Is Power Healthy? Adverse?

hurry through this part. Process the theme by postulating all kinds of questions; refine them until a final question takes shape (see Figure 3).

Expand into activities. Hook into the theme (and the question) and produce myriad activities that are triggered by the theme. "Web" the theme out to the various curricular areas: math, science, social studies, language arts, art, music, health, PE, and technology (Fogarty, 1991). Witness the fireworks as teachers fire off a million possible activities for integrated learning. Let this initial burst generate more activities than you could

Figure 4
Middle School Theme

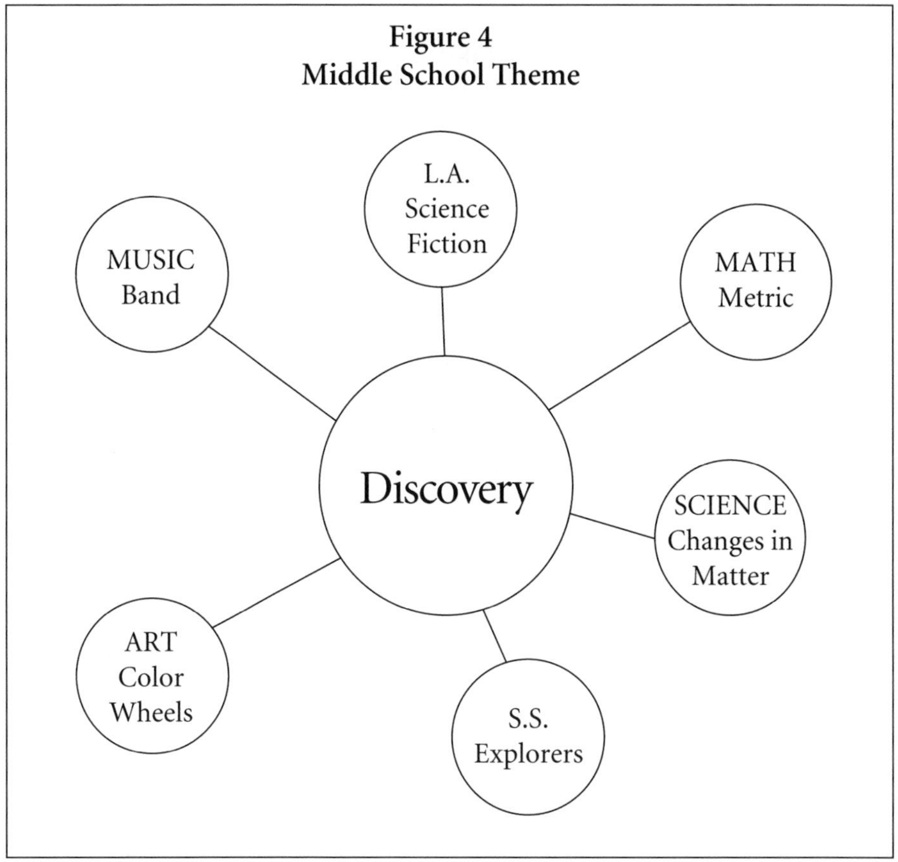

ever do. Include activities that involve the spectrum of multiple intelligences (visual/spatial, verbal/linguistic, logical/mathematical, musical/rhythmic, bodily/kinesthetic, intrapersonal, and interpersonal). Let the good times roll as you recall, borrow, and invent appropriate and appealing activities for youngsters. And, of course, include student choices and interests in an expanded and elaborated web (see Figures 4 and 5).

Select goals and assessments. Armed with the aims, goals, and objectives that comprise valued learner goals, take time to focus on the traditional curricular areas in the web—math, science, social studies, etc.—and examine each of the activities for

Figure 5
High School Theme

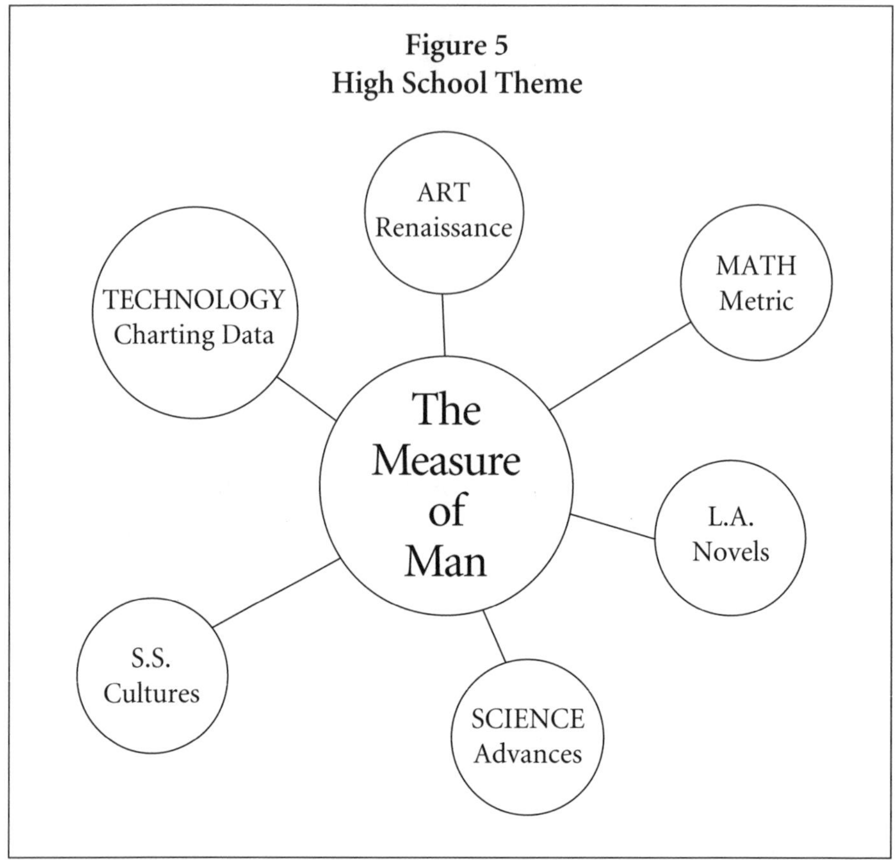

alignment with expected goals. Use this step to selectively abandon and judiciously include activities. Once you have an organizing theme or question, you can literally generate hundreds of activities. The task, now, is to refine the thematic unit with only those activities that truly target significant goals. Each activity, in whatever subject area, needs to be rich enough to provide fertile ground for thoughtful learning and mindful production. Once the activities are refined and aligned, assessment is easily determined through authentic measures such as portfolios and performances (see Figure 6).

IN CLOSING

Themes may not be as easy as one, two, three but they are as easy as T-H-E-M-E-S! Remember, themes are fun, inviting, and doable! Just do it!

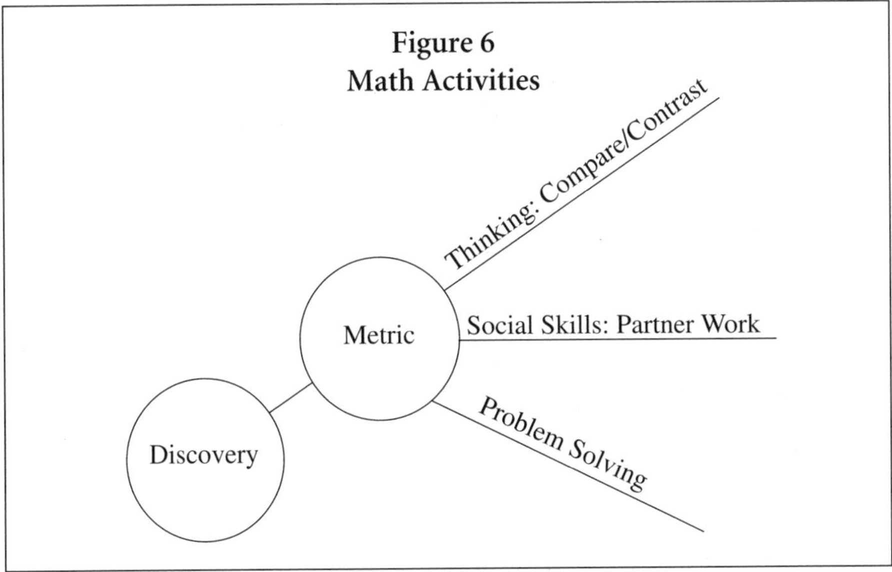

Sports; Myself; Skeletons; Music, Ballet, and Drama; Games Around the World; Antarctica; Fair-Weather Friends; Hobbies and Collections; Collectibles; Superheroes; Presidents; Choices; Honesty; The Farm; Industrialization; The Paper Chase; Science Fiction; Family Living; The Computer Age; The Arts; Islands; The Written Word; The News; The City; Opera; Famous Battles; The Newspaper; Headline News; Superstitions; Legends; Texas; Mexico; Egypt; Favorite Places; The Oregon Trail; Custer; The Moon; Hemingway; The American Dream; The Young and the Old; Bridges; Currency; Language; A Picture Is Worth a Thousand Words; Caring; Animals at Work; The Critics' Choices; Film; Human Connections; Archeology; Humor; Drugs: Beneficial or Harmful; Addiction; Plants; The Senses; Magnets; Both Sides of the Issue; The Research Search; Famous People; Fame or Fortune?; Competition; Cooperation; Leadership; Tongue Twisters; Fables; Tall Tales; Riddles; Controversy; The Garden; Witches, Ghosts, and Goblins; A Sign of the Times; Flowers; Celebrations of Life; Anecdotes; Afterthoughts; The Universe; Truth; Moral Dilemmas; Ethics; Pigs; The Rain Forest; Evolution; Night and Day; Why Do People Develop Habits?; There's No Place Like Home; The Ugly American; Tourists; The Sky Above; Pollution; Handicaps; Fantasy; The Middle East; Faces; Clowns; Masks; Faulkner; The American Novelist; Leverage; Debate; Cartoons; The Changing Tide; Megatrends; Warm Fuzzies; Creative Features; Frogs, Toads, and Princesses; Fairy Tales; The World of Work; Ways of Knowing; Man Through Art; Happiness; Picture This; Every Ending Is a Beginning; Short Cuts; Fashion; Prey; Talk, Tales, and Tidbits; Seasons; Wheels and Whachamacallits!

Figure 7
Illustrated Themes:
Using the Webbed Model for Thematic Teaching

Think of themes:

Friends	People, Places, Things	Argument and Evidence
The World	The Arts	Inventions
Animals	Old Favorites	Cultures
Harmony	Time After Time	Neighbors

Hone the list:

Topics	Concepts	Problems
Dinosaurs	Patterns	Hostages
Bears	Cycles	Health Care
Environment	Conflict	School Funding
Plants	Change	

Extrapolate the criteria:

Criteria for a Fertile Theme
1. Relevant to students
2. Many resources available
3. Broad enough for all curriculum areas
4. Intrigues teachers and students

Manipulate the theme:

Environment	→ Feast or Famine?
Citizenship	→ How am I a Good Citizen?
Creativity	→ Why Does Man Create?
The American Dream	→ Fantasy or Reality?
Desert	→ How Dry Is the Desert?

Expand into activities:

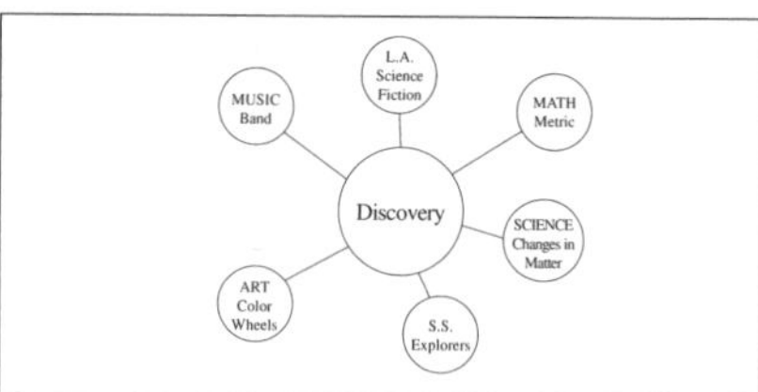

Select goals and assessments:

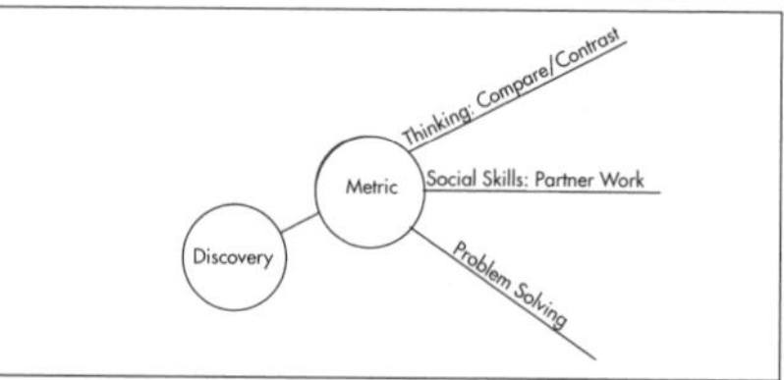

REFERENCES

Beane, J. A. (1993, September). Problems and possibilities for an integrative curriculum. *Middle School Journal*, pp. 18–23.

Burke, K. A. (1994). *The mindful school: How to assess authentic learning.* Palatine, IL: IRI/Skylight Publishing.

Caine, R. N., & Caine, G. (1991, October). Understanding a brain-based approach to learning and thinking. *Educational Leadership*, pp. 66–67.

Fogarty, R. (1991). *The mindful school: How to integrate the curricula.* Palatine, IL: IRI/Skylight Publishing.

Fogarty, R. (1990). *Keep them thinking: Level II.* Palatine, IL: IRI/Skylight Publishing.

Fogarty, R., & Bellanca, J. (1989). *Patterns for thinking: Patterns for transfer.* Palatine, IL: IRI/Skylight Publishing.

Fogarty, R., Perkins, D., & Barell, J. (1992). *The mindful school: How to teach for transfer.* Palatine, IL: IRI/Skylight Publishing.

Jacobs-Hayes, H. (1991, September). The integrated curriculum: What it is, why your students need it. *Instructor*, pp. 22–23.

Maute, J. (1989, March). Cross curricular connections. *Middle School Journal*, pp. 20–22.

Vars, G. (1991, October). Integrated curriculum in historical perspective. *Educational Leadership*, pp. 14–15.

Williams, R. B. (1993). *More than 50 ways to build team consensus.* Palatine, IL: IRI/Skylight Publishing.

Developing Teacher Teams

by Robin Fogarty

Teacher teams are essential for meaningful school reform (Goodlad, 1984; Fullan, 1991). As districts and boards across this continent strive to restructure schools with a learner-centered focus, an integrated, more holistic curriculum design appears boldly on many agendas (Virginia, Kentucky, Ontario, British Columbia).

This curriculum restructuring from the inside out requires a reconceptualization of many of the structures of schools today. One such structure that comes under scrutiny is the isolation of the teaching staff (Lortie, 1975).

If integrated learning is becoming a reality in our schools, it is because teachers are talking to each other.

If integrated learning is becoming a reality in our schools, it is because teachers are talking to each other—thinking and planning, reflecting and evaluating (Schlechty, 1990; Barth, 1990). In order to begin the professional dialogue among learned colleagues, there is a series of questions to be answered: Do we want to organize our schools by teacher teams and student clusters, as Goodlad (1984) suggests, to create schools within schools for easier focus on a learner-centered philosophy? If so, how do we create the teams, build the trust, assemble the clusters, and get them started? Once the teams are functioning, how do we keep them working productively and help them overcome obstacles? How do we facilitate team meetings with effective process strategies? How do we help teams resolve conflicts, come to agreements, and celebrate their success? Only when we address these questions can we experience the change from discipline-based curricula to a more integrated approach.

SKUNKWORKS: MANAGEABLE CHUNKS

Skunkworks! That is the word Peters and Waterman (1982) use in their landmark book, *In Search of Excellence*, to describe the ad hoc operations set up by innovative employees who make things happen in a particular area. Skunkworks are small teams of people, manageable chunks of the organization who "just do it." If we are to integrate curricula in our nation's schools, maybe we too must recognize and honor the skunkworks, the existing teacher collaborators who are already making it happen. Perhaps we must make the decision to create more manageable chunks in our organization. Maybe that is exactly what we need (Goodlad, 1984).

When teachers know that they have responsibility for the total learning experience of a group of students, they rally to the cause.

Consider radically reshuffling the deck by putting staff on teacher teams and assigning clusters of students to the teams for long-term innovative approaches to the business of schooling. While this is part of the middle school concept (Merenbloom, 1991), Goodlad (1984) heralds the idea of student clusters or schools within a school for K–12. Now, that is an idea! The decision to reorganize for schools within a school is the first in a series of decisions that lead to a more integrated approach to learning.

Teacher teams and student clusters set the stage for the professional dialogues that supersede any real integration of curricula. When teachers know that they have responsibility for the total learning experience of a group of students, they rally to the cause.

Teachers start sharing and planning in creative ways that cross the curricular lines as they involve the learner in rich learning episodes (Jacobs, 1989; Merenbloom, 1991; Little, 1981). The learners become the focus of the team planning, the common denominator for various subject-matter contents and curricular concerns.

FORMING THE TEAMS: TOP DOWN OR BOTTOM UP?

Once teams and clusters become restructuring priorities, other practical considerations come into play: Who forms the teams?

Do teachers have a voice in the make-up of the team or cluster, or are the decisions made from above?

Let's look at an option that reflects best practices currently in effect. For example, one middle school might choose neither a top-down nor a bottom-up mode. Instead, it could take the middle road. Before the teams are formed, all staff members participate in an informal sociogram in which they list staff members they prefer to team with and those whom they feel they are unable to work with on a long-term basis. Armed with that information, the principal organizes teams of four to six members. All teaching staff members are assigned to base teams as diverse in make-up as possible. That diversity includes gender, areas of expertise, years of experience, professional credentials, and teaching styles.

In this example, teams, team facilitators, or team coaches are formed for the three-year cycle of student clusters that span the sixth, seventh, and eighth grades. The teams move from grade to grade with their cluster. This guarantees long-term relationships for teacher team building and more long-term, holistic, integrated learning experiences for the students.

Sample teams from this scenario might include staff from the following disciplines.

Team X: Math, science, social studies, art, PE, and reading

Team Y: Computers, math, social studies, language arts, science, and gifted

Team Z: Music, science, math, language arts, social studies, and L.D.

The teams are formed with as much diversity as possible in academic areas since each team is ultimately responsible for all content for the students in their cluster. Teams may, at times, bring in an expert from another team if they need special consultation or content-specific instructional ideas.

BEGINNING THE CONVERSATION: IT'S A START!

Consider a staff retreat before the first year of integration that focuses on *team-building* activities that create the familiarity and trust needed for effective teamwork. Staff members participate in a variety of activities, with a skilled facilitator (Fullan, 1983), that create the ties that bind. They settle on team names, symbols, and mottoes or slogans (Scearce, 1992) and participate in a high-stakes performance with their newly created lyrics in a Song-A-Rama. For example, one team might call themselves "The Wrestling Team" because they are wrestling with ideas. They, in turn, can make a symbol of a wrestler's arm lock and create the motto, "We wrestle with ideas," as well as create a song to the tune of "Row, Row, Row Your Boat." While these antics seem superfluous to some, the humor, collegiality, and sense of "teamness" that result speak for themselves (Williams, 1993).

Staff members participate in a variety of activities that create the ties that bind.

A second tier of retreat activities focuses on beginning the conversations among team members as they reveal their expertise as valued members of a diverse and rich team. Attention is given to both formal and informal strengths and interests. For example, while one team member might be valued for her skills as a mathematics teacher, her hobby as a pilot of a Piper Cub could also spark possibility thinking. Another teacher on this team might reveal a pen name and his authorship of several published pieces, as well as his academic expertise in the field of American literature. All talent areas are mentally logged for later reference.

This *team inventory* is followed by still a third tier of retreat interactions in which the teams work on a shared vision that connects to the school or district mission. For example, one team might use the inductive model of goal setting called "Cardstorming," as described by Williams (1993). At this point, the teams might also carve out significant outcomes implied in that team vision. These might include a long-term integrated project such as an opera production that highlights learning in languages and the arts and teamwork.

There are three distinct types of interactions. The first type is characterized by high-powered, team-building antics that give a jump start to the groups so they start trusting each other and acting like a team with a common focus. The second type begins the conversations and steadies the pace for appreciation of the diverse talents on the team. Finally, the third type of interaction accelerates the team vehicle to a comfortable cruising speed for the year's plans that lie ahead. All are appropriate for the journey that is about to begin.

Before the retreat ends, teams have accomplished some initial bonding, taken an inventory of the particular team talents and expertise, created a shared vision, and slated significant outcomes for their first term.

IT'S A PROCESS: THE CONVERSATION CONTINUES

It is one thing to go on a retreat, away from the hustle and bustle of everyday routines, and be enthusiastic about your new team and cluster. It is quite another thing to keep that same energy level in the midst of the action with students, schedules, and scholarship.

If there is a fatal flaw in teacher teams, it is the use, abuse, and overuse of team meetings.

After some initial training in working as a team to integrate curricula, teams need to focus on specific reasons for meeting. If there is a fatal flaw in teacher teams, it is the use, abuse, and overuse of team meetings. Teams need to be instructed in how to conduct effective meetings. Specifically, they need to learn how to set agendas, make decisions, and come to consensus. In addition, teams must decide what kinds of things can be done before and after the team meeting (or outside the context of the meeting) to keep their time together as short and productive as possible. In addition, teams need to discuss strategies and team-generated guidelines that will govern their work together.

For example, a team may agree on the following guidelines:

1. Begin on time.
2. Review the agenda.
3. Stay on task.
4. Use task roles for members.
5. Come prepared.
6. Make sure all participate.
7. End on time.

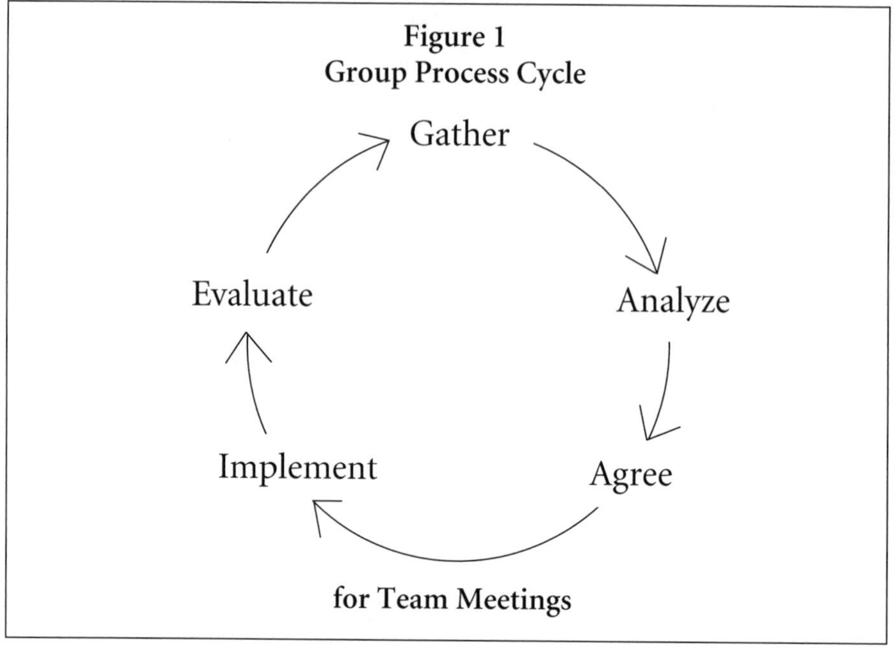

Figure 1
Group Process Cycle
for Team Meetings

Figure 2
Agenda

1. **Purpose:** Select a theme.
2. **Gather Ideas:** Brainstorm lists.
3. **Analyze:** Categorize lists.
4. **Agree:** Select one theme (discuss).
5. **Implement:** Go back and have students generate questions about the theme.
6. **Evaluate:** Find pluses and minuses of the session.
7. **Set Time:** To gather student questions and meet again.

Also, teams need specific methods and processes for gathering ideas, analyzing input, reaching agreement, and implementing and evaluating the results (see Figure 1).

To visualize this process in action, imagine a team meeting early in the fall to begin to integrate curricula through a thematic instructional unit. The following agenda is set at the beginning of the session (see Figure 2).

The team meeting might go as follows: The meeting starts on time. The team selects arbitrary roles for the process—recorder, reporter, observer, encourager, and discussion leader—just as teachers do in the classroom with cooperative learning groups. Team members brainstorm one hundred theme ideas. To reflect on the ideas, they categorize the one hundred themes into topics, concepts, or problems. Their discussion of criteria reveals several considerations, including relevancy, availability of resources, and keen interest of both students and teachers. The team members agree to select three candidate themes: one topic theme (e.g., natural disasters), one concept theme (e.g., change), and one problematic theme (e.g., our polluted earth). They also decide that a first step toward implementation is to take the three ideas to the students and have them generate essential questions for each. The team members plan to make a final theme selection by examining the student questions. After a brief discussion of the process they used for the meeting, they set the next meeting for a week later and adjourn at the agreed-upon time.

Of course, each meeting differs. Some are whole-team meetings, while others involve only members that need to meet for particular reasons. Most meetings are scheduled for the designated block time, but some are arranged by the participants on their own time. Meetings are the backbone of team planning. Effective teams understand how to maximize these times together. They organize for specific member input and for follow-up that can easily be done away from the meeting. Emergency meetings are kept to a minimum, but the team meets as it needs to—sometimes to resolve emerging conflicts or poll the group if rifts are obvious.

Team members need to remind each other that too many meetings and too much time take their toll. Remember, there is life after school, and the caution is to be reasonable. As one teacher says, "Integrating curricula is so entangling, it's like spaghetti; once you get in, you can't get out. Teachers need an out!"

GUIDE ON THE SIDE: FACILITATING THE TEAM

Facilitation involves a number of different tasks, including making schedules, facilitating meetings, finding resources, resolving conflicts, and orchestrating celebrations. Scheduling may mean formally meeting with the "authorities" and building in a block of time for teams to meet (Merenbloom, 1991; Goodlad, 1984). Alternatively, it may simply mean helping the teams and or team members carve out informal chunks of time for teachers to begin the conversation about curriculum integration.

In addition, once teams are formed and functioning at a basic level, they need continued and ongoing skill training in group processes, coaching and support, and genuine feedback on their meetings. This is where the facilitator takes on the role of guide on the side (Schlechty, 1990) for true team development. The facilitator may: (1) guide the choice of models for curriculum integration (Fogarty, 1991; Jacobs, 1989), knowing what level of sophistication various teams have; (2) coach the team in process skills (Williams, 1993; Scearce, 1992; Fullan, 1993; Joyce & Showers, 1983), including consensus-seeking strategies and conflict-resolution techniques (Williams, 1993); and (3) provide valid feedback and appropriate support, as indicated by the growth of the teams (Joyce and Showers, 1983).

Team facilitators are needed as trouble-shooters to help groups get unstuck when they are land-locked over an issue.

The site facilitator or team coach is always a visible, accessible resource person to whom teams may look for help. This may be the building principal, staff developer, or teacher who has opportunity for frequent interactions. Teams may also seek expert opinions, outside consultants and specialists, guest speakers, relevant materials, networking opportunities, or any number of other viable services. While the facilitator may not be able to fulfill all the roles, he or she certainly can be there to move the process along, especially until teams are ready to take certain responsibilities on as their own.

Team facilitators are needed as troubleshooters to help groups get unstuck when they are landlocked over an issue (Williams, 1992). Although teams are taught conflict resolution skills throughout the year in ongoing staff development offerings, teams sometimes need an outside mediator (or arbitrator) if they are to continue to function and develop (Williams, 1992;

Schmuck and Schmuck, 1988). "Guide on the side" implies that the "sage leaves the stage" (Schlechty, 1990) and takes a parallel position to the team itself. However, there are moments when an unbiased decision is the only way to dislodge the logjam that sometimes occurs in even the highest-functioning groups.

Finally, the facilitator ensures that teams celebrate their successes in some way (Scearce, 1992; Johnson, 1979; Schmuck, 1988). This is sometimes a missed phased in the process, but is a crucial element if teams are to develop to a sophisticated level for long-term involvement.

THREE-RING CIRCUS: THE TEAMING CONFERENCE

An added element to the long-range goal of building teams for curriculum integration is the idea of a teaming conference. Just as the retreat serves a special purpose in the initiation of teamwork, the teaming conference serves as a particular purpose, too. It is a high-profile event that permits massive training opportunities in skills and strategies that all school teams need. This might occur in the spring, for example, when the teaming conference focuses sessions on leadership, cooperative skills, process strategies, trust-building techniques, thematic teaching, thinking skills, learning styles, multiple intelligences, total quality, and developing significant outcomes and assessment procedures.

A teaming conference acts much like a leadership academy in which specific training is available. Teams attend the sessions that meet their immediate needs and concerns. For example, one team may want an in-depth session on thematic instruction, while another team may need training in cooperative learning. The conference allows for individual choice.

In addition, a teaming conference offers opportunities for sharing ideas and networking with other teams. After all, teams learn as much from other teams as they do from a facilitator. This conference idea gives working teams assurance that ongoing support and training are there for the long run. It is but one platform for team growth and development. However, to avoid the one-shot, smorgasbord approach to staff development (Joyce and Showers, 1983), additional, ongoing sharing and training opportunities are also a part of the larger plan.

Figure 3
Finding a Meeting Time

Purchased time	summer vacation or vacation planning
Borrowed time	Four days x fifteen-minute early arrival = one hour on Friday
Common time	block scheduling
New time	teacher incentives for their time
Freed-up time	parent volunteers or senior citizens
Tiered time	lunch/brunch or breakfast club
Found time	student teacher or unexpected time
Better-used time	faculty and department meetings/memos
Rescheduled time	back to back
Released time	professional development days

Extrapolated from *Time for Reform* by Purnell and Hill and NEA Center for Innovations.

A FINAL WORD: IT'S UP TO US

Until teachers begin the conversation across disciplines and between grade levels, curriculum integration is not likely to happen. To start the process, teacher teams must become a reality. Teachers must have frequent formal and informal opportunities to talk to each other in professional dialogues about curricular concerns.

Figure 3 provides food for thought as teams struggle with the challenge of finding time to meet. Just by being creative with the possibilities suggested by the list, time can be made for team meetings and planning—if they are real priorities.

For conversation to begin, decisions include whether or not to have school teams and student clusters, how to form the teams, ways to begin conversation across the disciplines, how to train the skills and facilitate the process, and when and how to troubleshoot for the teams. These decisions are determined by our teams. Yet, two questions remain: Are we ready to begin the conversation about who will integrate the curricula? Are we ready to make the critical decisions about teacher teams?

REFERENCES

Barth, R. S. (1990). *Improving schools from within: Teachers, parents and principals can make a difference.* San Francisco: Jossey-Bass.

Bellanca, J., & Fogarty, R. (1991). *Blueprints for thinking in the cooperative classroom* (Second Edition). Palatine, IL: IRI/Skylight Publishing.

Bellanca, J., & Fogarty, R. (1986). *Catch them thinking: A handbook of classroom strategies.* Palatine, IL: IRI/Skylight Publishing.

Bennett, B., & Rolheiser-Bennett, C. (1992). A restructuring journey. In Costa, A., Bellanca, J., & Fogarty, R. (Eds.), *If minds matter: A foreword to the future, Volume 1* (pp. 103–123). Palatine, IL: IRI/Skylight Publishing.

Bloom, B. S. (Ed.) (1984). *Taxonomy of educational objectives: The classification of educational goals, handbook 1: Cognitive domain.* New York: Longman.

Eisner, E. (1985). *The educational imagination: On the design and evaluation of school programs* (Second Edition). New York: Macmillan.

Fogarty, R. (1991). *The mindful school: How to integrate the curricula.* Palatine, IL: IRI/Skylight Publishing.

Fogarty, R., & Bellanca, J. (1986). *Teach them thinking: Mental menus for 24 thinking skills.* Palatine, IL: IRI/Skylight Publishing.

Fullan, M. (1991). *The new meaning of educational change.* New York: Teachers College Press.

Fullan, M. (1989). *The meaning of educational change.* New York: Teachers College Press.

Gibbs, J. (1987). *Tribes.* Santa Rosa, CA: Center Source.

Glasser, W. (1990). *The quality school.* New York: Harper & Row.

Goodlad, J. I. (1984). *A place called school, prospects for the future.* New York: McGraw-Hill.

Jacobs, H. H. (1989). *Interdisciplinary curriculum: Design and implementation.* Alexandria, VA: Association for Supervision and Curriculum Development.

Johnson, D. W., & Johnson, R. T. (1979). Conflict in the classroom: Controversy and learning. *Review of Educational Research, 49,* 51–70.

Joyce, B. R., & Showers, B. (1983). *Power and staff development through research and training.* Alexandria, VA: Association of Supervision and Curriculum Development.

Krupp, J. A. (1982). *The adult learner: A unique entity.* Manchester, CT: Adult development and learning.

Krupp, J. A. (1981). *Adult development: Implications for staff development.* Manchester, CT: Adult development and learning.

Little, J. W. (1981, April). *School success and staff development in urban desegregated schools: A summary of completed research.* Boulder, CO: Center for Action Research.

Lortie, D. C. (1975). *School teacher: A sociological study.* Chicago: The University of Chicago Press.

Loucks-Horsley, S., Phlegar, J., & Stiegelbauer, S. (1992). New visions for staff development. In Costa, A., Bellanca, J., & Fogarty, R. (Eds.), *If minds matter: A foreword to the future, Volume 1* (pp. 149–162). Palatine, IL: IRI/Skylight Publishing.

Merenbloom, E. Y. (1991). *The team process: A handbook for teachers.* Columbus, OH: National Middle School Association.

Peters, T., & Waterman, R., Jr. (1982). *In search of excellence: Lessons from America's best-run companies.* New York: Harper & Row.

Purnell, S., & Hill, P. (1992). *Time for reform.* Santa Monica, CA: RAND.

Sarason, S. (1990). *The predictable failure of educational reform.* San Francisco: Jossey-Bass.

Scearce, C. (1993). *100 ways to build teams.* Palatine, IL: IRI/Skylight Publishing.

Schlecty, P. C. (1990). *Schools for the 21st century: Leadership imperatives for educational reform.* San Francisco: Jossey-Bass.

Schmuck, R. A., & Schmuck, P. A. (1988). *Group processes in the classroom.* Dubuque, IA: W. C. Brown.

Vars, G. (1991, October). Integrated curriculum in historical perspective. *Educational Leadership*, pp. 14–15.

Williams, R. B. (1993). *More than 50 ways to build team consensus.* Palatine, IL: IRI/Skylight Publishing.

Vignettes: Integrating Curricula

by Robin Fogarty

The mission *impossible* is manifested in the concept of *school restructuring.* School restructuring seems much like the restructuring of a tree into a tree house. The existing vertical structure is solidly in place. Scraps are used to improvise a structure that is designed to keep people out. The tree house is functional but it is bound by the limitations of the original structure. Much like the restructured school, the results are often neither visible nor laudable.

On the other hand, the mission *possible* is in *reconceptualizing our schools.* Reconceptualizing schooling is more like building a sand castle. The natural resources are plentiful and the ever-expanding horizontal design is inherent. As the vision of the sand castle begins to take shape, it invites others into the process. Soon, many interested parties dig in, on hands and knees, and become energized by the creativity that is underway. The results are almost always visible and often times applauded.

The difference between *restructuring schools* and *reconceptualizing schooling* is critical.

The difference between *restructuring schools* and *reconceptualizing schooling* is critical. The vision of a sand castle is appealing; it engages our spirits as well as our skills. To better understand the reconceptualization process, three schools share their visions of sand castles. Each has a distinct and clear mission of schooling that guides every action of the educator-architect. Each has a mission made possible by the collaborative efforts of all involved. And they are energized by their belief in what they are doing. See what you think. Are these missions *impossible?* Do they burden teachers with unfounded mandates? Or are these missions *possible?* Do they renew the spirit and the skills of teachers?

MISSION POSSIBLE: INTEGRATION OF THE ARTS

Music, art, and dance permeate the interior of the one-hundred-year-old building that houses a school dedicated to the arts on Chicago's west side. Entering the school, one is greeted by an enormous mural of young African-American and Hispanic figures, reminiscent of the force of human activity depicted in Rembrandt's *The Night Watch.* The mural lines the unbannistered wall of the stairwell that leads to the main hallway. The skillful sophistication of the figures belies the tender ages and shy demeanor of the student-artists. It's difficult to take your eyes away as you move on down the hall in the direction of the main office.

The mission is . . . to integrate the visual and performing arts into the lives of all the students.

The mural, however, is just the beginning. It's a sign of things to come. Everything at this school is done in a big way; everything is filled with energy and drama. The halls are as wide as a two-lane highway; the classrooms have huge floor-to-ceiling windows; and the famed skylight of stained glass is awesome in the art wing. But, the mission is the biggest of all: to integrate the visual and performing arts into the lives of all the students.

"Unheard of!" you say, when you realize that this is not a magnet school of selected or solicited students, but an inner-city, neighborhood school in the heart of gang territory. "A school of the arts? Isn't that a bit high-brow under the circumstances? Isn't this a mission impossible?" Well, you don't know this principal and her staff.

This is a woman who, without warning, sends tickets to her staff in the mail with instructions to catch a train at a designated time. Playing along, the teachers arrive at the station, find the train, and board through the first car. Suddenly, they see their fearless leader, slumped over in a seat, with a knife in her back. And the mystery ride begins.

This marvelously engaging team-building stunt is just one of the crazy and innovative ways that the teacher group has learned to become an unstoppable team. A staff retreat, made possible by a $5,000 cash award, brought the teachers together, voluntarily, for a weekend to sort out their ideas, develop a shared vision, and crystallize their mission. Emerging from that first retreat with ongoing meetings, trainings, and networking partnerships, an integrated model of schooling began to take shape.

Driven by the vision of curriculum and instruction, incorporated with the visual and performing arts, an integrated scheme develops (Fogarty, 1991). In this design, traditional disciplines such as math, science, social studies, and language arts use the vehicle of the arts to carry the subject matter content into meaningful learning experiences. Figure 1 shows an integrated learning design.

Figure 1
Integrated Learning Design

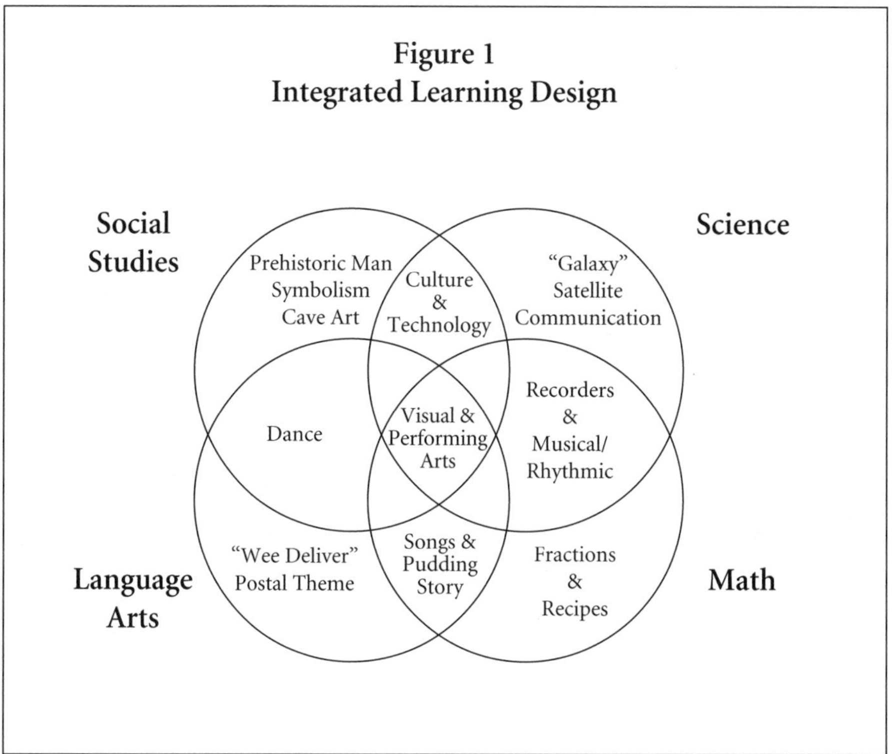

As students study a social studies unit on cultures and symbols, cave art is authentically displayed in an actual-size paper maché cave that is housed in the art gallery on the third floor. Music fills the air. Students embrace the songs and dances of the studied cultures as the rhythm and beat of global villages rock the walls of the school.

The satellite dish on the flat-roofed school proclaims the school's commitment to technology as an integrative thread.

In another room, the sweet, harmonic sound of recorders drifts into the hallway. Very young students, paired to share music stands, gingerly play these simple instruments as an entrée into the formal band program. Here the saying goes, "Everyone will learn to read music and play the recorder. And when they're big enough and get their two front teeth, they can join the band."

"Wee Deliver," a schoolwide theme, sponsored by the U.S. Postal Service, dictates zoning the halls of the school à la the federal zip code system: Disney Town 16025, Star Park 11789, Curiosity Heights 31452, and Motown 21879. The theme creates a natural forum for continued and purposeful writing across the curriculum and across the grade levels. Stamps, designed by the children, are featured each month from a different classroom. Student workers interview for the positions in the post office, which entail early morning sorting and delivery routes. Student responsibilities include training new inductees and maintaining new stamp releases. Although this began as a one-year theme, the principal emphasizes that the school's postal service is now an integral part of the children's lives, and it will continue each year in tandem with the other selected themes.

Technology is an additional integrative thread at this school. Cable hookups throughout the school begin in the teacher's resource room. A cable and wire branch out from a central source resembling the tentacled outreaches of an oversized octopus. This center is referred to as the Heart Room of the school as the programming pulses through the various classrooms. The satellite dish on the flat-roofed school proclaims the school's commitment to technology as an integrative thread. One third grade classroom, as part of the Galaxy

Project, communicates by fax with twenty-nine schools across the United States. Regional and cultural diversities are natural outgrowths of study in this high-tech communication network.

While the impetus for this school's mission is embedded in the concept of integration of the arts, science technology and mathematical reasoning fall easily under that organizational umbrella. Mathematical concepts, logic, and relevant scientific application are inherent in everything the children do. In one lesson, they use their knowledge of fractions to create pudding from a converted recipe, which in turn acts as a springboard for a science experiment on the changes of matter. In another classroom, students calculate their weight on the various planets as they read a book about other cultures, the climate, and how people need people.

Just as in any K–8 building across the continent, children's artwork wallpapers the walls. But, here, the art decoration goes beyond the norm. For in addition to a large, third-floor art gallery that houses an array of ever-changing exhibits and displays of authentic children's art, the school lunchroom also echoes the mission of the arts integration theme. Modeled after any fine dining establishment, soft music serenades the student patrons of this frequented lunch spot. As one enters the main dining room, two large pictures adorn the back wall, and a painting of a muscle man looks down from the side. Spotted with potted plants, half-walls divide the space. The seating arrangements resemble the careful sectioning of a well-managed restaurant.

This school is the reality of a mission made *possible* by the creativity, ingenuity, and hard work of an unstoppable team of dedicated teachers, parents, and staff. While the integration of the arts is a mission possible, it is also one that is, by its nature, a dynamic, ever-evolving concept. An emerging schema that guides the integrative learning is sketched here (see Figure 2). But, further refinement is inevitable. You can count on it.

MISSION POSSIBLE: INTEGRATION OF LIFE SKILLS

Escorted by the PE Division Head, interested parties are ushered down the main hallway to a stairwell that leads past the gym to the lower-level, "health club" atmosphere. In a center, caged area, one notices a group of students using the exercise equipment: bicycles, weight machines, a stair stepper, and a

Figure 2
Integration of the Arts—Mission Possible

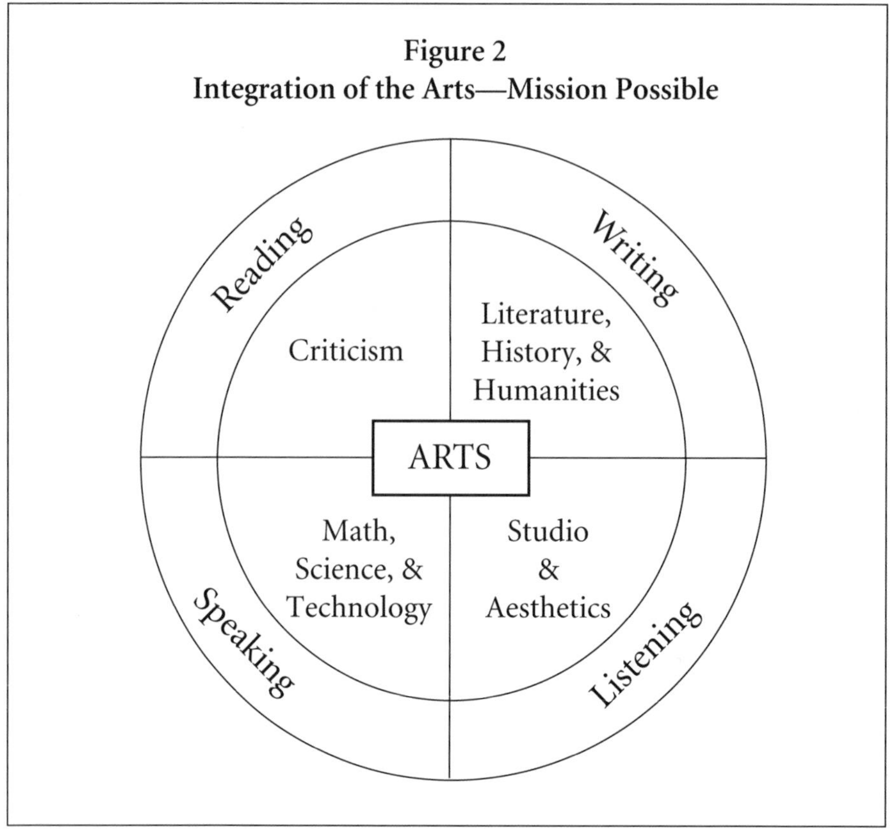

cross-country ski machine. Other students are running, jogging, and walking around the quarter-mile track that circles the center cage. In another area, a student intern leads a small group in stretching and toning routines.

Adjacent to the workout area, a large office, sprinkled with teachers' desks and lined with shelves of loose paper handouts, houses the various instructors. One young teacher leads a freshman through the orientation procedures by walking her through a series of evaluations: fat content, endurance, agility, flexibility, cardiovascular limits, and the usual height, weight, and body type assessments. Using this information, the student sets a ten-week goal to either lose weight, break her mile record, train for a marathon, or simply maintain a particular metabolism rate. Together they develop a physical-fitness plan based on the particular problem or to challenge the student.

In the meantime, students in the upstairs gym participate in a field hockey drill as part of their two-day-a-week, more traditional PE program. Boys and girls together scramble up and down the court as they practice the rudiments of the game.

Based on the enthusiastic responses of both teachers and students to this problem-solving approach to health and fitness, the faculty launched the idea of threading life skills across all the curricular areas. Embracing problem solving as their primary life-skill strategy, the faculty is introduced to a simple, generic model, I-D-E-A-L, through a series of staff development offerings: mini-workshops during the lunch hour, after-school sessions, and more in-depth release-time trainings for interested volunteers. With in-district leadership of educators committed to staff development and the support of key department people and administrators, the training tasks get done.

Supporting the problem-solving goal, large laminated posters adorn the walls in every classroom. The I-D-E-A-L model permeates the climate and, more importantly, the instructional focus of this high school (see Figure 3).

Problem Solving Becomes the Thread

In a rare and refreshing approach to traditional sequenced math and biology classes, an energetic team of five math teachers decides to realign their math content to coincide with relevant applications that occur naturally in the biology classes. Breaking radically from the standard scope and sequence that follows the algebra–geometry–trigonometry format, these creatively thinking math experts meet with the biology team.

Figure 3
The I-D-E-A-L Model

Identify the problem.
Describe your alternatives.
Evaluate your alternatives.
Act on your plan.
Learn from your experiences.

Through scheduling initiatives that cluster students and assign a cluster to the math and science team for the four years, innovative curriculum designs get underway as the conversations across disciplines begin.

The dialogue leads to commonsense connections between the two content areas as students are introduced to the math concepts that apply to their work in the science lab. Although not all members of the two departments are ready for this sort of radical shift in content, certainly the problem-solving approach is at work in a worthy pilot project. Giving consideration to long-term change, four years seem sufficient to gather the necessary data to evaluate the approach.

As team members explain, "We're not happy with the math program the way it is. We're losing a lot of kids at the upper levels and their skills seem lost and isolated from practical applications."

"While we understand that not everyone thinks this is a good idea, we're ready to go."

"We know we're going to need solid data to convince others, but we think that by working with the same group of kids over the four years, we'll get to know them well enough to ensure success for all students in our cluster. Of course, it will have to show on their ACTs and SATs if we're to convince others, but we feel pretty confident that we've got a good, solid plan here."

In still another area, integration of life skills is the target of a course called Family Living, directed by a two-teacher team well-grounded in business education, home arts, social studies, and psychology. Budgets, babies, and the business of daily living are the concerns in this lively class.

The following activity begins their day.

"O.K., roll the dice. Let's see if these young marrieds are about to have a baby. Remember, if seven or eleven comes up, you'll be the lucky parents of a newborn baby girl or boy."

"Well, here goes, Marla. Keep your fingers crossed," yells David as he tosses the dice onto the tabletop.

"Congratulations! You're the proud parents of a baby boy! Now, don't forget, you'll need to complete the birth certificate, revise your budget, and plan for the baby's arrival home."

After the excitement dies down, small groups disperse to the various designations. One couple, at the computer, displays a spreadsheet that contains budget figures. Another group works out low-budget, nutritious meals for the week, and yet another couple makes decisions about furnishing an apartment.

"Teaming is the best vitamin my teaching has had in a long time. I'm so energized for this class, I can't believe it."

"How's it going? Are you able to purchase everything you'll need?" one teacher asks.

"Well, the money's going faster than we thought. There definitely won't be a television in our kitchen."

"What about the essentials, like a toaster, kitchen utensils, bedroom furniture, and linens?"

"Oh, yeah! We've got the basics covered. We're just trying to stretch it to include the 'wanna gets' too. But, it's not looking very promising."

Following the tour through this diverse sea of problematic situations, the two teachers expound on the benefits and serendipitous effects on themselves as teachers.

"Teaming is the best vitamin my teaching has had in a long time. I'm so energized for this class, I can't believe it."

"I feel the same way. Working with a colleague this closely has provided an unbelievable boost to my spirit . . . and skills. It's really fun to be able to share all the things the kids think of, with someone who knows them as well as I do. I'll team every chance I get."

While numerous examples of problem solving abound in the school, one other collaborative effort illustrates the level of commitment the staff has to its mission of integrating life skills through the curriculum. In addition to problem solving as a thread, a three-year plan also includes two other priorities that the faculty has agreed to: (1) developing student responsibility and self-esteem as integral parts of the mission, and (2) reading across the curriculum. Both threads have been introduced over time. The teachers give their approval:

"Jurassic Park! Perfect! What a timely theme for us to use with the students. It bridges biology and literature and sets up a viable platform for theorizing and hypothesizing."

"And the kids are crazy with dinosaur fever because of the movie. It's relevant and interesting to them. It really is a good idea for both the problem-solving thread and the reading goals."

"In fact, we can even include the responsibility piece as we talk about the responsibilities that accompany man's scientific advances."

"It really is timely, too, because we can feed off the movie and have the kids analyze the similarities and differences between the book and the film."

"Not only that, but I'm excited about having teachers use science fiction as a problem-solving method."

"Well, it looks like we've got our start. Let's get to work."

In one last example of a rich model for threading life skills into the high school content, the journalism teachers use the school newspaper as the vehicle to carry the technology skills of word processing and desktop publishing. In the process of putting the paper to press, students must make many decisions about the production process, just as they would in a real-life career as a newsperson.

Without a doubt, over the past three years this high school has turned its vision of schooling into a mission *possible.* Students are enabled to grow and mature with skills they'll use not just for a test, but for a lifetime (see Figure 4).

MISSION POSSIBLE: INTEGRATION OF THE MULTIPLE INTELLIGENCES

Submitted and approved by their board of education, educators at a suburban elementary school have turned the challenge of an expanding student population into a mission of collaboration and innovation.

Committed to Gardner's theory of multiple intelligences, teachers at this recently reopened elementary school in western Illinois web the curricular content to seven different ways of knowing. Veteran and novice teachers alike express an interest in developing schooling around the multiple intelligences.

Figure 4
Integration of Life Skills—Mission Possible

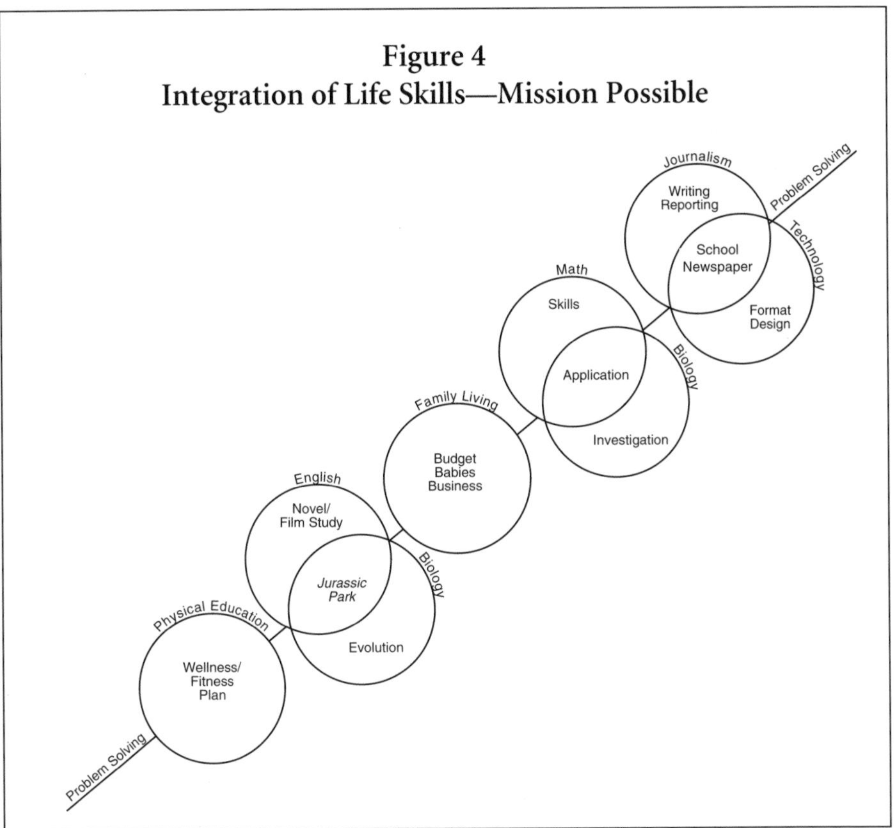

In each of the classrooms, explicit connections are made from a theme or lesson focus to authentic learning projects and episodes that include all seven identified intelligences:

1. the word-related pair: verbal intelligence and musical intelligence
2. the object-related trio: bodily intelligence, spatial intelligence, and mathematical intelligence
3. the personal-related intelligence pair: interpersonal intelligence and intrapersonal intelligence

A look in a primary classroom tells one part of this mission *possible.* Sweet and melodic guitar music drifts down the hall as one approaches this primary classroom. Perched on a high wooden stool, the teacher leads the singing as the children's voices build to an enthused and robust crescendo. Then, as if someone literally opens a can of worms, the milieu of bodies wiggle and squirm in delight at the impromptu applause of the first grade visitors.

Guided by the teachers, youngsters make their way to their assigned areas. The morning's next activity builds from the musical intelligence and includes strategies of other intelligences.

"Now, children, in your small groups, please recall the 'Old Favorite' story that you've read and chart your information on the story map. Be sure to include as many details as possible as you collect your information. And don't forget to draw your pictures to help tell your story." (Notice how the teacher taps into several intelligences: interpersonal, verbal/linguistic, and visual/spatial. See Figure 5.)

The children immediately start talking enthusiastically about the stories and slot in the information needed. A visual tour of the room reveals a museum of the children's collectibles. Each one has created an exhibit of old favorites collected over time and the display includes Barbie dolls, trolls, dinosaurs, teddy bears, car and coin collections, marbles, bottle caps, and

Figure 5
"Old Favorite" Story Map

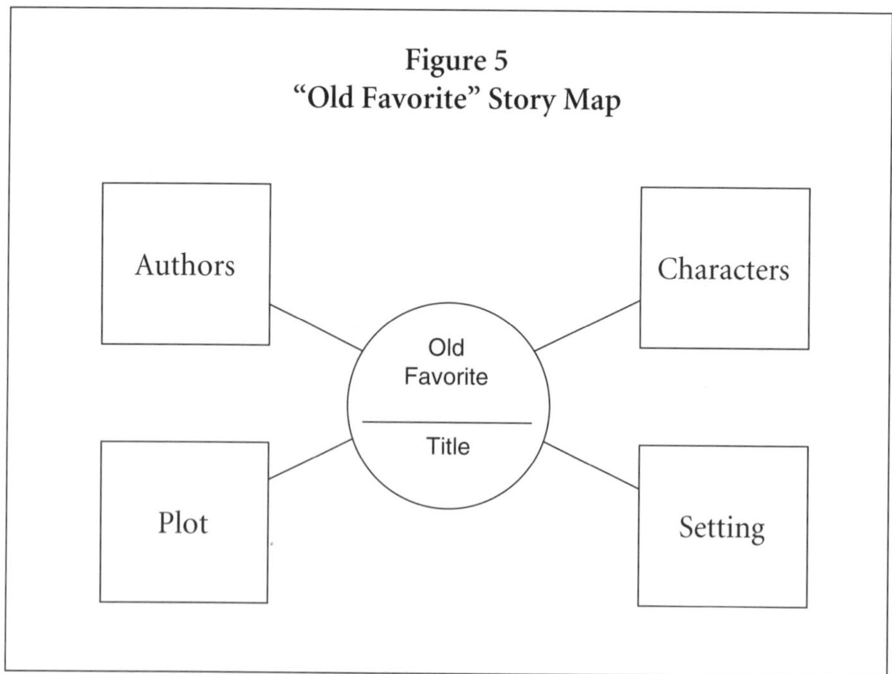

baseball cards. The intrapersonal intelligence is definitely in action here, as students exhibit their personal collections and expose their private feelings.

On the windowed wall, atop the metal bookcases, shoeboxes line the outer edges of this busy and noisy classroom. Each scene, carefully constructed with colored paper and household props that include toothpicks, toilet paper spools, and plastic figures, depicts the favorite stories of the children. In this whole language classroom, the mission to integrate the multiple intelligences into the lesson is not just one possible way—it is the most natural way.

Moving to the upper-elementary levels, two other classrooms epitomize Gardner's theory of teaching and learning with the multiple intelligences. One involves a sixth grade science unit on cells, while the other targets thinking and theory making in a fifth grade unit on evolution. With the science/health content focusing on cells, the creative teacher orchestrates an innovative, hands-on project for an active learning experience.

In cooperative groups, students design a working model that demonstrates the process of cell diffusion. Each team uses its combined creativity to build and explain its invention. The energy and enthusiasm in this classroom bubbles through the room as students engage their bodily/kinesthetic, logical/mathematical, and verbal/linguistic intelligences (see Figure 6).

"Remember, your model must show the sequence of what happens as the cell membrane acts as a guard, letting certain things in and keeping other things out."

Moving toward a group of four chattering boys, the teacher suggests, "Compare your model to actual cell diffusion. Use your organized ideas on the Venn diagram to help you explain your model."

"Well, we used golf balls and marbles. The marbles, because of their smaller size, slip through the tube easily, while the golf balls are effectively stopped."

"It's just like you said; the cell diffuses some things and stops or guards against others."

"Yeah! It works just like it's described in the science book."

Figure 6
Multiple Approaches

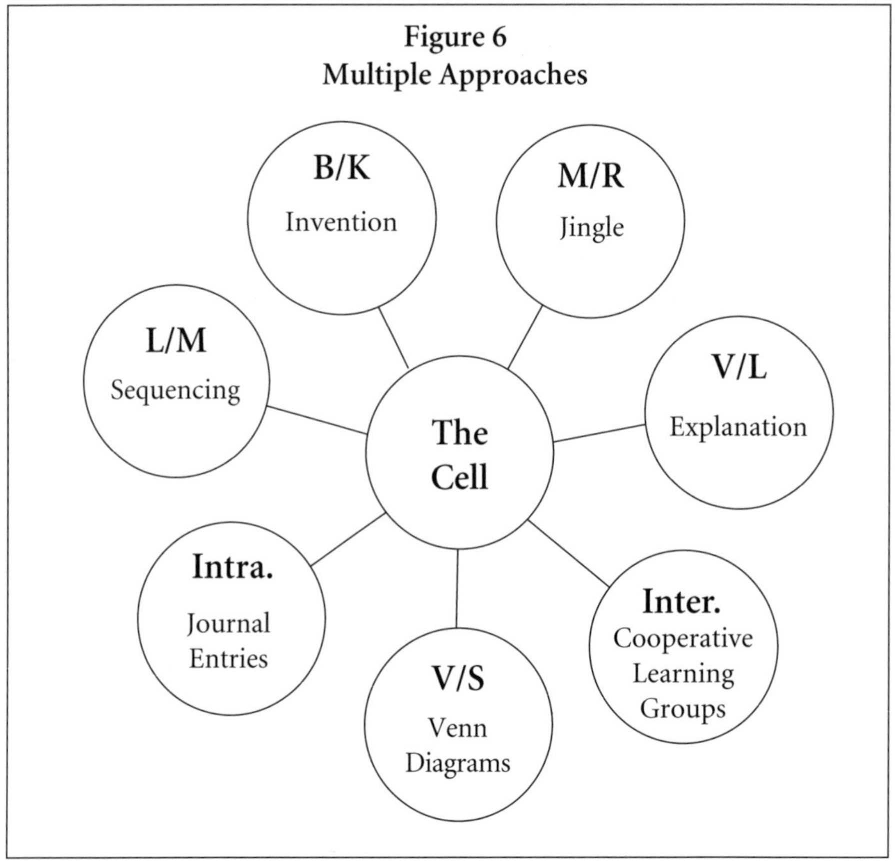

Pleased with the students' apparent understanding of the concept of cell diffusion, this sixth grade teacher assigns the next part of the project.

"For tomorrow, you are to present a jingle that explains and advertises your inventive model of cell diffusion. Be as creative as you can and use rhythms, beat, and melody to promote your model."

One group begins to work:

"O.K.! Now, we need to find a familiar song and then write the lyrics to fit the melody."

"How about something everyone knows, like 'Jingle Bells'?"

"That might work. Listen." (The student sings to the melody of "Jingle Bells.") "Cell diffusion, cell diffusion, cell diffusion all the way. Oh, what fun . . ."

"I've got another idea. Let's each work on this at home. Then we can come in a little early and select and learn the song that we like best. This way, we'll all have to know how cell diffusion works because we'll have to put our ideas in the song."

The teacher comments while passing by the group, "That's a good idea. I'm really proud of the way this team has shown its use of all seven intelligences. Be sure to appreciate each other with some words of thanks."

Down another hallway, fifth graders theorize with this launch question: What happened to the dinosaurs?

"Well, this is just a theory, but our group thinks that the continental shift (draws diagram on the board) brought with it colder climates, which in turn affected the food supply."

"Yeah, and when the food chain was interrupted, the dinosaurs eventually died out."

"That seems pretty logical. Does any other group have a plausible cause for the extinction of the dinosaurs?"

"Our team thinks that the plant-eating dinosaurs ate poisonous berries, and as they died off, the meat-eating dinosaurs soon had no food source."

"We think that the dinosaurs were caught in a plague of some sort. Maybe a bug bit them—like the mosquitoes that spread malaria—and the sickness eventually wiped out the entire population."

In their efforts to create logical theories, students use their multiple intelligences in a natural flow of learning (see Figure 7): the logical/mathematical intelligence is revealed in their reasoning sequences, while the verbal/linguistic is also tapped into in the justification process. In addition, the cooperative learning groups give students opportunities to work together in interpersonal efforts.

Not evidenced in the student dialogue, but orchestrated by the teacher, additional activities tap the other intelligences identified by Gardner. For example, following the theory-making session, students use their visual/spatial intelligence with Venn

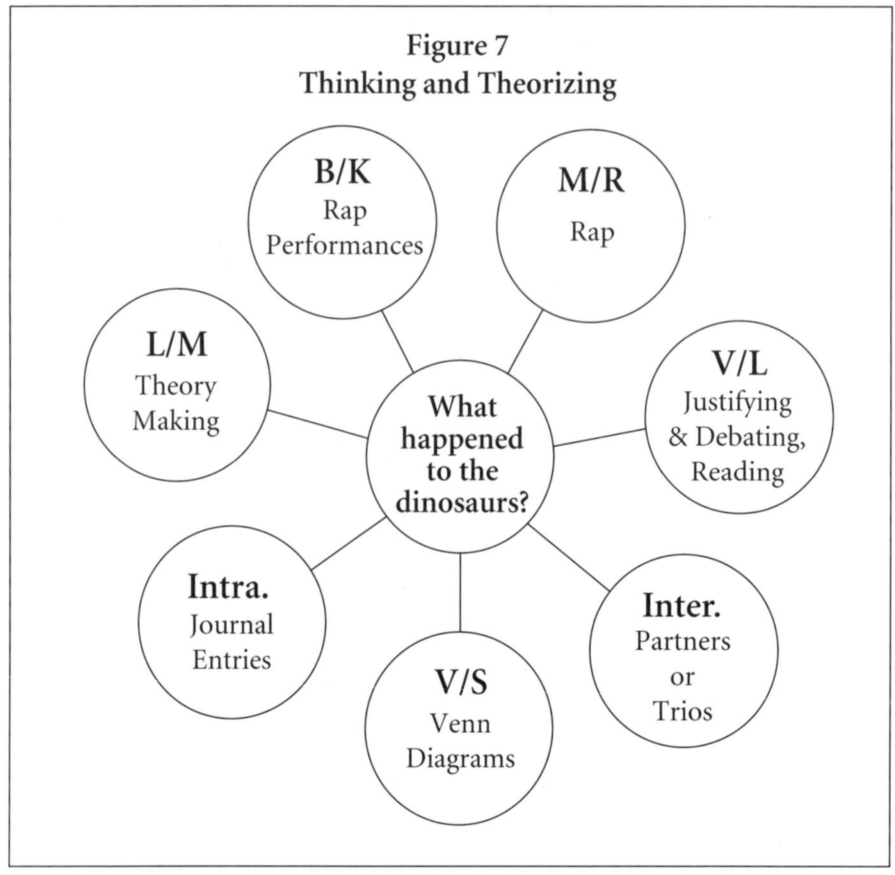

diagrams to compare and contrast their theory to the one in the text.

Journal writing is an introspective process incorporated to help students reflect on their learning and learn about the intrapersonal intelligence, as well as to relate ideas from class discussions to their readings.

As a dramatic, high-energy finale to the unit, each group creates a rap song about their theory-making process. Carefully delineated theory-making strategies are presented in rap with appropriate hand and body motions to complete the fully developed performance. One group raps with its musical/rhythmic intelligence.

"We can synthesize,
We can prioritize,

We can dramatize, and
we can even hypothesize.
But most of all—
We love to theorize!
Theorize! Theorize!
That's our favorite exercise."

Whether it be a whole language unit called "Old Favorites," using analogy to build models of cells, or an exercise in forming personal theories about intriguing phenomena, multiple intelligences make one school's mission a mission *possible.* Using our seven ways of knowing, learning becomes a logical outgrowth of our natural abilities.

IN CONCLUSION

The work of these innovative educators clearly shows how the sand castle of our minds can become a reality in our schools. The missions are diverse—integration of the arts, threading life skills into content lessons, and organizing brain-compatible learning through the multiple intelligences. The visions have never been more clear, and it is the clarity of the ideas that makes these missions possible. When we know where we're headed and when we make the decision to go forward, nothing is impossible.

Perhaps, inspired by the stories of these schools, you too can envision your school's "sand castle." If you can, accept the mission—and make the impossible possible!

REFERENCES

Brandt, R. (1987/1988, December/January). On discipline-based art education: A conversation with Elliot Eisner. *Educational Leadership,* pp. 6–9.

Burke, K. (1994). *The mindful school: How to assess authentic learning.* Palatine, IL: IRI/Skylight Publishing.

Chapman, C. (1993). *If the shoe fits . . . : How to develop multiple intelligences in the classroom.* Palatine, IL: IRI/Skylight Publishing.

Costa, A. L. (1991). *The school as a home for the mind.* Palatine, IL: IRI/ Skylight Publishing.

de Bono, E. (1992). *Serious creativity: Using the power of lateral thinking to create new ideas.* New York: Harper Collins.

Eisner, E. (1979). *The educational imagination.* New York: MacMillan.

Feuerstein, R. (1980). *Instrumental enrichment.* Baltimore: University Park Press.

Fogarty, R. (1991). *The mindful school: How to integrate the curricula.* Palatine, IL: IRI/Skylight Publishing.

Fogarty, R., & Bellanca, J. A. (1987). *Patterns for thinking: Patterns for transfer.* Palatine, IL: IRI/Skylight Publishing.

Gardner, H. (1993). *Multiple intelligences: The theory in practice.* New York: Basic Books.

Gardner, H. (1983). *Frames of mind: The theory of multiple intelligences.* New York: Basic Books.

Gardner, H. (1982). *Art, mind, and brain.* New York: Basic Books.

Perkins, D. N. (1992). *Smart schools: From training memories to educating minds.* New York: The Free Press.

Section 2

Thoughtful Instruction . . . Teaching with Rigor and Vigor

There are one-story intellects, two-story intellects, and three-story intellects with skylights. All fact collectors, who have no aim beyond their facts, are one-story men. Two-story men compare, reason, generalize, using the labors of the fact collectors as well as their own. Three-story men idealize, imagine, predict—their best illumination comes from above, through the skylight.—Oliver Wendell Holmes

Teaching *for*, *of*, *with*, and *about* thinking is the key to the thoughtful classroom. To critically and creatively challenge youngsters, to engage their minds and ignite their spirits is the mission of schooling. The five articles in this section reveal ways that skillful teachers can teach with rigor, vigor, and passion.

"Capture the Vision: Future World, Future School" attempts to create an image of life beyond the schoolyard walls. Within this worldly context, viable strategies are outlined to provoke thoughtful classroom behavior. Using Toffler's (1970) future school predictions, the implications for cooperative learning, metacognition, and problem solving as key instructional elements in all schools are convincingly conveyed.

The second article, "Cognition in Practice," examines the research base supporting the thoughtful classroom. Included in this survey are several theoretical positions. These include the research on teaching explicit thinking skills, cognitive organizers, metacognition, and transfer.

The cornerstone piece for thoughtful instruction is "Educating Teachers for Higher-Order Thinking: The Three-Story Intellect." Through a historic tracking of the thinking skills movement, a logical path for teaching teachers how to teach thinking is revealed. Based on the three-story intellect described by Holmes, a progressive plan unfolds.

Multiple intelligences also provide an avenue for thoughtful instruction. Grounded in Gardner's (1983) theory, the fourth article, "Multiple Intelligences: Integrated Instruction," surveys the seven frames of mind and suggests how these might look in the classroom as teachers tap into the talents of all children.

This section concludes with "Vignettes: Teaching Thinking," a series of five thoughtful instruction classroom examples. Circling back to the key to the thoughtful classroom—teaching for, of, with, and about thinking—five teachers are metaphorically presented. The guide, the wizard, the coach, the weaver, and the counselor represent varying levels of the thoughtful classroom.

This section only scratches the surface in terms of the complex interactions necessary for truly thought-provoking instruction. Yet, the selections give a flavor of the many ingredients required to help kids think, create, and problem solve.

REFERENCES

Gardner, H. (1983). *Frames of mind.* New York: Basic Books.

Toffler, A. (1970). *Future shock.* New York: Bantam Books.

Capture the Vision: Future World, Future School

by Robin Fogarty and James Bellanca

The year 2000 is less than a decade away. By then, the body of learnable information will have doubled four times since 1988. Students who will graduate from high school in the twenty-first century are in the classroom today. Just as Gutenberg's press revolutionized what and how students learned four centuries ago, the microchip will continue to alter teaching and learning in the next century. Schooling in the electronic age may bear little resemblance to the linear print classroom so familiar to us.

Schooling in the electronic age may bear little resemblance to the linear print classroom so familiar to us.

What will schooling look like in the year 2000? By updating the works of Toffler, Naisbitt, Ferguson, Cetron, Kearns, Doyle, and Osborne with a study of the most current headlines, demographic data, and observations of technological developments already commonplace in the home, school, and workplace, we can sketch a portrait of the future school with three emerging trends: *interpersonal interaction, idea innovation,* and *information interpretation.* By analyzing each trend with a future learner's perspective, we can forecast implications for education. The trend of interpersonal interaction suggests the growing need for *learning how to relate;* idea innovation calls for an increased emphasis on *learning how to learn;* and information interpretation for *learning how to choose.* Together, the three trends give us a vision of what is ahead for today's students in the world of tomorrow.

From *If Minds Matter: A Foreword to the Future, Vol. 1*, pp. 13–23. © 1992 by IRI/Skylight Publishing, Inc.

Figure 1
Interpersonal Interactions: Future World

People	Politics
Single-Parent Family	Economic Interdependence
	Currency
Women Working	Trade
Corporate Mobility	Political Interdependence
	Super Powers
Baby Boom Echo	Third-World Countries
Rising Elderly Population	Cultural Interdependence
	Pacific Influence

INTERPERSONAL INTERACTION

The first trend, *interpersonal interaction*, shows society shifting from "me" to "we." Learning to interact and cooperate with culturally and socially diverse peers becomes the first key to school success. Shifts in demographics and politics mandate this change (see Figure 1).

People

In the United States, fewer than one in three families can be described as traditional nuclear families. The number of working women, the mobility of the corporate family, the single-parent household, and blended families created from remarriages continue to increase in number each year.

Also, the rising number of immigrants is changing the composition of neighborhoods. By the year 2000, more than half the school-age children in American cities will be from minority groups. The African-American population, Hispanic citizens, and an increasing number of Asian families will spread out from the inner cities to take jobs and residences in suburban villages.

By the year 2000, the elderly population will exceed thirty-two million people. As the health care industry uses technology to stretch the average life-span to eighty-one-plus years, elderly people stay in the job market longer, travel more, and provide an increasing number of voluntary services.

The overriding implication for the Future School is for students to learn how to relate in new and different ways.

Politics

At the national and global levels, we see the politics of interpersonal interaction reaching into every sector of society. Economic interdependence becomes more apparent in world trade and in the international stock indices. The export/import balance has effects around the world as we saw during the energy crisis. Currency prices make the news daily as the mark, yen, and pound influence the U.S. dollar. "Buy American," even in the American auto industry which championed the phrase, makes less sense as more major auto parts are imported and as partnerships between the "Big Three" and non-American automakers become commonplace.

With the end of the Cold War, the United States and Russia no longer control the world scene. Third-world countries, totalitarian governments, and terrorist groups all have an impact on global politics. The shrinking globe, made smaller by high-tech transportation and communication innovations, brings conflicts from around the world into our family rooms.

Culturally, economically, and politically, the Pacific influence continues to gain entry into all realms of our society. Business, real estate, trade, and education feel the impact of the Pacific wave. As the economic rivalry between the United States and Japan increases, concerns about trade wars and security differences grow.

Implication: Learning How to Relate

As we analyze the implications of this first trend, interpersonal interactions, the overriding implication for the Future School is for students to learn how to relate in new and different ways. With the rapid turnover of people in their lives, students in tomorrow's schools will need help in finding ways to accelerate

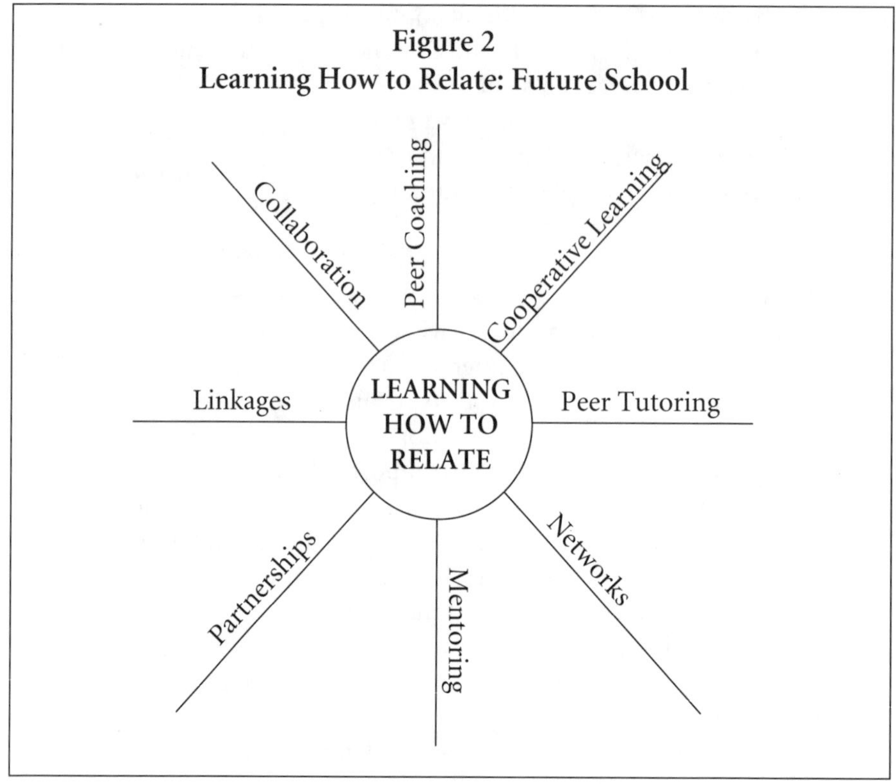

friendship formation, bond to stable forces in their lives, and develop the skills of collaboration. In the Future School, we will see a greater emphasis on these collaborative models (see Figure 2).

Cooperative learning teaches interactive social skills and provides peer bonding in the classroom. As students increase their capabilities to relate constructively with peers from more diverse cultural and socioeconomic groups, academic achievement, school-liking, and self-esteem will improve. Entire schools will develop a cooperative culture that immerses adults and young learners in collaborative learning.

Peer tutoring helps students learn from each other, both formally and informally, in their own age groups and across age groups and cultures. Not only will tutoring provide a practical tool for classroom teachers to help at-risk and slower-learning students, it will provide a rich opportunity for students to develop bonds with their peers.

Collaborative coaching teams and problem-solving teams help teachers and administrators work together to improve both instructional content and methodology for a student body with a wide range of cultural backgrounds, learning styles, and readiness to learn.

Networks of professionals from within districts and across district and state lines will meet face to face, communicating with colleagues in other states and countries through computers and satellites. Likewise, students will use electronic links to talk with peers around the country and across oceans or study cultures first-hand through video.

Mentoring programs bring experts of all ages in contact with each other. Schools will tap the expanding senior citizen pool for help in solving problems created by the demands of diversity. Without needing to leave their homes, students will use dial-help cable TV for homework assistance from elderly volunteers, teachers, and peers.

School-business partnerships at local, state, and national levels will expand ties between education and industry. Industry will provide an increasing number of fiscal and human resources to help schools better prepare students for the ever-changing work world.

Colleges and universities improve teacher preparation and the overall quality of schools. Research on how to improve schools and specialized continuing education programs for educators will strengthen the bonds between higher education and the K–12 community. Students, parents, and teachers will communicate through video and computer lines directly with experts on campus.

International exchange programs will introduce more students to the diverse cultures of the world. Students will work in teams to study the range of cultures that they find in their classrooms, to travel internationally, to explore ways to develop new perspectives for resolving conflict and creating harmony, and to continue the dialogue back home.

IDEA INNOVATION

The second trend, *idea innovation*, reveals the shift from the industrial society to the technological society. As information multiplies at rates faster than we can imagine, the need for a primary focus on learning how to learn becomes preeminent. An analysis of this trend brings us face to face with the high-tech/high-touch phenomenon. Here we quickly discover a unique irony endemic to an age in which technology creates more information than the human mind can digest. To the degree that impersonal technology and the information flood restructure our lives, interpersonal as well as intrapersonal interactions grow in importance. For each high-tech discovery, pressure mounts for a high-touch balance in which communication, positive relationships, and cultural understanding are essential (see Figure 3).

High-Tech

The high-tech explosion is best recognized in the wonderland of computers. Both hardware and software innovations are developing at such a rapid pace that it becomes an overwhelming task, if not an economic impossibility, to keep abreast of the most current developments.

As fast as new innovations appear in computer hardware, the advances in software are more surprising. Leading in the latest software creations is artificial intelligence. Programmers, most notably in the military and medical fields, are creating expert systems to solve highly specialized problems. In the business world, training design has shifted from print materials to multimedia interactions. Breakthroughs in software already in use emulate the decision-making processes of surgeons and anesthetists at the operating table, architects at the drawing board, and bio-engineers in the laboratory. Complementing the new developments in software are a variety of other innovations in electronics, communications, engineering, and production. In electronics, parallel processing systems are increasing the speed of intricate calculations for solving highly complex problems. Microchips are becoming smaller, faster, and more powerful. Already our autos, phone systems, and grocery store checkout registers are dependent on the microchip.

In the communications field, lasers, fiber optics, satellites, super conductors, and digital screens, all in concert with macrocomputers, are changing the speed, accuracy, and availability of long-distance and on-the-spot transactions. We can send an instantaneous picture of anything thousands of miles across

Figure 3
Idea Innovation: Future World

High-Tech

Computers	Lasers
Parallel Processing	Fiber Optics
Artificial Intelligence	Satellites
Genetic Engineering	Super Conductors
Bio-Chemistry	Digital Electronics
Plastics	Robotics
Polymers	

High-Touch

Physical Fitness
Nutrition
Environmental Concerns
Visualization
Eastern/Western Philosophies
Sports Motivation

continents and oceans on a fax machine. Back home, we can witness a laser light reading the coding bars on clothing, hardware, and food purchases. In the hospital operating room, we learn that the laser beam is making the surgical knife obsolete.

Technological breakthroughs in manufacturing and production are just as noteworthy. In manufacturing, high-impact plastics and polymers, microwave processing, and molecular engineering are revolutionizing the plant. In the future, we can expect new cars to be almost one hundred percent plastic.

We cannot discuss high-tech manufacturing without including robotics. Not only are these electronic helpmates taking over the dangerous, high-risk tasks, but also the repetitive assembly line jobs that require "six sigma" precision performance. In bio-medical plants, robots can stamp out millions of specially designed plastic containers, fill each with a precise formula and test content quality without the touch of a single human hand. Most amazing is that such robots in one major health products firm reduced wasted formula by 60 percent. In that same plant, robots are not replacing human workers as once feared. Instead, robots are increasing the demand to retain workers who can control the machines, analyze data, and suggest how to improve the product. As a result, higher quality is assured for the consumer. Visits to new manufacturing facilities in electronics, auto production, and aeronautics corroborate this trend.

Genetic engineering is providing some of the most eye-opening innovations. Within the next decade, genetic engineers foresee a form of genetic family screening that will be part of routine physical exams. Soon after a child's birth, doctors will correct defective and disease-bearing genes. Similarly, genetic engineers continue to make breakthroughs in food production. Their experiments are planned to double or triple the nutritional capacity of a single fruit or vegetable. Yes, we can build a better tomato.

High-Touch

This high-tech wave, which throws people into an electronic world of push-button devices, a world in which they spend their days interfacing with a computer screen instead of other human beings, has caused a backlash called high-touch. In the high-touch world, more and more people seek a fulfillment of human needs. This search emerges as a concern with physical fitness, health, nutrition, and general well-being.

High-touch is visible in the growing effort to balance economic and environmental concerns. Protesters step forward to battle over clean air and clean water. Worldwide and local organizations help save endangered species. Neighborhood groups band together to prevent corporations and local governments from building chemical and nuclear waste producing plants in their backyards.

We see another sign of high-touch in the emerging attention given to the body/mind connection. Corporations sponsor stress clinics and whole-health seminars. Drug and alcohol prevention programs have become as prevalent in professional sports leagues as in elementary schools. Eastern religion marries Western philosophy as professional athletes, Olympic stars, and high school heroes discover sports motivation and sports psychology. Physical training is complemented with visualization and meditation and the psyche is tapped to create the mental edge of champions.

High-touch is also evident in the concern for the values of family and life. Presidential candidates argue which party platform most supports the family. Right-to-life groups battle pro-choice advocates. Legislators struggle with ways to finance daycare, ways to support senior citizens, and ways to ease the problems of the homeless. TV stations, newspapers, professional athletes, foundations, and community agencies band together to battle drug and alcohol abuse.

By learning how to learn, students will develop . . . the key survival skill for the twenty-first century.

Implication: Learning How to Learn

As we examine the implications of *idea innovation*, the spotlight falls on the need for learning how to learn. By the year 2000, the likelihood of increased job and career changes and a longer lifespan argue for a focus on life-long learning. Students will face an increasing demand to learn, unlearn, and relearn. By learning how to learn, students will develop what may best be described as the key survival skill for the twenty-first century (see Figure 4).

To prepare students adequately for this shifted emphasis, we must view intelligence from its broadest perspective. Gardner's theory of multiple intelligences is one alternative. It suggests that schools might best reorganize so that all students have the fullest opportunity to develop all of their intelligences:

- *Logical/Mathematical* uses skills of analysis and reasoning . . .
- *Musical/Rhythmic*, formerly referred to as musical talent . . .
- *Verbal/Linguistic* includes reading, writing, and speaking . . .
- *Visual/Spatial* uses keen perceptual skills...
- *Bodily/Kinesthetic* develops the physical ways of knowing . . .
- *Intrapersonal* embodies the philosophy of "knowing thyself" . . .
- *Interpersonal* governs the range of social skills . . .

Figure 4
Learning How to Learn: Future School

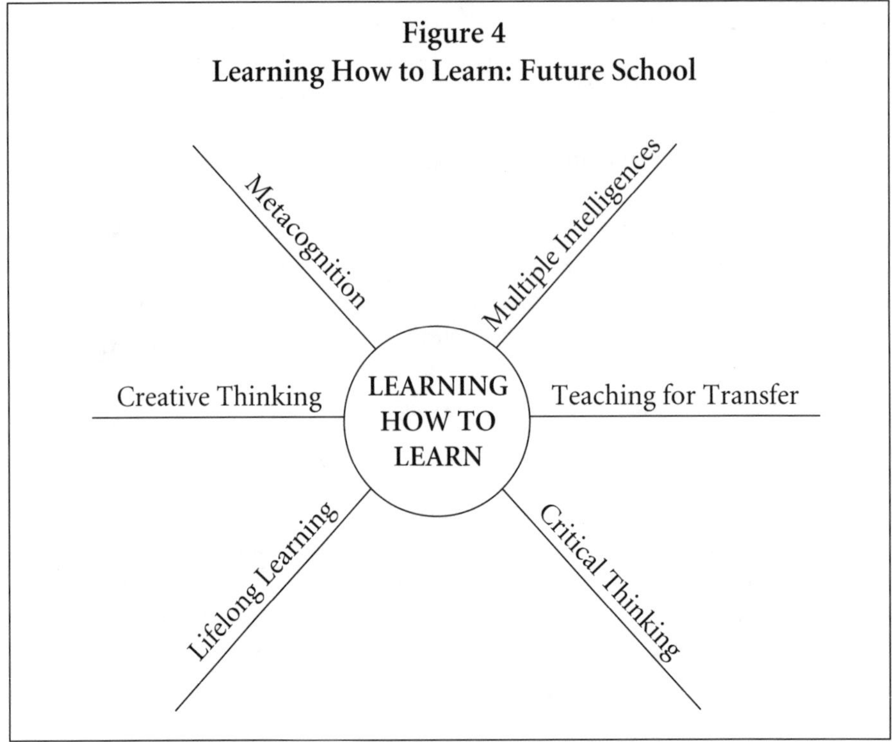

The following thinking skills or processes must also be developed:

- *Critical thinking skills* of analysis and evaluation . . .
- *Creative thinking processes* of generating and producing ideas . . .
- *Metacognition*—the awareness and control over your own thinking—a necessary focus for lifelong learning.

Many will argue that schools already do these things. They will also argue that they teach children to think and problem solve. There is no doubt that some do, but not to the degree or with the emphasis that the changes in the future world indicate are needed. For instance, most schools do teach for the verbal and the mathematical intelligences. The other intelligences, however, are tangential to the central curriculum. The changes we see in the high-tech/high-touch revolution suggest the need for a more central and purposeful focus on all seven.

Furthermore, when we examine what is currently taught for mathematical and verbal improvement and how it is taught, there is serious question about the focus.

The current focus, at least as revealed by the test results we are seeing nationally, has merely tinkered with the need for more skillful critical and creative thinking, problem solving, and metacognition. To be sure, a small number of classrooms are addressing this need in a serious way. However, even many of these see thinking and problem solving as tangential to the "real" curriculum. When we speak of the need for students in the Future School to learn how to learn, we don't mean this is something that would be nice to do if there is time. Rather, teaching students how to learn must take first priority, forming the core of the new curriculum. The substantive implication is that the school day will be reorganized around teaching for multiple intelligences. Such a reorganization will have little impact if it does not lead to substantive changes in the preoccupation with covering pages of a printed text in the linear curriculum. The myopic insistence on teaching methods that do more of the same thing must go.

The goal of the future curriculum is to provide the confidence for applying thinking and problem solving.

A curriculum, supported by electronic technology, that insists on inquiry, transfer, and creative problem solving will emerge. In this future curriculum, critical thinking skills such as analysis and evaluation, creative thinking skills such as forecasting and dealing with paradox, and a command of how to problem solve will help all students, not only the gifted, develop greater control over their own learning. As students master new mind tools (the techniques that enable any learner to gather, analyze, and apply data more skillfully) and those thinking skills that are the heart of the Future School's curriculum, they will become the commanders of information. Whatever the content, whatever the situation or problem, the goal of the future curriculum is to provide the confidence for applying thinking and problem solving. This means that the focus in the classroom will change from the teacher as storehouse of wisdom to the teacher as facilitator of student thinking.

INFORMATION INTERPRETATION

The third trend, *information interpretation*, concerns the shift from an either/or society to a world of multiple choices. Learning how to choose becomes the dominant need as lifelong learners improve their decision-making capabilities. Integrally related to the other trends, it starts with the multitude of options that every individual faces in the information society. Instead of the simple either/or choices that presented themselves in the past, multiple choices have become the norm. By all analysis of the future, the multiple-choice trend will continue to intensify as data feed on data to create more data.

The technological society bombards itself with choices. In terms of products, there was a time when a person could buy a pair of gym shoes, aspirin, or any personal product without the need to research the multitude of specialized models, bottles, and fragrances. Today the choice is more complex: shoes for running, shoes for tennis, shoes for aerobics, shoes autographed by your favorite athletic star. Add pain killers with aspirin, weak strength non-aspirin, extra strength aspirin substitutes, generic aspirin, and a multitude of brands. Don't forget the choice of the right size, brand, flavor, color, endorsement, and odor of perfume, hair spray, deodorant, shaving cream, or nail polish.

Just as the options bombard the consumer with product choices, the same dizzy array blasts the consumer in the service sector. In air transportation: Which airline? Which flight? Which route? Which fare bargain? Which class? If not air, is bus, car, or train a better choice? The maze becomes so mind-boggling that many resort to the easiest and safest choice: "just pick something for me."

The confusion that faces the consumer with product and service choices is mild compared to what awaits her in the information world. The barrage of available media is almost unmanageable by the most skillful of decision makers. The selection of packages for word processing or desktop publishing presents an endless software parade. The barrage makes the search for the right package burdensome and confusing.

The ultimate challenge, however, comes not in deciding which item to buy from the smorgasbord of services, products, and information. It comes with the emerging moral and ethical decisions created by the shrinking globe and advancing

Figure 5
Learning How to Choose: Future School

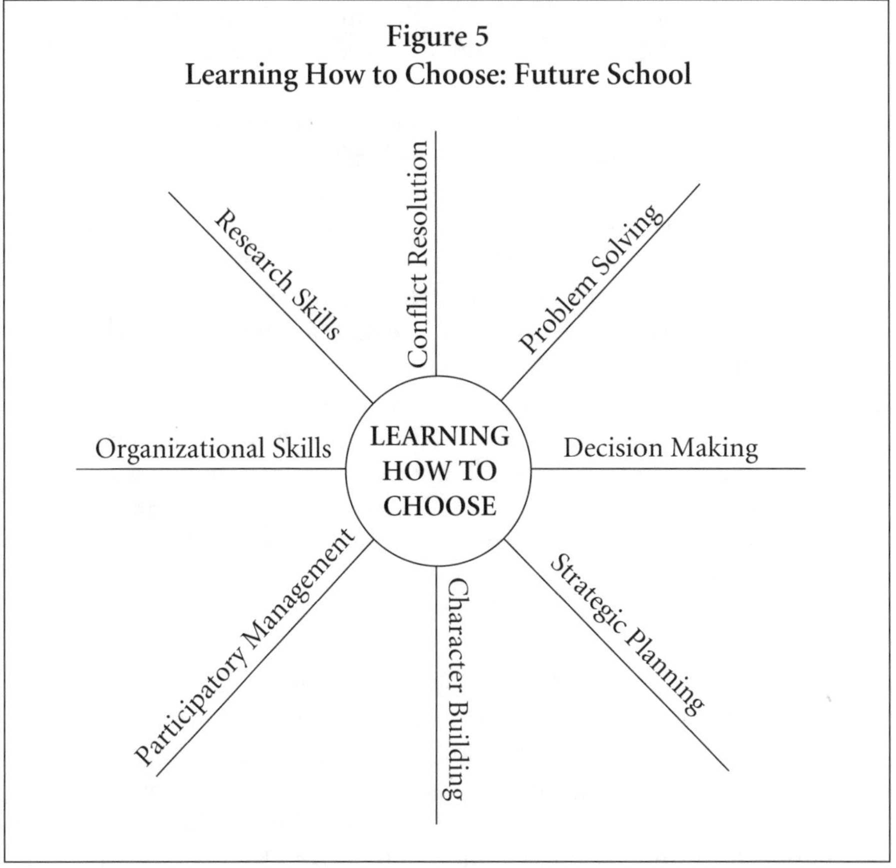

technologies. Genetic engineering, life support systems, organ transplants, mechanical organs, nuclear power, legal and illegal drugs, and other issues await legal clarification.

Implication: Learning How to Choose

The multiple-choice snowstorm that is blanketing today's students suggests that the Future School must give greater attention to training students in how to make choices (see Figure 5). It is necessary to include some of the following in the Future School's curriculum:

Creative problem solving in which students learn to tackle real and fictional problems and translate the process to the challenges they face every day: drugs, alcohol, gang pressure, abuse, and first careers;

Decision-making skills that will help students examine alternatives, take a stand, and support decisions with well-evaluated data;

Research skills with technical and non-technical media for searching out and evaluating needed information;

Conflict resolution skills to provide students with the capability to solve problems, negotiate, and compromise at the right times;

Character-building programs to help students understand moral and ethical issues and acquire skills for making reasoned judgments; and

Strategic planning for those who frame the curriculum and provide the instruction. The Future School must provide time for training and development, time for strategic planning with an emphasis on site-based, participatory management, and time for teamwork and community involvement in systemic patterns of change.

SUMMARY

As we ponder these trends of the Future World and the implications of the Future School, it seems appropriate to note the comment of futurist Daniel Burris who described the flow of innovation in society. Burris notes that innovations are available first to the military, where most of the research and development begins. Next, the innovation flows to the medical world where it is refined and tested. Then, innovations flow to business and industry, where further creative adaptations take place to meet client specifications. In turn, the toy makers target the innovation and mass produce simulated versions. Finally, the flow of innovation trickles down into the schools—sometimes many years after the innovation has been totally implemented in these other sectors (see Figure 6).

It is paramount that educators create school missions with a vision of the future.

Why is the school the last to know? What can educators do to change this flow? First, they can move to a future-oriented paradigm. It is paramount that educators create school missions with a vision of the future. The data are available. The predictions are clear. With the gift of creativity, they can develop plans

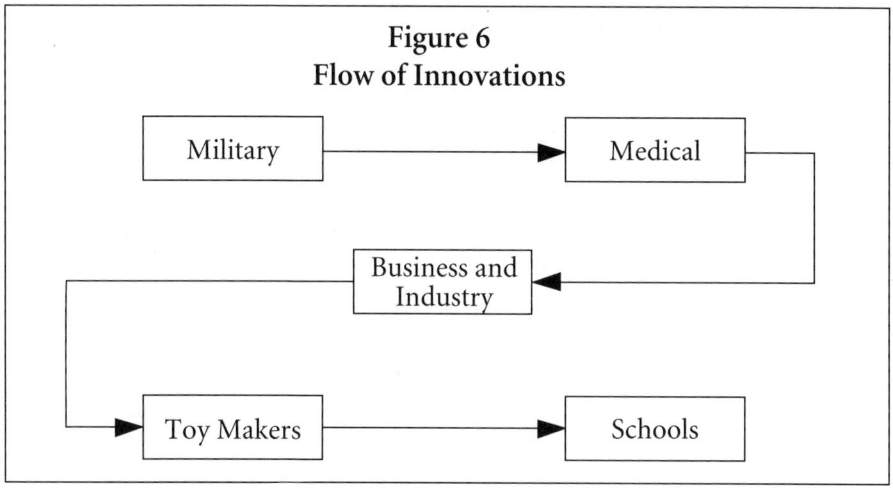

Figure 6
Flow of Innovations

that are visionary in nature, plans that have change built in. These plans will make the three major trends the central guide to restructuring the school. Looking back to see how educators can stay with a curriculum and instructional method designed for an agricultural society will only help perpetuate the failures of the past. Doing more of what was tried in the good old days, even doing that better, has not worked. Educators must position education in the future tense. They must create a future vision as they look into tomorrow with tomorrow's eyes.

WHAT CAN SCHOOLS DO?

To best prepare today's students for tomorrow's world, there are seven important considerations. First, to see tomorrow through tomorrow's eyes, educators can *refocus the curriculum*. Instead of seeing learning as the act of pouring out-of-date information into empty heads, they can focus the future on learning as an act of processing and applying information. The curricular content must put thinking, decision-making, and problem-solving skills at the center of the students' day. Aided by a host of technological tools, students must have the opportunity to extend their learning well beyond the limited curriculum found in schools today. If state offices of education must prescribe time limits to the curriculum, they must give preeminence to thinking skills. When those same offices prescribe state tests, the tests must show how well students predict, analyze, and infer, and how skillfully they solve problems, make beneficial decisions, and apply what they have learned.

Second, schools can *shift instructional focus* from methods that are designed to improve rote work to methods that are more appropriate to the mastery of a high-tech curriculum. In this context, cooperative learning, explicit thinking skill instruction, inquiry, and regular use of the computer become integral requirements for every teacher's instructional repertoire.

Third, educators must decide how they will *provide electronic hardware and software* as key learning tools in every classroom. In the primary grades, children can master the basic skills, aided and tutored by the computer. In high school, students can use software to simulate decision making, learn biology, write poetry, wordprocess, or make business forecasts and spreadsheets. Instead of spending tens of thousands of dollars on dated, consumable workbooks and expensive print textbooks, strategic planning must allow for laser technology, hardware/software purchases and repurchases, and equipment repair that will make the computer as common as the pencil in the classroom. The goal is an electronic school in which a variety of high-tech tools enrich teaching and learning and speed students' access to and use of information.

Fourth, *emphasize staff development.* As Cetron (1988 and 1985) and Kearns and Doyle (1988) have pointed out, business and industrial leaders are unhappy with the $25 billion spent to teach workers basic skills that should have been taught at school. Not only do we see today's teaching corps lacking the key skills for working with the at-risk populations, we see too little attention and far too little money being provided to help teachers gain skills to use software, laser video, cooperative learning, and the other instructional methods essential to the classroom of the twenty-first century. Staff development efforts must increase. A five-percent budget allocation should be standard for the Future School. Ten to fifteen percent may be necessary to provide the amount and quality of training programs that teachers need in order to learn the new knowledge and skills dictated by the high-tech curriculum.

Fifth, students can go outside the school walls for many of the resources they need. Forming *partnerships and networks*, recruiting senior citizen volunteers, and relying on business and industry for expertise in management, training and development, and knowledge of the high-tech work world can only expand the resource pool.

Sixth, schools can investigate a variety of alternatives for *restructuring the learning experience.* With the existing capability of the computer to track student progress, give feedback, and guide new directions in any learning task, there is strong reason to expect that the egg-crate structure of the nineteenth-century schoolhouse with one teacher for each class is as out-of-date as the Model T.

Seventh, we can recognize that the tools now exist for *restructuring the Future School,* so that the future becomes the present tense. There are many ways, but is there a will?

REFERENCES

Bellanca, J. (1988). *Team stars.* Palatine, IL: IRI/Skylight Publishing.

Burris, D. (1985). *Future view: A look ahead.* Burris Research Associates.

Cetron, M. (1988). *The great job shakeout.* New York: Simon & Schuster.

Cetron, M. (1985). *Schools of the future.* New York: McGraw Hill.

Costa, A. (1984, November). Mediating the metacognitive. *Educational Leadership,* pp. 57–62.

Ferguson, M. (1980). *The aquarian conspiracy.* New York: J. P. Tarcher.

Gardner, H. (1983). *Frames of mind.* New York: Basic Books.

Johnson, R., & Johnson, D. (1986). *Circles of learning.* Alexandria, VA: Association for Supervision and Curriculum Development.

Kearns, D., & Doyle, D. (1988).*Winning the brain race.* San Francisco: ICS Press.

Lazear, D. (1991). *Seven ways of knowing.* Palatine, IL: IRI/Skylight Publishing.

Machado, L. A. (1980). *The right to be intelligent.* Oxford: Pergamon Press.

Naisbit, J. (1982). *Megatrends.* New York: Warner Books.

Parnes, S. (1975). *Aha! Insight into creative behavior.* Buffalo, NY: D.O.K. Publishers.

Perkins, D. N. (1986). *Knowledge as design.* Hillsdale, NJ: Lawrence Erlbaum.

Rico, G. (1983).*Writing the natural way.* Boston: J. P. Tarcher.

Schlechty, P. C. (1990). *Schools for the 21st century.* San Francisco: Jossey-Bass.

Sternberg, R. (1984, September). How can we teach intelligence? *Educational Leadership,* pp. 38–48.

Toffler, A. (1970). *Future shock.* New York: Bantam Books.

Cognition in Practice

by Robin Fogarty and James Bellanca

Cognitive instruction research embodies four distinct areas of study: explicit skill instruction, cognitive organizers, metacognition, and transfer of learning. Each of these areas has its own body of literature as well as works that encompass all four areas.

EXPLICIT THINKING SKILLS

A steady current of experts favor explicit skill instruction for the thinking curriculum. In some areas, consensus among the many thinking skills advocates embodies these beliefs (Costa, 1985a):

- Thinking is most often taught indirectly, but a direct approach is needed.
- Learning how to think is not an automatic by-product of studying certain subjects.
- Students will not learn to think better simply by being asked to think about a subject or topic.
- Youngsters do not learn how to engage in critical thinking by themselves.
- There is little reason to believe that competency in critical thinking can be an incidental outcome of instruction directed, or apparently directed, at other ends.
- Instructions for the skills must be direct and systematic prior to, during, and following students' introduction to the skills and use of them in the classroom.

However, there seem to be two obstacles impeding the momentum of a stronger flow toward consensus on how to teach thinking explicitly. The first obstacle is a philosophical issue that must be addressed before the second obstacle can even be

---

Figure 1
Thinking Skills Programs

	Pros	Cons
Thinking Infused into Content	• Easy transfer • Carries content	• Teachers may be unskilled in the teaching skills
Thinking Taught Separately	• Spot and slot for thinking • Targeted to test and grade • Easy staff development	• No time • No transfer

approached. This primary issue is the debate over whether explicit thinking skills should be taught separate from or infused into the existing subject area curriculum. There are, of course, pros and cons for each instance (see Figure 1).

Although both approaches are successfully implemented in various settings, we favor the infused model. Our focus is always and foremost on the *transfer of learning* for all children, and the infused model eases the way for fruitful transfer, creative application, and relevant student use throughout the curriculum. The separate model seems to reinforce for students the "little boxes" theory of curriculum: in little boxes, math is not art, art is not science, and thinking is not any of these—the curricula are fragmented.

However, once the decision has been made in terms of how to deliberately include thinking in the curricula, the next obstacle stubbornly emerges: How does one know which program is best? An overview of the spectrum of thinking models provides some food for thought. Just as in cooperative learning, the various programs tend to cluster into four distinct categories: the conceptual models, the strategic approaches, the curriculum

Figure 2
Clusters of Thinking Skills Programs

CONCEPTUAL MODELS
- Patterns for Thinking: Patterns for Transfer—*Fogarty and Bellanca*
- Tactics in Thinking—*Marzano*
- Dimensions in Thinking—*Marzano*
- Thoughtful Education Training Series—*Hansen, Silver, and Strong*
- Teaching for Intelligent Behavior—*Costa*
- Models of Teaching—*Joyce and Weil*

CURRICULUM PACKAGES
- Philosophy in the Classroom—*Lipman, Sharp, and Oscanyan*
- Instrumental Enrichment—*Feuerstein*
- HOTS—*Pogrow*
- SOI—*Meeker*
- Great Books—*Will*
- Future Problem Solving—*Torrence*
- Odyssey—*Harvard Project Zero*
- Critical Thinking—*Black and Black*

STRATEGIC/SKILLS APPROACH
- Cognitive Research Trust (CoRT)—*de Bono*
- Catch Them Thinking—*Bellanca and Fogarty*
- Start Them Thinking—*Fogarty and Opeka*
- Teach Them Thinking—*Fogarty and Bellanca*
- Synectics—*Gordon*
- Strategic Reasoning—*Upton*
- Practice Strategies for Teaching Thinking—*Beyer*
- Project Impact—*Winocur*

MODEL BUILDING WITH PROTOTYPES
- Knowledge as Design—*Perkins*
- Keep Them Thinking I, II, III—*Opeka, Fogarty, Bellanca*
- Breakthroughs—*Jones*
- Guided Design—*Wales, Nardi, and Stager*
- Connections—*Perkins et al.*
- Creative Problem Solving—*Parnes*
- Cooperative Think Tank—*Bellanca and Fogarty*

packages, and the model-building designs. Figure 2 presents the thinking skill programs as they cluster in patterns.

The major categories that delineate the four types of thinking skills programs have definite characteristics that distinguish one from the other. Each program has a flavor of its own, yet each category is also easily recognized by its distinguishing critical attributes.

Conceptual Models

In the conceptual models, broad guidelines set the framework within which more specific ideas are set forth. For example, in Patterns for Thinking: Patterns for Transfer, the four broad guidelines framing the program are teaching *for, of, with,* and *about* thinking: setting the climate *for* thinking, teaching the explicit skills *of* thinking, structuring interactions to teach *with* thinking, and teaching metacognitively *about* thinking. Within that framework, specific thinking skills and strategies are used to demonstrate the conceptual model.

Likewise, in Models of Teaching, Joyce and Weil conceptualize instructional models into families: information processing, personal, social, and behavioral. Within that framework, specific models are explored. For example, within the personal family the synectics approach is elaborated. It begins with a scenario that presents the model, followed by an introduction to the basic structures, theory, demonstration, practice, and feedback. It ends with coaching and extended application that help teachers learn the instructional techniques.

The strategic/skills approach . . . provides tried-and-true, teacher-tested techniques that are ready for immediate use.

While conceptual models allow great freedom on the part of the teacher for innovative and highly relevant content-specific use, less skilled or less confident staff may find the freedom within the conceptual structure too ambiguous.

Strategic/Skills Approach

The strategic/skills approach, on the other hand, provides tried-and-true, teacher-tested techniques that are ready for immediate use. In the strategic/skills approach, a menu of specific and fully delineated methods are presented to the teacher for explicit instructional use.

Usually, these strategies/skills are introduced in what is often called a content-free lesson. In reality, this content-free lesson does indeed have a content focus. However, the content is usually familiar, almost generic in nature. It is used merely as a vehicle to carry the strategy or skill under study. For example, in teaching the explicit thinking skill of classification, the familiar content focus might be on solids, liquids, and gases. Using these generic categories, the classification skill, not the science, becomes the focus of the lesson.

Similarly, in teaching the strategy PMI (plus, minus, interesting), de Bono uses the generic or familiar content of buses. The initial lesson requires students to generate pluses, minuses, and interesting aspects of buses that have no seats. Again, by using content that is simple and well known, the emphasis can be placed on the PMI strategy itself.

While the strategic/skills approach usually has immediate appeal to practitioners because it easily applies directly to the classroom, caution must be taken that the strategies and skills lessons are not merely used as a cutesy Friday afternoon activity. If the strategy or skill is used only once as modeled in the teacher training, it is an *activity*. If, however, teachers introduce the strategy or skill as modeled, practice it in another situation, and transfer it into still another situation, then and only then can we call it a *strategy*. An activity is a one-time shot. A strategy is placed in our repertoire of instructional techniques, our tool kit to be used over and over, whenever appropriate.

An activity is a one-time shot. A strategy is placed in our tool kit to be used over and over, whenever appropriate.

Curriculum Packages

Curriculum packages provide a ready-made set of materials for classroom use. These materials are, more often than not, specifically designed for explicit instruction as separate and disparate pieces in the classroom. While the curriculum package provides a neat and tidy unit for deliberate placement in the instructional day, a spot and a slot for explicitly addressing thinking skills and strategies, often the subsequent transfer needed for continued and relevant use does not occur.

Examples of the curriculum packages might include Feuerstein's Instrumental Enrichment, in which specific and strategic thinking techniques are taught through pencil-and-paper tasks. By metacognitively processing and talking about how students approached a particular task, future application and transfer are mediated for the students.

Another curriculum package is Lipman, Sharp, and Oscanyan's Philosophy for Children, in which skillfully written, highly motivating, and extremely relevant scenarios are used to engage students in Socratic dialogue. Using the fictional situations as springboards, further discussion is encouraged as students attempt to draw philosophical principles into other academic situations or into life's circumstances.

While curriculum packages have strong appeal because of their completeness as a package, their use can be limiting if transfer is not addressed with vigor.

Model Building with Prototypes

The final cluster of thinking skills programs, model building with prototypes, provides a generic piece or model as a prototype. That is, the generalizable model is presented through a content-specific lesson, with the implicit understanding that it is a model and should be used as such. Transfer to other content is built in explicitly. Examples of model building with prototypes are the Breakthroughs program by Jones and Knowledge as Design by Perkins.

In the Breakthroughs program, for example, a lesson on garbage is presented in a fully designed, ready-to-use lesson format. However, in model building a specific prototype is set up. The lesson features specific strategies for modeling collaborative learning, reciprocal teaching, and cognitive mapping. The expectation is that although garbage is the lesson's content focus, the real lesson extends beyond that with definite attention to instructional methodology.

Perkins' Knowledge as Design uses the same model-building approach. Perkins poses four questions that can be applied across content, subject matter, and life situations:

- What is its purpose (or purposes)?
- What is its structure?
- What are the model cases of it?
- What are arguments that explain and evaluate it?

Through these four questions, a model for thinking emerges. Perkins claims these questions can be applied to ecology, Boyle's law, the Bill of Rights, and to understanding a common screwdriver.

THINKING SKILLS PROGRAMS

Briefly, without belaboring the decision-making processes that must be employed to reach consensus, there are some major considerations to weigh in the selection of a program (see Figure 3).

Figure 3
Pros and Cons of Thinking Skills Programs

Type	Pros	Cons
Conceptual Models	• Deep understanding results in creative application • Can easily adapt, mix, and match the best from many models	• Full commitment to long-term change from building or district • Needs explicit attention to transfer
Strategic/Skills Approach	• Easy for teachers to learn • Immediate application • Transfer power inherent (if noted explicitly)	• Can appear cutesy • Superficial activities rather than generic, transferable strategies for the instructional repertoire
Curriculum Packages	• Stand alone • Spot and slot in curriculum • Teacher's preparation minimal	• Narrow in focus • Needs (and often overlooks) attention to transfer • Separated from content; more to teach
Model Building with Prototypes	• Procedural learning or heuristics taught and modeled for easy application and transfer • Straightforward approach with transfer built in	• Can be narrow in focus • Transfer embedded but can be slighted

Considerations for Selecting a Program

- What is the purpose of the program?
- Should an explicit thinking skills program be introduced separate from or infused into the subject matter content?
- What are the experiences and competencies of the teachers?
- What are the available resources in terms of time and funds for training and materials?
- What is the commitment level for long-term change toward cognitive instruction?
- What kinds of results are expected?

How to Teach the Skills

After consideration of these key issues, program selection becomes easier. By targeting needs and expectations, several programs will seem more appropriate than others. Once the final choice is made, the subsequent decisions on how to teach the skills fall into place. A model of what is required to teach explicit thinking skills, according to Beyer (1987), is provided in Figure 4.

The research on the need for explicit attention to thinking in the curriculum is clear. Knowing that...

...schools do make a difference (Edmonds, 1979);

...intelligence is modifiable (Feuerstein, 1980);

...learners can monitor and control their own performance (Brown, 1978); and

...learners are active, strategic, planful, and constructive (Anderson, Hiebert, Scott, & Wilkinson, 1984),

then cognitive instruction must include explicitness in both the thinking skill and the transfer of the thinking skill.

COGNITIVE ORGANIZERS

The concept of cognitive organizers is rooted in Ausubel's (1978) theory of meaningful reception learning. Simply put, Ausubel believes that information is naturally stored hierarchically in the brain. For instance, highly generalized concepts seem to cluster together, followed by less inclusive concepts, and finally specific facts and details.

Ausubel advocates the idea of the advance organizer in which information is graphically displayed prior to the reading of the text. In Ausubel's terms, this advance visual depicts information in hierarchical order and is called a *structured overview* (see Figure 5).

The structured overview always shows vocabulary in relation to more inclusive vocabulary. However don't think of the cognitive structure as passive. It is really quite dynamic. As new information and experiences are assimilated by the learner, it is reorganized cognitively and the graphic display reflects the shifts.

Figure 4
How to Teach Explicit Skills

1. Examples (or products)
2. Introduction to components of the thinking skill in a systematic manner
3. Demonstration of the basic attributes of the skill
4. Discussion of the operation and how to do the operation
5. Opportunity for related practice and feedback
6. A broadening of the skill beyond the original components
7. Generalization of the skill with application in a variety of situations

Explicit Skill Instruction Model

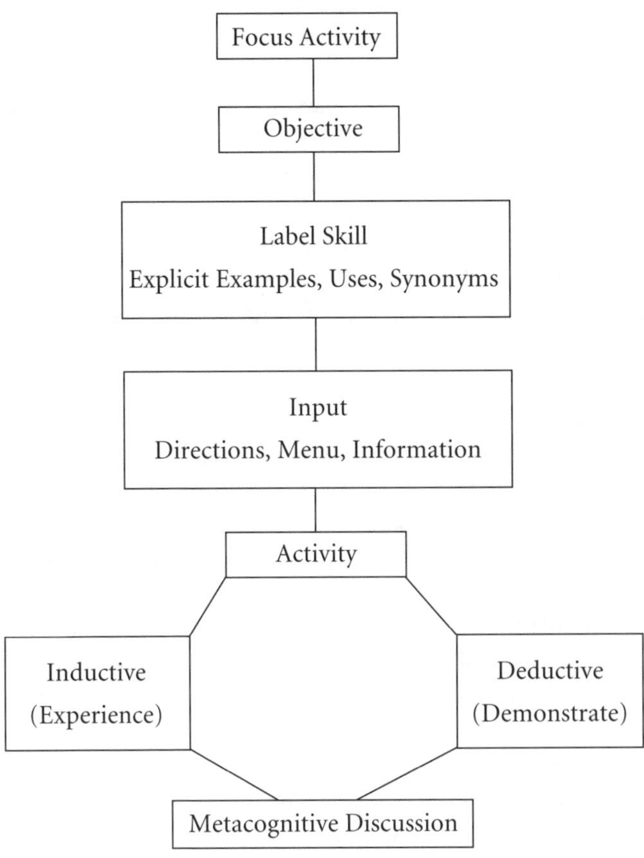

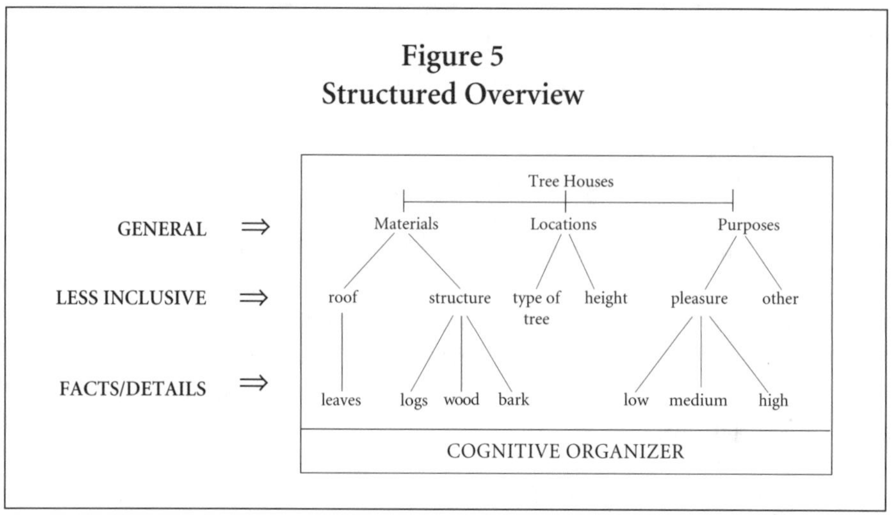

Mapping

Cognitive maps, or organizers, as studied by Armbruster and Anderson (1980), Dansereau et al. (1979), Davidson (1982), and Vaughn (1982), demonstrate success in improving the retention of information. Lyman and McTighe (1988) demonstrate the use of cognitive maps in a discussion of theory-embedded tools for cognitive instruction. They suggest that the ability to organize information and ideas is fundamental to thinking. Graphic displays or cognitive maps aid in the development of organizational skills for students of all ages and abilities across all content.

Cognitive organizers provide a holistic picture of the concept, complete with relationships and interrelationships. Lyman and McTighe suggest that cognitive maps help students:

- represent abstract or implicit information in more concrete forms,
- depict the relationships between facts and concepts,
- generate elaborate ideas, and
- relate new information to prior knowledge.

Maps and Minds—Together

From kindergarten to college, cognitive organizers are employed to help students organize, retain, and assimilate concepts and ideas. Perhaps the most widely used cognitive organizer is the web, which targets a concept and provides structures for analyzing attributes. Other types of maps include sequence chains, vector charts, story maps, analogy links, flow charts, matrices, Venn diagrams, and ranking ladders. These cognitive organizers provide frameworks for class or small-group discussions and written work. According to Lyman and McTighe (1988), when used in conjunction with think-pair-share cooperative strategies and metacognitive cues, these cognitive maps are even more powerful in helping students learn.

Perhaps most important, the use of cognitive organizers provides a deliberate technique for allowing students to interact personally with the information. These theory-embedded tools, called maps, make the thinking visible for both the students and the teacher. Ausubel suggests that learning is easier for a person whose knowledge is clear, stable, and organized. Cognitive organizers facilitate just that sort of thinking—clear, stable, and organized.

METACOGNITION—A SUPERORDINATE KIND OF THINKING

According to Swartz and Perkins (1989), metacognition refers to knowledge about, awareness of, and control over one's own mind and thinking. Costa (1985a) calls this thinking about thinking. Marzano and Arredondo (1986) also speak of awareness and control over one's own thinking, while Brown(1978) describes the metacognitive process in relationship to the reading process.

They allude to the good reader who reads and reads and reads and suddenly hears a little voice inside his or her head saying, "I don't know what I just read." The words on the page had been read; they had been spoken in the mind, but in a "word-calling" sense, no meaning had been conveyed. Suddenly, the reader becomes aware of this deficit. Good readers realize they have lost contact with the context of the text, and their minds signal them to adapt a recovery strategy: reread the beginning of the paragraph, recall a thought, scan the text for key words, etc.

On the other hand, poor readers read and read and read and never know they don't know. They don't notice that they

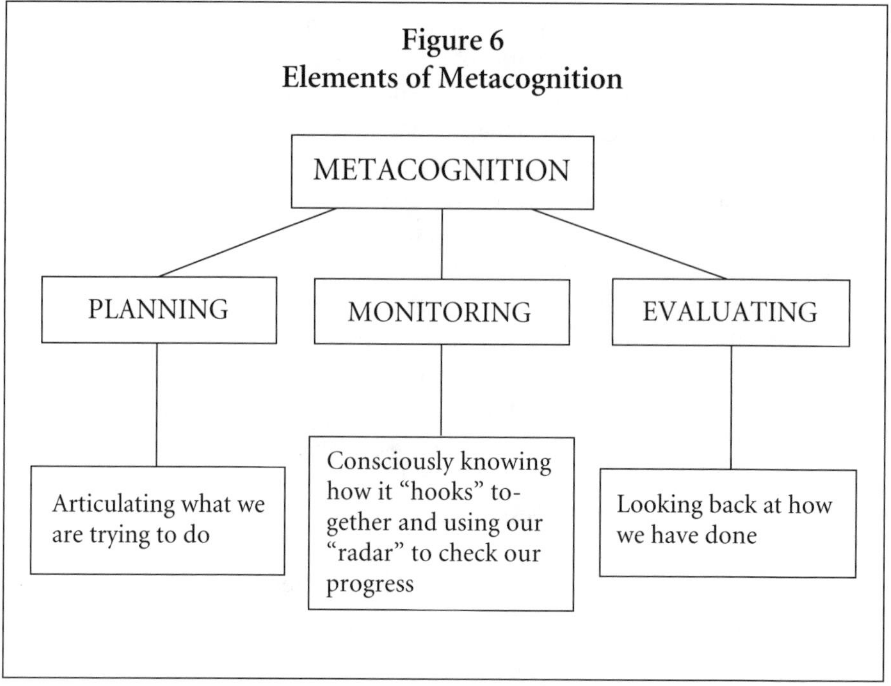

are getting no meaning from the text because they never have gotten meaning from text. They word-call in their minds, but they are nonreaders in the real sense of reading.

Learning to understand and articulate our own mental processes is a necessary link to fruitful transfer—or as Costa suggests about metacognition, having the ability to know what we know and what we don't know and wondering why we are doing what we are doing. That's the metacognition we want to promote for all learners.

More specifically, planning, monitoring, and evaluating the learning activity are the components of metacognitive processing. Students become aware of their own thinking and what goes on inside their heads when they are thinking prior to, during, and after a learning activity (see Figure 6).

In the current writings about metacognition, Swartz and Perkins (1989) gauge the sophistication of thinking by four distinctive levels that are increasingly metacognitive in nature (see Figure 7).

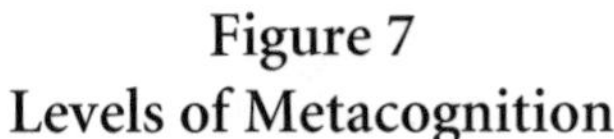

Figure 7
Levels of Metacognition

Tactic Use:	Doing a kind of thinking without thinking about it
Aware Use:	Conscious of when one is doing a certain kind of thinking
Strategic Use:	Organizing thinking by conscious strategy
Reflective Use:	Reflecting upon thinking before, during, and after the process; pondering how to proceed and how to improve

(4) Reflective Use
(3) Strategic Use
(2) Aware Use
(1) Tactic Use

A sophisticated example of paying explicit attention to metacognition is seen in Whimbey's model (1975) of paired partner think-alouds. In this strategy, a problem solver thinks aloud as he or she works through a situation. The monitor cues thinking aloud with specific questions or prompts. Thus, instead of tacitly solving the problem, unaware of the strategies used, awareness is brought to a conscious level. In addition, over time, strategic use is mapped out by both the problem solver and the monitor as problem-solving patterns emerge. Reflective use is inherent in the think-aloud technique. In fact, all four metacognitive levels are clearly evidenced in the strategy.

By using metacognitive prompts we can help students monitor and direct their own thinking as they move toward reflective thinking. Beyond teaching about thinking, metacognitive questions also promote the kind of metaphorical thoughts, generalizations, and mindful abstractions that Perkins and Salomon (1988) suggest are powerful bridges for complex transfer.

In addition, Beyer (1987) elaborates on a cueing technique to prompt metacognition. Beyer suggests the following questions to foster metacognitive behavior:

- What am I doing?
- Why am I doing it?
- What other way can I do it?
- How does it work? Can I do it again or another way?
- How would I help someone else do it?

These questions and similar questions lead students to examine their own thinking and behavior in ways that press the generalization process. The following are additional lead-ins that may be discussed within the group or reflected upon individually in a log entry:

- How is __________ like __________________?
- I wish I'd known this when ________________.
- Next time, I am going to...

Mrs. Potter's Questions (Fogarty & Bellanca, 1989) are standard metacognitive questions that promote reflective thinking and foster future applications. They are suggested for repeated use to process student thinking during cooperative learning tasks in the classroom.

As the story goes, Mrs. Mimi Potter was Jim Bellanca's "critic" teacher when Jim was completing his student teaching in Champaign-Urbana, Illinois. In this high school English class, regardless of what lesson Jim taught or how successful the lesson seemed, Mrs. Potter would always sit Jim down and ask him to reflect on these questions:

- What were you trying to do?
- What do you think went well?
- What would you do differently next time?
- Do you need any help?

In the self-analysis and in answering these four questions, Jim was asked to reflect on his own teaching behavior for future transfer and successful use. Inadvertently, in Jim's own teaching situations, he discovered that he began asking the very same questions of his students. In turn, they became reflective about their own thinking and behavior in his classes. Mrs. Potter's

Figure 8
A Metacognitive Tool

Affective: How did it feel?

P(+)	
M(-)	
I(?)	

Questions can be posted and used repeatedly as reminders of the metacognitive nature needed for the transfer process. They can easily become part of the processing that follows a cooperative task.

In addition, Beyer (1987) suggests modeling direct instruction of a thinking skill and thinking guides to promote planning, monitoring, and evaluating. A viable tool that students can readily use to assess their own behavior is a strategy based on de Bono's (1970) PMI chart. In this procedure, students look at the affective, cognitive, and metacognitive levels for processing their thinking. This evaluation is tied directly to the learning situation (see Figures 8 and 9).

Regardless of the means or measures used for the metacognitive process, the evidence is clear that explicit attention to the metacognitive—the stuff beyond the cognitive answers—promotes transfer and application of knowledge, skills, concepts, and positive attitudes in novel situations.

BO PEEP, LOST SHEEP, AND THE GOOD SHEPHERD—TALES OF TRANSFER

Isn't all learning for transfer? The question is so generic to the teaching/learning process, one wonders why talk of transfer has become this seemingly unending tale of controversy and confusion. To transfer learning means to use what is learned in one situation in another situation that is either quite like the initial

Figure 9
Levels of Processing

Cognitive: Assessing answers or strategies	**Metacognitive:** Why bother? How can I use this?
What answer did you get?	Can I: Duplicate?
What else?	Replicate?
Tell me more.	Integrate?
Give an example.	Map?
Please illustrate.	Innovate?

learning situation or even perhaps quite different from the situation in which the learning originally took place.

That seems quite straightforward. In learning to drive one car, we, in essence, transfer that learning to driving all cars. In learning to survey a book, we learn the art of survey as an overview methodology. Of course, we learn things so we can use that learning in other places. Learning has relevance and usefulness.

However, as the tale of transfer unfolds, the complexity of the issue becomes more evident, and the concern for transfer takes on added dimensions. On the one hand, experts over the past twenty-five years seem to agree that there is a natural dichotomy to this concept called transfer. There appears to be transfer that is simple and another type of transfer that is more complex. The research suggests many terms to describe this dichotomy. For the simple transfer there is simple (Fogarty, 1989), near (Wittrock, 1967), horizontal (Joyce & Showers, 1983), automatic (Perkins, 1986), low road (Perkins & Salomon, 1988), similar (Hunter, 1973; Beyer, 1987), spontaneous (Sternberg, 1984), and practiced (Feuerstein, 1980). For the complex transfer there is complex (Fogarty, 1989), far (Wittrock, 1967), vertical (Joyce & Showers, 1983), mindful (Perkins, 1986), high road (Perkins & Salomon, 1988), cued

Figure 10
Dichotomy in Tranfer

Low Level	High Level
simple	complex
near	far
horizontal	vertical
automatic	mindful
low road	high road
similar	cued
spontaneous	guided and scaffolded
practiced	mediated

(Beyer, 1987), guided and scaffolded (Sternberg, 1984), and mediated (Feuerstein, 1980) (see Figure 10).

This distinction between simple and complex transfer seems to be fairly easy to sense and deal with. Yet there is another dichotomy in thinking about transfer that takes precedence over all else. In fact, to explore the division in thinking, the controversy over whether transfer is best served with generalized teaching rather than with teaching that has a content-specific focus, we must look historically into the issue.

Bo Peep Theory

"Leave them alone and they'll come home wagging their tails behind them." According to Perkins (1986), this represents the standard instructional practice today. It is the basic position that holds the educational community in its grip at the present time—teach the content, give students practice that is both immediate and spaced over time, and the transfer of learning is sure to follow.

For example, by teaching students the periodic table of the elements and giving them practice in recognizing and analyzing the atomic structure of the elements, it is presumed that this factual information somehow transfers into relevant application. With sufficient and varied practice, this may actually occur. Then again, it may not. It may also be presumed that students who learn the periodic table of the elements also somehow transfer concepts about patterns, symbolic notation, and charting information by simply working with the actual table in fact-oriented tasks. While there is some possibility of the first presumption occurring as a result of varied practice, there is slim possibility of the second type of transfer occurring. Bo Peep has lost her sheep here.

Lost Sheep Theory

In fact, according to Fogarty, Perkins, and Barell (1991), over time, transfer has become the "lost sheep" of the education community. Let's unravel the tale from the beginning to see how this lost sheep theory has evolved to the point that it somehow overrides all other evidence.

Historically, the educational dogma dictating curricula adhered to the idea that Latin, geometry, and the like train the mind. However, in the early 1900s, Thorndike and others presented convincing evidence that suggested that training the faculties indeed did not transfer in generalized ways. These researchers favored schooling in which the initial learning situation simulated as closely as possible the anticipated transfer situation. In fact, they advocated learning that encompassed identical elements for the two situations. Training would be specific and transfer would occur.

Diametrically opposed to that view was the position advocated by Polya in the early 1900s that a general, generic, heuristic approach to problem solving in math was the key to the transfer of learning in diverse settings. The arguments for transfer from specific, similar contexts versus transfer from generalizable heuristics began. Unfortunately, buried within the embers of the fading controversy is one illuminating fact. Neither side—context-bound, specific training nor generalizable principles and rules—shows overwhelming and convincing evidence of transfer.

Perkins' summation: "Transfer ain't that great, right now. We're not getting the transfer we want." In fact, the transfer is so lacking and so rare that transfer has become what Perkins now calls the lost sheep of education. The attitude is if it doesn't work, if we can't seem to get the transfer we want, then let's just do better in highly focused subject-oriented lessons. Thus, transfer has been ignored. If transfer can't be there, it's not a big issue. Let's just teach well what we can teach.

Good Shepherd Theory

Fortunately, the transfer embers, close to becoming forgotten ashes, have recently been stirred by the winds of curricular change. A number of voices from the thinking skills movement are focusing on the transfer issue again, igniting sparks of urgent concern and emerging agreements. While the controversy surrounding transfer as context-bound or transfer as generalizable remains a somewhat unresolved issue, agreements about transfer of learning do show evidence of promise for the educational community.

In both context-bound teaching and a general heuristics approach, transfer must be shepherded.

Teaching Latin does not seem to transfer inherently in terms of a more disciplined mind, yet it is now agreed that Latin may not have transferred because Latin had not been taught to cultivate transfer. And while teaching general heuristics such as steps to math problem solving do not seem to transfer into problem-solving steps in the writing process even though transfer had been expected, intricate and powerful implications have emerged from work in both areas.

In essence, what current transfer research suggests is that when teachers pay attention to transfer in contextual learning situations, transfer does occur. And when general, bare strategies are accompanied with self-monitoring techniques, transfer does in fact occur. In both context-bound teaching and a general heuristics approach, transfer must be shepherded.

Thus, there is Perkins' good shepherd theory: when transfer is provoked, practiced, and reflected on, transfer is fairly easy to get. Transfer can be mediated. With the good shepherd theory comes new hope for transfer. And with that new hope, of course, comes a new responsibility toward teaching for transfer—for after all, isn't all learning for transfer?

Figure 11
Transfer Tactics

	Anticipatory	Retrieval
High Road	• abstracting rules • anticipating applications	• reflect by generalizing the problem • focus retrieval in one particular context • make metaphors
Low Road	• immediate practice • varied practice • matching lesson target and outcome	• varied practice performed over time

Hugging and Bridging for Transfer

To get transfer, to change Perkins' summation "transfer ain't that great, right now" to "transfer is greater than ever, right now," a close look reveals two critical elements that foster the transfer phenomenon. Perkins and Salomon (1988) refer to low-road, automatic transfer and high-road, abstracted transfer. They further describe two mediation strategies for low-road/ high-road transfer which they label *hugging* and *bridging.*

Hugging means teaching so as to better meet the conditions for low-road or automatic transfer. Bridging means teaching to better meet the conditions for high-road transfer by mediating the needed processes of abstraction and making connections (Perkins & Salomon, 1988).

While Beyer refers to mediation as cueing what to do, when to do it, and how to do it, his cues take the content lesson's thinking skills into new contexts. Perkins et al. (1989) further suggest that anticipatory tactics and retrieval tactics promote transfer (see Figure 11).

The Transfer Curriculum

In looking at the transfer of learning by adult learners in staff development programs, Joyce and Showers (1983) suggest that

Figure 12
Teacher Levels of Transfer

Ollie the Head-in-the-Sand Ostrich OVERLOOKS  Does nothing; unaware of relevance and misses appropriate applications; overlooks intentionally. (resists) *"Great session but this wouldn't work with my kids or content" ... "I chose not to... because..."*	**Dan** the Drilling Woodpecker DUPLICATES  Drills and practices exactly as presented; Drill! Drill! Then stops; uses as an activity rather than as a strategy; duplicates. (copies) *"Could I have a copy of that transparency?"*
Laura the Look-Alike Penguin REPLICATES  Tailors to kids and content, but applies in similar content; all look-alike, does not transfer into new situation; replicates. (differentiates) *"I use the web for every character analysis."*	**Jonathan** Livingston Seagull INTEGRATES  Raised consciousness; acute awareness; deliberate refinement; integrates subtly with existing repertoire. (combines) *"I haven't used any of your ideas, but I'm wording my questions carefully. I've always done this, but now I'm doing more of it."*
Cathy the Carrier Pigeon MAPS  Consciously transfers ideas to various situations, contents; carries strategy as part of available repertoire; maps. (associates) *"I'm using the webbing strategy for everything."*	**Samantha** the Soaring Eagle INNOVATES  Innovates; flies with an idea; takes it into action beyond the initial conception; creates, enhances, invents; takes risks. (diverges) *"You have changed my teaching forever. I can never go back to what I used to do. I know too much. I'm too excited."*

while horizontal transfer shifts directly into the classroom teaching situation, vertical transfer requires adaptation to fit the conditions. High-road transfer requires understanding the purpose and rationale of the skill and know-how to adapt it with executive control. Still, looking at adult learners, Fogarty (1989) suggests a continuum of transfer behavior within the dichotomy of simple and complex transfer. The learner levels, originally indicative of adult creative transfer, are also similarly applied to student transfer as depicted in Figures 12 and 13.

Figure 13
Student Levels of Transfer

Ollie the Head-in-the-Sand Ostrich OVERLOOKS  Misses appropriate opportunity; overlooks; persists in former way. *"I get it right on the dittos, but I forget to use punctuation when I write an essay."* (Doesn't connect appropriateness.)	**Dan** the Drilling Woodpecker DUPLICATES  Performs the drill exactly as practiced; duplicates. *"Yours is not to question why—just invert and multiply."* (When dividing fractions, has no understanding of what she or he is doing.)
Laura the Look-Alike Penguin REPLICATES  Tailors but applies only in similar situation; all look alike; replicates. *"Paragraphing means I must have three 'indents' per page."* (Tailors into own story or essay, but paragraphs inappropriately.)	**Jonathan** Livingston Seagull INTEGRATES  Is aware; integrates; combines with other ideas and situations. *"I always try to guess (predict) what's going to happen next on T.V. shows."* (Connects to prior knowledge and experience.)
Cathy the Carrier Pigeon MAPS  Carries strategy to other content and situations. Associates and maps. *Parent-related story—"Tina suggested we brainstorm about our vacation ideas and rank them to help us decide."* (Carries new skills into life situations.)	**Samantha** the Soaring Eagle INNOVATES  Innovates; takes ideas beyond initial conception; risks; diverges. *"After studying flow charts for computer class, student constructs a Rube Goldberg type invention."* (Innovates; invents; diverges; goes beyond and creates something novel.)

Awareness of the learner's transfer level and monitoring of that transfer through appropriate cueing questions seem to promote creative transfer, which is increasingly complex. For example, for the learner who is simply duplicating the learned skill or strategy, which is a somewhat low level of transfer, the teacher might cue with a question such as, "Can you think of an adjustment you can make so that this idea is useful in another context?" This cue may be enough to spark movement toward

Figure 14
Transfer Cueing Questions

OVERLOOKING
Think of an instance when the skill or strategy would be inappropriate.
"I would not use ________ when__________."

DUPLICATING
Think of an opportunity when you could have used the skill or strategy.
"I wish I'd known about ________ when __________."

REPLICATING
Think of an adjustment that will make your application of __________ more relevant.
"Next time I'm going to __________."

INTEGRATING
Think of an analogy for the skill or strategy.
"__________ *is like* ________ *because both* __________."

MAPPING
Think of an opportunity to use the new idea.
"A strategy to carry across is ____________."

INNOVATING
Think of an application for a real-life setting.
"What if ________."

replicated transfer in which learners personally tailor the idea to suit their needs.

This reflective questioning based on transfer levels is analogous to a student who always draws figures in an identical way, almost as if they were produced in a cookie-cutter fashion. Simply by suggesting that the learner might change the eyes or hair on the figure, or even the size of it, the teacher propels the student toward creative divergence and more complex transfer. The metacognitive reflection questions can be self-monitored or peer-monitored with both adult and student learners. Note the shifts that are required as one wrestles with the transfer cueing questions in Figure 14.

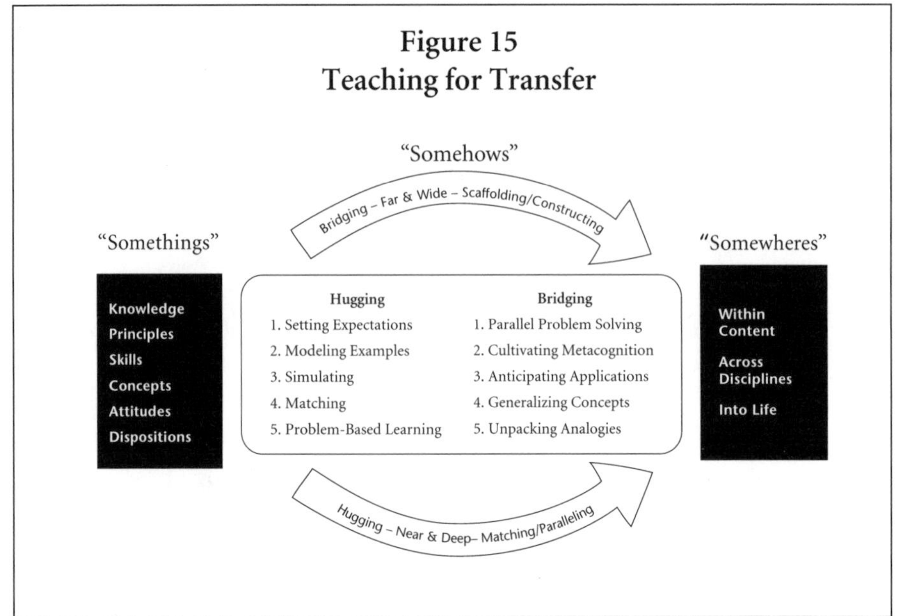

Shepherding Transfer

Some of the current thinking on transfer is addressed by Perkins et al. (1989). They look at the topic of teaching for transfer as the key to more thoughtful instruction. By focusing curricula on the "somethings" to be transferred (the knowledge, skills, concepts, principles, attitudes, and dispositions) and the "somewheres" that teachers want them transferred to (within content, across disciplines, and into life), instruction is expertly tailored by mediating the "somehows" of the hugging and bridging strategies.

By working with the model of somethings to transfer somewhere, the instructional strategies of the somehows take on greater emphasis in the teaching/learning situation. In essence, the curricula is shaped with the pieces, which have what Fogarty calls transfer power, and teaching for transfer becomes an explicit part of the lesson (see Figure 15).

Knowing that the Bo Peep theory leads only to the loss of one of the key aspects of the learning situation, the transfer of learning, and knowing that by ignoring transfer as the lost sheep of the instructional cycle, we again miss the essence of learning, which of course is the transfer, use, and application of learning in new settings. Knowing that if we pay attention to transfer and guide it like a good shepherd herds sheep, then we will take learning to new heights for learners of all ages and in all situations—knowing all this, we can pay attention to transfer, for isn't all learning for transfer?

CONCLUSION

The four realms of cognitive research tie together to provide practitioners with the tools to teach for thoughtfulness. Based on the context of teaching for transfer, these tools provide rich opportunities for teachers to shift from a conceptually poor recall agenda to a fertile format for mindfulness.

REFERENCES

Adams, M. et al. (1986). *Odyssey: A curriculum for thinking.* Watertown, MA: Mastery Education Corporation.

Anderson, R., Hiebert, E., Scott, J., & Wilkinson, I. (1984). *Becoming a nation of readers: The report of the commission on reading.* Washington, DC: The National Institute of Education.

Armbruster, B., & Anderson, T. (1980). *The effect of mapping on the free recall of expository test.* (Technical Report 160). Champaign-Urbana: Center for the Study of Reading, University of Illinois.

Ausubel, D. (1978). *Educational psychology: A cognitive view.* (2nd ed.). New York: Holt, Rinehart, & Winston.

Bellanca, J. (1990). *Keep them thinking: Level III.* Palatine, IL: IRI/Skylight Publishing.

Bellanca, J., & Fogarty, R. (1990). *Blueprints for thinking in the cooperative classroom.* Palatine, IL: IRI/Skylight Publishing.

Bellanca, J., & Fogarty, R. (1986). *Catch them thinking: A handbook of classroom strategies.* Palatine, IL: IRI/Skylight Publishing.

Beyer, B. K. (1987). *Practical strategies for the teaching of thinking.* Boston: Allyn & Bacon.

Black, H., & Black, S. (1987). *Building thinking skills: Books 1–3.* Pacific Grove, CA: Midwest Publications.

Brown, A. L. (1978). Knowing when, where, and how to remember: A problem of metacognition. In R. Glaser (Ed.), *Advances in instruction psychology* (1). Hillsdale, NJ: Lawrence Erlbaum.

Brown, A., & Campione, J. (1990). Communities of learning and thinking, or a context by any other name. *Human Development, 21,* 108–125.

Costa, A. (Ed.). (1985a). *Developing minds.* Alexandria, VA: Association for Supervision and Curriculum Development.

Costa, A. (1985b). *Teaching for intelligent behavior: A course syllabus.* Orangevale, CA: Search Models Unlimited.

Crabbe, A. B. (1989, September). The future problem solving program. *Educational Leadership,* pp. 27–29.

Dansereau, E., et al. (1979). Development and evaluation of a learning strategy training program. *Journal of Educational Psychology, 71*(1), 64–73.

Davidson, J. (1982, October). The group mapping activity for instruction in reading and thinking. *Journal of Reading,* pp. 53–56.

de Bono, E. (1973). *Lateral thinking: Creativity step by step.* New York: Harper & Row.

de Bono, E. (1970). *Lateral thinking.* New York: Harper & Row.

Edmonds, R. (1979, October). Effective schools for the urban poor. *Educational Leadership,* pp. 15–18.

Feuerstein, R. (1980). *Instrumental Enrichment.* Baltimore: University Park Press.

Fogarty, R. (1990). *Keep them thinking: Level II.* Palatine, IL: IRI/Skylight Publishing.

Fogarty, R. (1989). *From training to transfer: The role of creativity in the adult learner.* Doctoral dissertation, Loyola University of Chicago.

Fogarty, R., & Bellanca, J. (1989). *Patterns for thinking: Patterns for transfer.* Palatine, IL: IRI/Skylight Publishing.

Fogarty, R., & Bellanca, J. (1986). *Teach them thinking.* Palatine, IL: IRI/Skylight Publishing.

Fogarty, R., & Opeka, K. (1988). *Start them thinking.* Palatine, IL: IRI/Skylight Publishing.

Fogarty, R., Perkins, D., & Barell, J. (1991). *The mindful school: How to teach for transfer.* Palatine, IL: IRI/Skylight Publishing.

Gordon, W. J. (1961). *Synectics: The development of creative capacity.* New York: Harper & Row.

Hansen, J., Silver, H., & Strong, R. (1986). *Thoughtful education training series.* Moorestown, NJ: Hansen, Silver, Strong, & Associates.

Harvard University. (1983, October). *Project intelligence: The development of procedures to enhance thinking skills.* Final report. Submitted to the Minister for the Development of Human Intelligence, Republic of Venezuela.

Hunter, M. (1973). *Teach for transfer.* El Segundo, CA: Tip Publications.

Jones, B., Tinzmann, M., & Thelan, J. (1990). *Breakthroughs: Strategy for thinking* (series). Columbus, OH: Zaner-Bloser.

Joyce, B., & Showers, B. (1983). *Power in staff development through research and training.* Alexandria, VA: Association for Supervision and Curriculum Development.

Joyce, B., Showers, B., & Rolheiser-Bennett, C. (1987, October). Staff development and student learning: A synthesis of research and models of teaching. *Educational Leadership,* p. 17.

Joyce, B., & Weil, M. (1992). *Models of teaching.* Needham Heights, MA: Allyn & Bacon.

Lipman, M., Sharp, A., & Oscanyan, R. (1980). *Philosophy in the classroom* (2nd ed.). Philadelphia: Temple University Press.

Lyman, F., & McTighe, J. (1988, April). Cueing thinking in the classroom: The promise of theory-embedded tools. *Educational Leadership,* pp. 18–24.

Marzano, R., & Arredondo, D. (1986, May). Restructuring schools through the teaching of thinking skills. *Educational Leadership,* p. 23.

Marzano, R., Brandt, R., Hughes, C., Jones, B., Presseisen, B., Rankin, S., & Suhor, C. (1987). *Dimensions of thinking: A framework for curriculum and instruction.* Alexandria, VA: Association for Supervision and Curriculum Development.

Meeker, M. N. (1969). *The structure of intellect: Its interpretation and uses.* Columbus, OH: Charles E. Merrill.

Opeka, K. (1990). *Keep them thinking: Level I.* Palatine, IL: IRI/Skylight Publishing.

Parnes, S. (1975). *Aha! Insights into creative behavior.* Buffalo, NY: D.O.K.

Parnes, S. (1972). *Creativity: Unlocking human potential.* Buffalo, NY: D.O.K.

Perkins, D. N. (1986). *Knowledge as design.* Hillsdale, NJ: Lawrence Erlbaum.

Perkins, D. N., & Salomon, G. (1988, September). Teaching for transfer. *Educational Leadership,* pp. 22–32.

Perkins, D. N., Mirman, J., Tishman, S., & Goodrich, H. (1991). *Connections: A program for integrating the teaching of thinking with instruction in the subject matters.* Unpublished material prepared by Project Zero, Harvard Graduate School of Education, Cambridge, MA, in conjunction with the Regional Lab of the Northeast and Islands, Andover, MA.

Pogrow, S. (1990). *HOTS: A validated thinking skills approach to using computers with at-risk students.* New York: Scholastic.

Sternberg, R. (1984, September). How can we teach intelligence? *Educational Leadership,* pp. 38–48.

Swartz, R. J., & Perkins, D. N. (1989). *Teaching thinking: Issues and approaches.* Pacific Grove, CA: Midwest Publications.

Torrance, E. P. (1978). Giftedness in solving future problems. *Journal of Creative Behavior, 12,* 75–86.

Upton, R. (1985). *Strategic reasoning.* Bloomington, IN: Innovative Sciences.

Vaughn, L. (1982, February). Use the construct procedure to foster active reading and learning. *Journal of Reading.*

Wales, C., Nardi, A., & Stager, R. (1987). *Thinking skills: Making a choice.* Morgantown, WV: West Virginia University Center for Guided Design.

Whimbey, A. (1975). *Intelligence can be taught.* New York: E. P. Dutton.

Will, H. (1991). The junior great books program of interpretive reading and discussion. In A. Costa (Ed.), *Developing minds: Programs for teaching thinking* (rev. ed., Vol. 2, pp. 57–58). Alexandria, VA: Association for Supervision and Curriculum Development.

Winocur, S. (1983). *Project impact.* Costa Mesa, CA: Orange County School District.

Wittrock, M. (1967). Replacement and nonreplacement strategies in children's problem solving. *Journal of Educational Psychology, 58*(2), 69–74.

Educating Teachers for Higher Order Thinking: The Three-Story Intellect

by Robin Fogarty and Jay McTighe

Vignette

History Teacher: I'm so frustrated with my class today. For homework, I asked them to compare the major campaign strategies of the two candidates. That seems straightforward enough. It's all over the media.

American Literature Teacher: Yes, it's certainly a current topic that they should be hearing lots about. So what happened?

History Teacher: You should see what they turned in. It's awful! Sometimes they just don't *think*.

American Literature Teacher: That's exactly right. They don't always think about what they're doing. It's almost as though they need to be taught *how* to think.

History Teacher: I always assume that by this age, kids know how to think. So when I ask them to compare two ideas in an essay question, I expect them to automatically outline similarities and differences—how the two ideas are alike and how they differ.

American Literature Teacher: But they simply tell one way they're different and think they're answering the question. They never fully explore the idea by comparing and contrasting many characteristics.

From *Theory Into Practice*, Summer 1993, pp. 161–169 (A theme issue on Teaching for Higher Order Thinking).

History Teacher: That's right. You've had the same experience, then? You know, we probably need to take some time to teach them strategies for thinking.

American Literature Teacher: You mean, teach them thinking skills?

History Teacher: Yes, but more than that. We need to actually demonstrate good thinking. They need the tools to work with so they can approach any question, any situation, and think it through.

Teachers everywhere are familiar with the dilemma in this scenario. They see student work that is lacking in thoughtfulness; they hear student responses that reveal faulty thinking; they struggle with the challenge of helping students use knowledge in meaningful ways. And they are moving gently from that standard. "Yes, but . . ." hesitation in the direction of a much needed, "What if . . ." exploration.

Cognitive instruction provides the ways to engage students in dealing with that content in a thoughtful manner.

Teachers are beginning to realize that their subject matter content is not the focus but the vehicle that carries the skills of critical and creative thinking (Swartz & Perkins, 1990). The content provides something to think about, but cognitive instruction provides the ways to engage students in dealing with that content in a thoughtful manner (or to meaningfully use content knowledge).

Seasoned teachers know their content well, understand child development, and have classroom management in hand. What they need and want more of is professional development in the area of cognitive instruction. They want to know how to teach students to think; how to develop the skills students will need as they encounter life's challenges.

The purpose of this discussion is to delineate the process by which teachers learn how to teach thinking in their classrooms. We have found the following quotation by Oliver Wendell Holmes (1872/1884) useful in considering the process of thinking and the process of training teachers to teach thinking.

> [There are] one-story intellects, two-story intellects, three-story intellects with skylights. All fact-collectors, who have no aim beyond their facts, are one-story men [sic]. Two-story men compare, reason, generalize, using the labors of the fact-collectors as well as their own. Three-story men idealize, imagine, predict; their best illumination comes from above, through the skylight.

Like Holmes's three stories, the evolution of the thinking skills movement occurred in three phases, which are described in the next section. The section that follows then shows how this three-phase process can illuminate the process of teaching teachers to teach thinking. The final section provides guidelines for staff development.

Examples of "first-story" thinking include skill development in classifying, comparing and contrasting, and analyzing for bias.

TRACKING THE THINKING SKILLS MOVEMENT

As noted above, the maturation process of the educational phenomenon called the thinking skills movement occurred in three phases. The phases are described below.

Phase 1: Thinking Skills

In the early 1980s, the idea of teaching thinking skills to all students (not just the gifted) was somewhat new. Perhaps influenced by the "basic skills" emphasis, advocates for cognitive instruction recommended that specific skills of thinking be identified and taught explicitly, using a direct instruction method (Beyer, 1983; Black & Black, 1985; Costa, 1981; Ennis, 1985; Guilford, 1979; Marzano & Hutchins, 1985; Meeker, 1976; Paul, Blinker, Adamson, & Martin, 1988; Sternberg, 1984). This parallels the first-story thinking stages of gathering knowledge and facts.

Examples of "first-story" thinking include skill development in classifying, comparing and contrasting, and analyzing for bias. Skills were taught within familiar content and practiced frequently before they were used in other content areas. The focus in this early stage was on developing some level of basic knowledge and student competency in using a targeted number of thinking skills. In fact, a number of "stand-alone" thinking skills programs, separate from traditional content areas (e.g.,

Odyssey, Adams et al., 1986; Project Impact, Winocur, 1983; Midwest Instrumental Enrichment, Black & Black, 1985; Cognitive Research Trust (CoRT), de Bono, 1983) became popular during this era.

Phase 2: Critical/Creative Thinking

Phase 2 of the nationwide movement paralleled the "second-story intellect" of Holmes's model. Proponents of cognitive instruction focused on the broad critical and creative macro-processes of thinking necessary for problem solving, decision making, and inventing (de Bono, 1983; Feuerstein, 1980; Fogarty & Bellanca, 1986; Gardner, 1983; Parnes, Nickerson, Perkins, & Smith, 1985; Paul et al., 1988; Pogrow, 1990; Taylor, 1968; Torrance, 1973). Even the terminology changed. Often, the word *skills* was dropped in favor of the encompassing concept: *thinking*. Emphasis was on active processing of information through reasoning within subject areas rather than through decontextualized, "content-free" thinking skill activities.

Graphic organizers serve to make the invisible visible by assisting students in generating and organizing ideas and information.

This stage of the thinking skills movement was enhanced by the incorporation of two instructional innovations: cooperative learning (Cohen, 1986; Glasser, 1986; Johnson & Johnson, 1986; Kagan, 1977; Kohn, 1986; Sharan & Sharan, 1976; Slavin, 1983) and visual representation of information and ideas with graphic organizers (Armbruster & Anderson, 1980; McTighe & Lyman, 1988; Vacca, 1981). Research and experience show that cooperative learning enhances thinking processes. Through cooperative learning, students articulate their thoughts to each other and thus engage in an interactive approach to processing information.

Graphic organizers serve to make the invisible visible by assisting students in generating and organizing ideas and information. Both cooperative learning and graphic organizers provide powerful, interactive, and organizational mind tools for helping students think more effectively about the content.

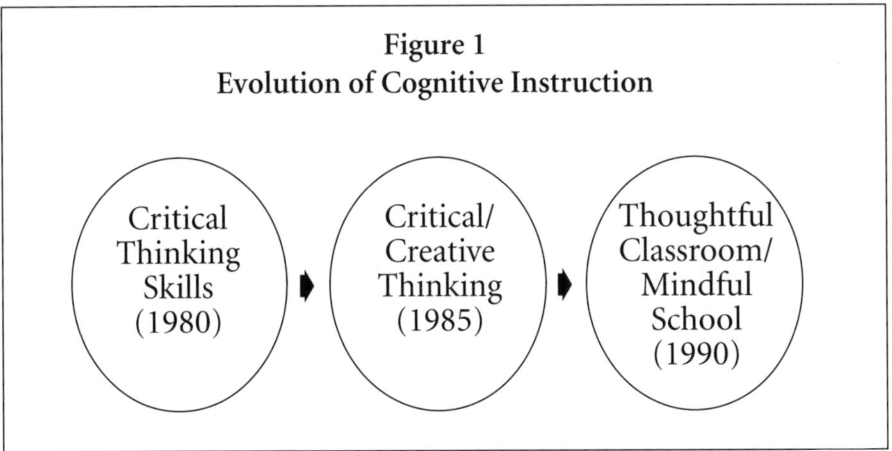

Figure 1
Evolution of Cognitive Instruction

Phase 3: Thoughtful Classroom/Mindful School

Phase 3 of the thinking skills movement (the current state of things) builds on Phases 1 and 2 but extends the application level and is characterized by metacognitive reflection about learning (Brown, 1982; Costa, Bellanca, & Fogarty, 1992a, 1992b; Feuerstein, 1980; Flavell, 1977; Fogarty & Bellanca, 1991; Fogarty, Perkins, & Barell, 1991; Swartz & Perkins, 1990). Concerned about moving thinking skills to a new level in which thoughtfulness is fostered in the integrated, holistic designs of curriculum and instruction, the third-story phase mindfully transfers thinking to novel situations (see Figure 1).

TEACHING THINKING AND THE THREE-STORY INTELLECT

The thinking skills movement passed through three levels of development: skill acquisition, critical and creative thinking process, and thoughtful application. Teaching teachers to teach thinking may parallel those same levels: explicit micro-skill instruction, active practice in problem solving and decision making, and mindful application and transfer across content and into life situations (Beyer, 1987).

First-Story Intellect: Skill Acquisition

To teach thinking, teachers must have an awareness of and competence with the specific skills of thinking. In Phase 1,

Table 1
Creative and Critical Thinking Skills

Creative Thinking Skills	Critical Thinking Skills
Brainstorming	Attributing
Visualizing	Comparing/contrasting
Personifying	Classifying
Inventing	Sequencing
Associating relationships	Prioritizing
Inferring	Drawing conclusions
Generalizing	Determining cause/effect
Predicting	Analyzing for bias
Hypothesizing	Analyzing for assumptions
Making analogies	Solving for analogies
Dealing with ambiguity and paradox	Evaluating

based on the direct instruction of an explicit thinking skill introduced by Beyer (1987), teachers can be introduced to cognitive instruction by identifying, defining, and learning about explicit thinking skills. To do this, in Beyer's model, teachers are made aware of thinking as an entity in itself and begin to take a self-inventory to determine which thinking skills are inherent in their subject matter content (specifically, which micro-skills are embedded in the tasks they already assign to students).

Examples of thinking skills (Fogarty & Bellanca, 1986) that include both the creative skills of generating and producing ideas and the critical skills of analysis and evaluation can be given to teachers (see Table 1). Upon examination of specific content areas, particular skills pop up over and over again in the curriculum. For example, the skill of classifying occurs consistently in the science curriculum; literature analysis relies on the skill of inferring; history calls for critical analysis or comparing cultures, events, and leaders; math demands strategic use of the skill of hypothesizing and proof; computer technology dictates skill application in sequential thinking; and design requires skill in visualizing. Of course, the list is unending, but the key is for teachers to identify the skills necessary to think about the content they are already teaching.

Figure 2
Teaching an Explicit Thinking Skill

Skill: inferring

Synonyms: assuming, deducing, implying

Definition: making an assumption based on subtle verbal and nonverbal clues, "reading between the lines," concluding or projecting based on premise or evidence

When to use: looking beyond the literal, sensing moods, evaluating points of view, seeing the hidden or implied meaning

Example: guessing mood from facial clues, body language, tone of voice

How to use: Identify literal level, face-value
Note verbal and nonverbal
Find evidence
Extend original interpretation
Restate revised interpretation

Once these skills are noted, individual teachers, or grade-level and department teams, can be asked to agree on the skills to teach with their content. This decision should be based on the desired learning outcomes and the nature and needs of the students (Davidson & Worsham, 1992). One approach is to introduce the thinking skills through a direct instructional model (Beyer, 1987), but become infused in the subject-matter lesson as the students process the data and information. To teach the skills, the teacher:

- names the skills and defines them
- elicits synonyms, as well as examples of their use
- provides an explicit model of the steps/strategies involved in using the skill
- talks about how and when to use the skills with special references to subject matter content
- plans for guided practice

Figure 2 provides an example of the skill, inferring.

Figure 3
A Venn Diagram of *The Old Man and the Sea*

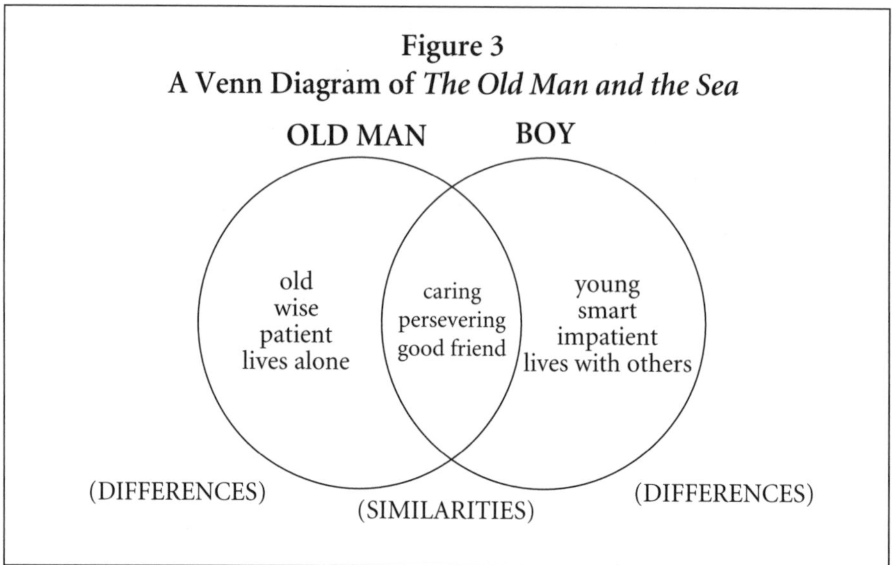

Second-Story Intellect: Making Meaning

Once teachers gain some knowledge of the explicit thinking skills, they can move directly into second-story thinking by learning how to provide opportunities for students to practice the skills with the appropriate processing tools—cooperative learning structures and graphic representations of their thinking (Bellanca & Fogarty, 1991). This is where students make meaning with the various mind tools available to them.

This is the shift from a direct-instruction model that focuses on skill development to the next level of the intellect where learners actively process the information in order to construct knowledge and meaning for themselves. Just as the thinking skills movement naturally advanced to this broader focus on thinking and reasoning, so, too, the teacher learns to move students to this next level when teaching them how to think.

In an example of second-story thinking, students are arranged in cooperative groups of three or four members, with each member assigned a role: materials manager, recorder, reporter, and observer. On large chart paper, the students record information from their text and/or notes in a Venn diagram (see Figure 3) to compare and contrast two characters from their reading. After ample time, the charts are discussed in the whole group by sampling each group's visual.

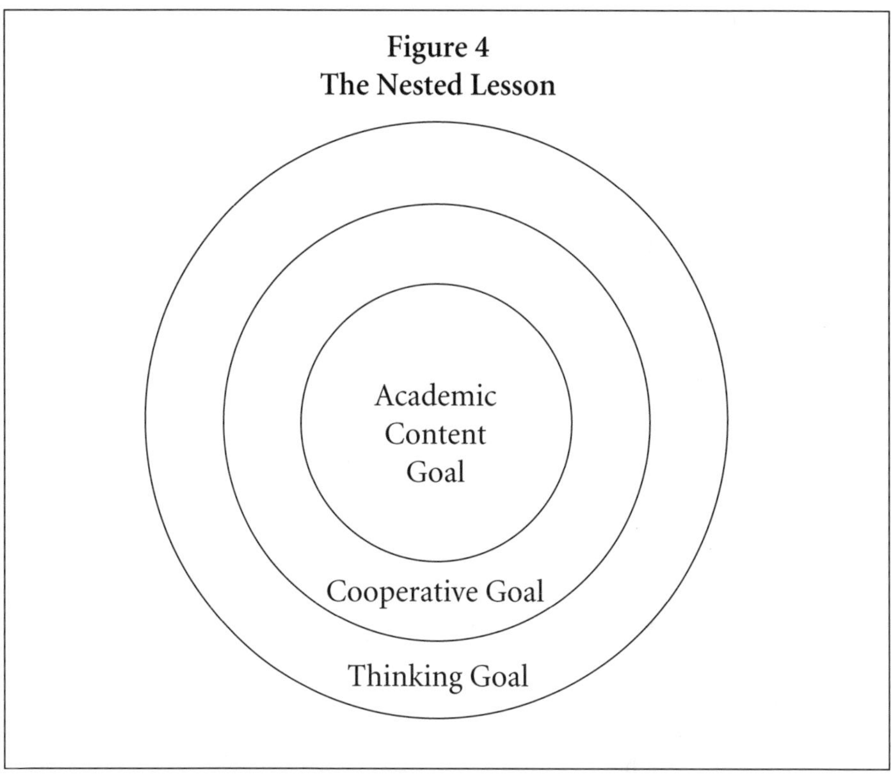

As part of this activity, a social skill such as "active listening" or "encouraging others" can be targeted for practice. Following the academic task, members discuss the social behavior of the group as well as their final product. In these mini-sessions following the team work, the focus is on team-building skills, communication, trust building, and conflict resolution (Johnson & Johnson, 1986).

This second-story intellect emphasizes the processing phase of teaching thinking using the "nested" model of instruction (Fogarty, 1991) in which the teacher learns to target three goals: an academic goal, a cooperative goal, and a thinking goal (see Figure 4). The academic goal is content based and is often at the center of the nest. The cooperative goals and the thinking goals are intertwined with the content goal to add complexity to the task and to provide teaching efficiency.

By targeting three goals simultaneously, the nested model structures for high-content, high-support, and high-challenge instruction. By using both cooperative learning strategies and the visual representation of the graphic organizers, teachers have two authentic tools by which to assess student development in the affective and cognitive realm (Costa et al., 1992a, 1992b; Kallick, 1989; Jeroski, Brownlie, & Kaser, 1990). Teachers can *hear* what student thinking sounds like in cooperative learning groups and they can *see* what student thinking looks like by using the graphic organizers. Both methods offer invaluable evidence of growth as students actively process content and build on prior knowledge and past experiences.

Second-story thinking, where teachers help students internalize and personalize the thinking skills while learning and using mind tools, lays the groundwork for third-story thoughtfulness that takes them beyond the skylight.

Third-Story Thinking: Transfer and Application

Third-story thoughtfulness requires mindful abstraction for application and transfer of learning. As teachers help students to anchor their learning using the deep processing methods structured into second-story thinking, students warehouse concepts, skills, attitudes, and strategies for lifelong use. The mind tools they learn are theirs forever—for creative use and adaptation in diverse academic and personal situations throughout their lives (Brown, 1978).

The thoughtful behaviors of third-story thinking are rooted in metacognitive reflection, or thinking *beyond* the cognitive—knowing what you know and what you do not know, what works well and what to do differently. Metacognitive reflection is manifested in the awareness and regulation of one's own behavior. It requires self-assessment and self-adjustment. Such reflection fosters more thoughtful behavior as students recognize and take control of their thoughts and actions.

For example, students meet in small groups at the beginning of math class to review their homework problems. They discuss only the ones with differing answers, trying to reconcile the differences. Only when agreement is reached do they turn in their papers. In this scenario, group members trace their problem-solving steps in an effort to find the best answer. Students may reason that they need to multiply at one point in the problem because they know the answer has to be a larger number.

Figure 5
Significant Curricular Outcomes

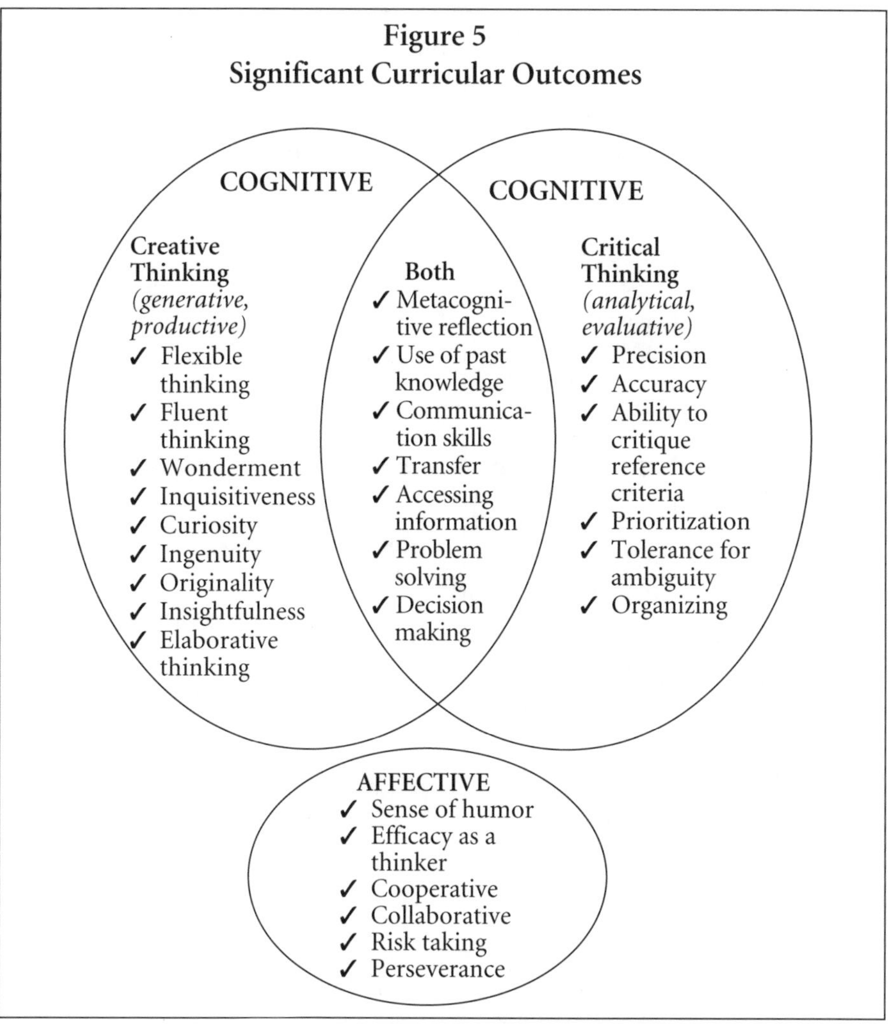

The focus is on being aware of one's thinking processes and, in turn, being privy to others' thinking strategies. The goal, of course, is to become better at problem solving. Thus, students develop awareness and control over their own thinking through reflection.

Third-story thoughtfulness is based on expected outcomes—outcomes that include lifelong habits of mind as suggested in the diagram in Figure 5 (Fogarty, 1992). Until teachers learn to ferret out significant outcomes and make them the focus of schooling, cognitive instruction remains at the first-story

Table 2
Teaching Thinking Using the Three-Story Intellect Model

	Focus	Intellect	Description	Researchers/ Authors
THIRD STORY	Thoughtfulness	THIRD-STORY INTELLECT Applying the skill(s) and process(es) in diverse academic and personal settings	Creative use and transfer of skill(s) and process(es) through metacognitive reflection	Barell; Beyer; Brown; Costa; Feuerstein; Flavell; Fogarty & Bellanca; Gardner; Presseisen; Resnick; Salomon & Perkins; Swartz & Perkins
SECOND STORY	Thinking	SECOND-STORY INTELLECT Processing skills through articulation and visualization	Intense student involvement to think and reason with the use of cooperative learning and graphic organizers	Armbruster; Anderson; Barell; Bellanca & Fogarty; Black & Black; Bloom; Cohen; de Bono; Ennis; Johnson & Johnson; Kagan; Lipman; Lyman & McTighe; Torrance
FIRST STORY	Thinking Skills	FIRST-STORY INTELLECT Gathering information and skill acquisition	Direct instruction in explicit thinking skill(s)	Black & Black; Beyer; Costa; de Bono; Ennis; Feuerstein; Fogarty & Bellanca; Hansen, Silver & Strong; Marzano & Arredondo; Paul; Pogrow; Whimbey & Whimbey

level of direct instruction/acquisition, dipping slightly into the second-story level of guided practice.

As teachers become more aware of the critical elements of the thoughtful classroom, they are better able to align the thinking elements with the district outcomes. The mindful school is a place where students can develop productive problem-solving strategies, mindful decision-making tactics, and creative, innovative thinking; where teachers, as architects of the intellect, design a curriculum that invites learners into a three-story intellect structure; and where, as capable apprentices, students gradually accept responsibility for their own learning as they develop their own third-story intellects (see Table 2).

ABOVE THE SKYLIGHT: GUIDELINES FOR STAFF DEVELOPMENT

> *One who learns from one who is learning drinks from a running stream.*—Indian saying

Students are learning how to think from teachers who are learning how to teach students to think. It may follow that the thinking processes teachers bring to the classroom carry a springlike freshness and the accompanying strangeness of something budding and new. To help teachers gain confidence as well as competence in teaching thinking, the following principles (see Bloom & Krathwohl, 1977; Costa, 1981; Marzano et al., 1988; Sternberg, 1984) become critical as we plan our professional development activities.

The messages teachers send through their actions influence students' attitudes toward learning and their perceptions of themselves as thinkers.

Establish a climate that encourages thoughtfulness. The messages teachers send through their actions influence students' attitudes toward learning and their perceptions of themselves as thinkers. In a rigid, controlling, "one correct answer method" classroom, students may be hesitant to question the teacher or offer innovative ideas. A thoughtful classroom, on the other hand, encourages inquiry and experimentation, values unique thinking styles, honors diverse points of view, and provides opportunities for students to choose products and methods.

Teachers of teachers have an important responsibility to establish a learning environment within their workshops and courses that invite thinking. The saying, "What you do speaks so loudly that I can't hear what you say," reminds teachers and teacher educators of the importance of their actions in supporting or inhibiting thoughtfulness.

Help teachers develop a framework of thinking. A search of the literature reveals a variety of theories and models reflecting different conceptions of thinking. For example, Bloom & Krathwohl (1977), Guilford (1979), Costa (1981), Sternberg (1984), and Marzano et al. (1988) have offered frameworks or taxonomies based on their own theoretical interpretations. The existence of these diverse views indicates that the "unified field theory" of thinking and cognition is not yet agreed upon. Nevertheless, a theoretical base is important since it provides a conceptual foundation for grounding teaching practices.

Staff developers and course instructors have the option of introducing a specific model of thinking or presenting two or more models from which teachers can select. They must then help teachers to internalize the chosen model and apply it within their curriculum.

Apply thinking skills and processes. The overt application of thinking skills and processes to curriculum content helps students extend and refine their knowledge. Likewise, this principle applies to teachers learning new ways to develop thinking abilities. Staff developers and course instructors "practice what they preach" when they involve teachers in *comparing* two lessons, *analyzing* commercial thinking skills materials, *making decisions* about appropriate assessment methods, or *developing* visual maps of the essential concepts in a unit of study. Not only do such activities promote thoughtful engagement, they provide instructional models that can be applied in the classroom.

The overt application of thinking skills and processes to curriculum content helps students extend and refine their knowledge.

Utilize cooperative learning strategies. Teachers who employ cooperative learning methods promote thinking because these collaborative experiences engage students in an interactive approach to processing information (Johnson & Johnson, 1986). Research on cooperative learning substantiates its benefits: greater retention of subject matter, improved attitudes toward learning, increased opportunities for "higher order" processing of information, and enhanced interpersonal relations among group members (Johnson & Johnson, 1986).

These same benefits may be realized when cooperative strategies are used during professional development sessions with teachers. The application of strategies such as think-pair-share, peer response groups (that react to teacher-developed unit plans or videotaped lessons), and brainstorming contributes to thoughtful, active learning on the part of the teachers while helping them internalize the finer points of these techniques. Likewise, peer coaching and collegial conferencing provide beneficial opportunities for analytical observations and thoughtful dialogue about instructional practice.

Encourage continuous reflection. Helping students to become reflective is a fundamental goal for teachers of thinking. The methods suggested for regular use in thinking classrooms are equally appropriate for teacher seminars and courses. By routinely asking teachers to examine their underlying beliefs about learning and to evaluate their teaching, the "third story" of the intellect is engaged. The use of learning logs/journals to record structured and free-writing responses is an especially effective means of encouraging reflection on instruction. In addition, staff developers and course instructors can demonstrate metacognition by thinking aloud as they explain their own instructional decision-making processes.

CONCLUSION

Just as we see the thinking skills movement follow its evolutionary path from skill acquisition, to meaning-making, and finally to application and transfer, we also see the same gradual process for teachers as they learn the skills of how to teach thinking. In turn, these teachers see their students experience the same stages as they develop fully their three-story intellects. Teachers, as architects of the intellect, leave a three-story legacy.

REFERENCES

Adams, M., Buscaglia, J., Herrnstein, R., de Sanchez, M., Swats, J., Huggins, A., Starr, B., Nickerson, R., Grignetti, M., Feehrer, C., Perkins, D., Laserna, C. (1986). *Odyssey: A curriculum for thinking.* Watertown, MA: Charlesbridge Publishing.

Armbruster, B., & Anderson, T. (1980). *The effect of mapping on the free recall of expository text.* Tech. Rep. No. 1609. Champaign-Urbana: Center for the Study of Reading, University of Illinois.

Barell, J. (1991). *Teaching for thoughtfulness: Classroom strategies to enhance intellectual development.* White Plains, NY: Longman.

Bellanca, J., & Fogarty, R. (1991). *Blueprints for thinking in the cooperative classroom* (2nd ed.). Palatine, IL: IRI/Skylight Publishing.

Bellanca, J., & Fogarty, R. (1986). *Teach them thinking.* Palatine, IL: IRI/ Skylight Publishing.

Beyer, B. (1983, November). Common sense about teaching thinking. *Educational Leadership,* pp. 44–49.

Beyer, B. (1984, March). Improving thinking skills—Defining the problem. *Phi Delta Kappan, 65,* 486–490.

Beyer, B. (1987). *Practical strategies for the teaching of thinking.* Boston: Allyn & Bacon.

Black, H., & Black, S. (1985). *Building thinking skills.* Pacific Grove, CA: Midwest Publications.

Bloom, B., & Krathwohl, D. (1977). *Taxonomy of educational objectives, Handbook I: Cognitive domain* (Reprint of 1956 editorial). New York: David McKay.

Brandt, R. (1984). Teaching of thinking, for thinking, and about thinking. *Educational Leadership, 42*(1), 3.

Brown, A. (1982, April). Inducing strategic learning from text by means of informed self control thinking. *Topics in Learning Disabilities, 2*(1), 1–17.

Brown, A. (1978). Knowing when, where, and how to remember: A problem of metacognition. In R. Glaser (Ed.), *Advances in instructional psychology* (Vol. 1; pp. 77–165). Hillsdale, NJ: Lawrence Erlbaum.

Cohen, E. (1986). *Designing groupwork.* New York: Teachers College Press.

Costa, A. (1981, October). Teaching for intelligent behavior. *Educational Leadership,* pp. 29–32.

Costa, A. (1984, November). Mediating the metacognitive. *Educational Leadership,* pp. 57–62.

Costa, A. (Ed.). (1985). *Developing minds: A resource book for teaching thinking.* Alexandria, VA: Association for Supervision and Curriculum Development.

Costa, A., Bellanca, J., & Fogarty, R. (Eds.). (1992a). *If minds matter: A foreword to the future (Vol. I).* Palatine, IL: IRI/Skylight Publishing.

Costa, A., Bellanca, J., & Fogarty, R. (Eds.). (1992b). *If minds matter: A foreword to the future (Vol. II).* Palatine, IL: IRI/Skylight Publishing.

Davidson, N., & Worsham, T. (Eds.). (1992). *Enhancing thinking through cooperative learning.* New York: Teachers College Press.

de Bono, E. (1969). *The mechanisms of the mind.* New York: Simon & Schuster.

de Bono, E. (1970). *Lateral thinking.* New York: Harper & Row.

de Bono, E. (1983, June). The direct teaching of thinking as a skill. *Phi Delta Kappan, 64,* 104.

Ennis, R. (1985). Goals for a critical thinking curriculum. In A. Costa (Ed.), *Developing minds: A resource book for teaching thinking* (pp. 68–72). Alexandria, VA: Association for Supervision and Curriculum Development.

Feuerstein, R. (1980). *Instrumental Enrichment.* Baltimore: University Park Press.

Flavell, J. (1977). *Cognitive development.* Englewood Cliffs, NJ: Prentice-Hall.

Fogarty, R. (1992). Beyond test scores: Tracking significant outcomes. *Cogitare, 6*(3), 2.

Fogarty, R. (1991). *The mindful school: How to integrate the curricula.* Palatine, IL: IRI/Skylight Publishing.

Fogarty, R. (1989). *From training to transfer: The role of creativity in the adult learner.* Unpublished doctoral dissertation, Loyola University of Chicago.

Fogarty, R., & Bellanca, J. (1991). *Patterns for thinking: Patterns for transfer.* Palatine, IL: IRI/Skylight Publishing.

Fogarty, R., & Bellanca, J. (1986). *Teach them thinking.* Palatine, IL: IRI/Skylight Publishing.

Fogarty, R., Perkins, D., & Barell, J. (1991). *The mindful school: How to teach for transfer.* Palatine, IL: IRI/Skylight Publishing.

Gardner, H. (1983). *Frames of mind: The theory of multiple intelligences.* New York: Basic Books.

Glasser, W. (1986). *Control theory in the classroom.* New York: Harper & Row.

Guilford, J. P. (1979). *Way beyond I.Q.: A triarchic theory of human intelligence.* New York: Cambridge University Press.

Hansen, J., Silver, H., & Strong, R. (1986). *Thoughtful education training series.* Morristown, NJ: Hansen, Silver, Strong, & Associates.

Hemingway, E. (1980). *Old man and the sea.* New York: Scribner. (Original work published 1952.)

Holmes, O. W. (1884). *The poet at the breakfast table* (19th ed.). Boston: Houghton-Mifflin. (Original work published 1872.)

Jeroski, S., Brownlie, F., & Kaser, L. (1990). *Reading and responding: Evaluation resources for your classroom.* (Vols. 1–2: Late primary and primary). Toronto: Nelson Canada. (Available in the United States from The Wright Group, Bothel, WA.)

Johnson, R. & Johnson, D. (1986). *Circles of learning: Cooperation in the classroom.* Alexandria, VA: Association for Supervision and Curriculum Development.

Jones, B. F. (1987). Strategic teaching: A cognitive focus. In B. F. Jones, A. S. Palincsar, D. Ogle, & E. Carr (Eds.), *Strategic teaching and learning: Cognitive instruction in the content areas* (pp. 33–63). Alexandria, VA: Association for Supervision and Curriculum Development.

Kagan, S. (1977). Social motives and behaviors of Mexican American and Anglo American children. In J. L. Martinez (Ed.), *Chicano psychology* (pp. 45–86). New York: Academic Press.

Kallick, B. (1989). *Changing schools into communities for thinking.* Grand Forks, ND: University of North Dakota Press.

Kohn, A. (1986). *No contest: The case against competition.* Boston: Houghton-Mifflin.

Lipman, M., Sharp, A., & Oscanyan, F. (1980). *Philosophy in the classroom* (2nd ed.). Philadelphia: Temple University Press.

Machado, L. (1980). *The right to be intelligent.* New York: Pergamon.

Marzano, R., & Arredondo, D. (1986, May). Restructuring schools through the teaching of thinking skills. *Educational Leadership,* pp. 20–26.

Marzano, R., Brandt, R., Hughes, C. S., Jones, B. F., Presseisen, B. Z., Rankin, S. C., & Suhor, C. (1988). *Dimensions of thinking: A framework for curriculum and instruction.* Alexandria, VA: Association for Supervision and Curriculum Development.

Marzano, R., & Hutchins, R. (1985). Thinking skills: A conceptual framework. Issue of "Noteworthy." Aurora, CO: Midcontinent Regional Educational Laboratory. (ERIC Document Reproduction Service No. 266 436).

McTighe, J., & Lyman, F. (1988). Cueing thinking in the classroom: The promise of theory-embedded tools. *Educational Leadership, 45*(7), pp. 18–24.

Meeker, M. (1976). *Learning to plan, judge, and make decisions* (A "Structure of intellect" series). El Segundo, CA: S.O.I. Institute.

Osborn, O. (1963). *Applied imagination.* New York: Scribner.

Parnes, S., Nickerson, R., Perkins, D., & Smith, E. (1985). *The teaching of thinking.* Hillsdale, NJ: Lawrence Erlbaum.

Paul, R., Blinker, A., Adamson, R., & Martin, D. (1988). *Critical thinking handbook: High school.* Rohnert Park, CA: Sonoma State University.

Perkins, D. (1986). *Knowledge as design.* Hillsdale, NJ: Lawrence Erlbaum.

Perkins, D., & Salomon, G. (1988, September). Teaching for transfer. *Educational Leadership,* pp. 22–32.

Perkins, D., & Salomon, G. (1989, January-February). Are cognitive skills context bound? *Educational Researcher, 18,* 16–25.

Pogrow, S. (1990). *HOTS: A validated thinking skills approach to using computers with at-risk students.* New York: Scholastic.

Presseisen, B., Sternberg, R., Kischer, K., Knight, C., & Feuerstein, R. (1990). *Learning and thinking styles: Classroom interaction.* Washington, DC: National Education Association and Research for Better Schools.

Resnick, L., & Klopfer, L. (Eds.). (1989). *Toward the thinking curriculum: Current cognitive research.* Alexandria, VA: Association for Supervision and Curriculum Development.

Seigel, H. (1980, November). Critical thinking as an educational ideal. *Educational Forum, 45*(1), 7–23.

Sharan, S., & Sharan, Y. (1976). *Small group teaching.* Englewood Cliffs, NJ: Educational Technology Publications.

Slavin, R. (1983). *Cooperative learning.* New York: Longman.

Sternberg, R. (1984). How can we teach intelligence? *Educational Leadership, 42*(1), 38–48.

Swartz, R., & Perkins, D. (1990). *Teaching thinking: Issues and approaches.* Pacific Grove, CA: Midwest Publications.

Taylor, C. (1967). Questioning and creating: A model for curriculum and reform. *Journal of Creative Behavior, 1*(1), 22–23.

Taylor, C. (1968, December). Be talent developers as well as knowledge dispensers. *Today's Education, 14*(8), 67–69.

Torrance, E. (1973). Can we teach children to think creatively? *Journal of Creative Behavior, 6*(2), 114–143.

Vacca, R. (1981). *Reading in the content areas.* Boston: Little, Brown.

Vygotsky, L. (1978). *Mind in society: The development of higher-order processes.* Cambridge, MA: Harvard University Press.

Wales, C. (1979, February). Does how you teach make a difference? *Engineering Education, 69*, 394–398.

Whimbey, A. (1975). *Intelligence can be taught.* New York: Innovative Science.

Winocur, L. (1983). *Project impact.* Costa Mesa, CA: Orange County School District.

Multiple Intelligences: Integrated Instruction

by Robin Fogarty and Judy Stoehr

It's not how smart you are, but how you are smart. This idea refers to Gardner's theory of multiple intelligences, which first appeared in his seminal piece, *Frames of Mind*, in 1983. Inspired by his work with brain-damaged veterans at Boston's Veteran Medical Center and with developing minds of children through his work at Project Zero at Harvard's Graduate School of Education, Gardner used what he had learned to formulate a theory advocating seven ways of viewing the world.

Rounding out the accepted and established intelligences of the *verbal* and *mathematical*, Gardner hypothesized that human potential encompasses *spatial*, *musical*, and *kinesthetic*, as well as *interpersonal* and *intrapersonal* intelligences. His comprehensive view of intelligence further suggested that while the seven intelligences are independent of one another, they do work together.

The mutiple intelligences theory allows one to assess the talents and skills of the whole individual.

Gardner postulated that his theory of seven intelligences would offer an alternative to the theory of intelligence as indicated by an intelligence quotient (IQ) score. The multiple intelligences theory allows one to assess the talents and skills of the whole individual rather than just his or her verbal and mathematical skills. Indeed, the theory of multiple intelligences does provide a more holistic, natural profile of human potential than an IQ test.

A closer look at the seven intelligences reveals the complexity Gardner's theory offers in terms of developing human

---

Figure 1
Gardner's Seven Intelligences

Visual/Spatial: Show Me!
Images, graphics, drawings, sketches, maps, charts, doodles, pictures, spatial orientation, puzzles, designs, looks, appeal, mind's eye, imagination, visualization, dreams, nightmares, films, and videos.

Logical/Mathematical: Why Bother?
Reasoning, deductive and inductive logic, facts, data, information, spreadsheets, databases, sequencing, ranking, organizing, analyzing, proofs, conclusions, judging, evaluations, and assessments.

Verbal/Linguistic: Who Says?
Words, wordsmiths, speaking, writing, listening, reading, papers, essays, poems, plays, narratives, lyrics, spelling, grammar, foreign languages, memos, bulletins, newsletters, newspapers, E-mail, FAXes, speeches, talks, dialogues, and debates.

Musical/Rhythmic: I Hear It!
Music, rhythm, beat, melody, tunes, allegro, pacing, timbre, tenor, soprano, opera, baritone, symphony, choir, chorus, madrigals, rap, rock, rhythm and blues, jazz, classical, folk, ads and jingles.

Bodily/Kinesthetic: Just Do It!
Art, activity, action, experiential, hands-on, experiments, try, do, perform, play, drama, sports, throw, toss, catch, jump, twist, twirl, assemble, disassemble, form, reform, manipulate, touch, feel, immerse, and participate.

Interpersonal/Social: Can We Talk?
Interact, communicate, converse, share, understand, empathize, sympathize, reach out, care, talk, whisper, laugh, cry, shudder, socialize, meet, greet, lead, follow, gangs, clubs, charisma, crowds, gatherings, and twosomes.

Intrapersonal/Introspective: What's in It for Me?
Self, solitude, mediate, think, create, brood, reflect, envision, journal, self-assess, set goals, plot, plan, dream, write, fiction, nonfiction, poetry, affirmations, lyrics, songs, screenplays, commentaries, introspective, and inspection.

potential. The human mind seems to receive and express ideas in myriad ways. These ways, or as Gardner terms them, intelligences, are listed in Figure 1.

VISUAL/SPATIAL INTELLIGENCE

The symbol of the film projector epitomizes the imaginary movies of the mind. As the mind conceptualizes ideas about its surrounding environment, it often employs the visual/spatial intelligence of images, pictures, and graphical representations. This intelligence might be referred to as the mind's eye—the lens that sees through visual metaphors and memory imprints.

Looks and Sounds Like

The visual/spatial intelligence looks like a child locking in place the final piece to a puzzle, a toppling tower of blocks, or an architect's rendering of a contractor's blueprints. It looks like Rodin's sculpture *The Thinker,* San Francisco's Golden Gate Bridge, the Leaning Tower of Pisa, and Old Faithful at Yellowstone National Park.

The visual/spatial intelligence embodies the talent of a designer/architect as well as the skill of a civil engineer. It manifests itself in CAD/CAM computer programs and software such as Aldus PageMaker. The visual/spatial intelligence provides mental pictures of road maps, faces, and places. Storyboard plans for film shoots, hopscotch grids on sidewalks, political cartoons, and Sunday comics are all products (partly) of the visual/spatial intelligence.

The sounds of the visual/spatial intelligence are heard in analogies or similes or metaphors: "His teeth were as white as pearls"; "Transfer of learning is like a bridge that connects two things"; or Carl Sandburg's famous line, "The fog comes on little cat's feet." Visual/spatial intelligence sounds like an eyewitness' testimony given at a trial, a radio announcer's voice giving a play-by-play description of a baseball game, or lingo used by a tour guide to describe the Austrian Alps.

Development

As with all of the other intelligences, the visual/spatial intelligence follows a progressive development. In fact, with early childhood programs, degrees of maturity are sometimes measured by the sophistication of a draw-a-person exercise. Drawings that go beyond a large oval head with eyes, nose, and mouth and include details such as five fingers on each hand, strands of hair, freckles, etc., receive a higher score because they indicate a greater developmental maturity.

The development of the visual/spatial intelligence is often evidenced in sketchbooks and lifetime works of artists, architects, or sculptors. Their early works often show immature execution, yet they also reveal strong signs of content and technique that later appear in their masterpieces. Practice, exercise, and explicit training are necessary for this intelligence to advance. As ideas are structured graphically in one's mind and a hierarchy of sorts is created from seemingly unrelated information (Ausubel, 1978), the novice advances toward more sophisticated and coherent imaging skills.

Notables

Leonardo da Vinci's sketchbooks leave no doubt that he qualifies not only as a true visionary, but also as a person with a strong visual/spatial intelligence. He sketched thousands of drawings of scientific phenomena, architectural renderings, and renowned anatomical drawings. His visual/spatial intelligence was so finely tuned that his work is unsurpassed even today. Other visual/spatial notables include Frank Lloyd Wright, Auguste Rodin, and Pablo Picasso.

Personal Profiles

Everyone possesses visual/spatial intelligence to some degree. Yet, some are not as tuned in as others to this channel of images, pictures, and graphics. They do not use a lot of metaphorical language, and they often write out directions rather than drawing a map. In general, these people rely on other intelligences to describe or understand the world. On the other end of the spectrum, there are some who have a more fully developed visual/spatial intelligence. They see through their mind's eye, visualizing phone numbers for quick recall, easily picturing how the kitchen will look with new wallpaper, or sketching thoughts in a concept map in order to see how ideas relate.

People reveal their visual/spatial intelligence in the language they use: "I see what you mean," "It looks good," "Show me," or "Do you see the big picture?" Visual/spatial intelligence is also noticeable in those who have a flair for matching outfits or a propensity for splashes of color or decorative jewelry.

Those high in the visual/spatial intelligence might say things like "The movie was better than the book" or "The comics are the first thing I read in the Sunday paper." Theirs is a world of images, pictures, and graphics. They are able to see themselves five years from now and set long-term goals; they remember faces and places, not streets and numbers.

The visual and performing arts must share center stage with other academic and vocational activities.

Implications

It is disturbing to see cuts in school programs involving the arts. The visual and performing arts must share center stage with other academic and vocational activities. Training, practice, and exercise in the visual/spatial intelligence is as important as these other activities, and all children deserve the opportunity to hone their skills and talents in this area.

For learners to massage this intelligence, classroom environments must reflect the value placed on it. Paints, crayons, pastels, clay, paper, paste and glue, markers, sand, water, scissors, tape, computer software, and color copiers are the tools of artists. From the primary classroom to the college lecture hall, these tools must be accessible for all to use, experiment with, and play with as they envision their world.

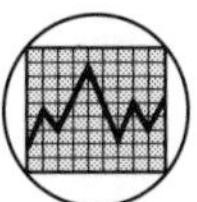

LOGICAL/MATHEMATICAL INTELLIGENCE

Pictured in the icon as a graph representing specific data, the logical/mathematical intelligence encompasses an entire range of reasoning skills. From the logic of Sherlock Holmes to the wisdom of Winston Churchill and from the cleverness of the Big Bad Wolf to the sound deductions of Archimedes, the logical/mathematical intelligence charts the data, information, and facts in the human mind.

Looks and Sounds Like

The following are all examples of what the logical/mathematical intelligence looks and sounds like: the reasoning of a scientific hypothesis, the logical progression of a computer program, the dichotomous classification of a species, the sequence of operations in mathematical equations, the cause-and-effect cycle of societal trends, the predictability of a plot in a novel, the patterned complexity of the periodic table of the elements, and the layered textures of an archeological dig. All of these things are sights and sounds of this incredibly *rigid*, yet incredibly *expansive* intelligence. Within this paradoxical intelligence, order reigns supreme.

Reasoning is the fourth "r" of the developing mind's critical skills of reading, 'riting, and 'rithmetic.

Development

Beginning with concrete manipulatives and hands-on learning, youngsters soon grasp the concept of one-to-one relationships and numeration. They advance from concrete ideas to representational ideas in the form of symbolic language, work equations, and formulas, and they learn about abstraction through the world of logic and numbers.

Reasoning is the fourth "r" of the developing mind's critical skills of reading, 'riting, and 'rithmetic. As learners construct knowledge and grapple with new ideas, they use their logical/mathematical intelligence to make sense of their world. It is the logical/mathematical mechanism in the mind that seeks order by analyzing and departmentalizing discrete pieces of information into chunks of meaning that can be abstracted into practical applications.

Notables

Perhaps the most frequently mentioned of all logical/mathematical notables is Albert Einstein. His theory of relativity, $E = mc^2$, symbolically represents a complex series of computations that embody a theory of the universe. Others include Polya (1945), who delineates the logic of the mind in his steps to problem solving, as well as Socrates, Plato, and Aristotle, who document the logistics of syllogistic language. More modern notables include Sherlock Holmes, Agatha Christie, and James Bond.

Personal Profiles

Personalities that exhibit a strong logical/mathematical intelligence enjoy lively discussions, relish the dialogue of controversy and argument, and are often comfortable with paradox and ambiguity. Students adept in this frame of mind understand the abstraction of calculus and the logic of statistics. They debate articulately, embrace the study of law, and are eager to analyze, chart, graph, and mathematically extrapolate data to its reasoned ends. They delight in opportunities to deduce and like nothing better than an end to a dilemma that resembles a neatly wrapped package.

Implications

The implications of this intelligence call attention to the need for rigorous curricula and vigorous instruction in the area of critical thinking, mathematical reasoning, and logic. Manipulating objects and working with concrete materials are important to this intelligence. It is also important to gradually move toward the symbolic realm of math, music, or language to secure abstract ideas. Discerning fact from fiction in literature, observation from interference in scientific investigation, and pure data from biased representation are exercises completed by the logical/mathematical mind. Encapsulated in this intelligence are the microskills of analysis, including comparison, classification, sequencing, and prioritizing. The ability to analyze, evaluate, and logically surmise are the essence of this intelligence.

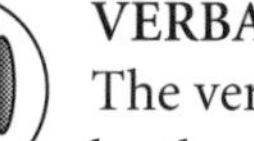

VERBAL/LINGUISTIC INTELLIGENCE

The verbal/linguistic intelligence is aptly symbolized by the megaphone, which embodies the ideas of speaking and listening. However, the power of the word, in its myriad forms, is truly at the heart of this intelligence. Thus, reading, writing, and other forms of communication, such as sign language, also reside under this umbrella.

Looks and Sounds Like

Art and science are the culturally valued targets of receptive language (listening and reading) and expressive language (speaking and writing), which are embedded in the verbal/linguistic intelligence. In the realm of receptive language, the verbal/linguistic intelligence looks like someone reading Fitzgerald's *The Great Gatsby,* Hemingway's *The Sun Also Rises,* Tolstoy's *War and Peace,* or one listening to a presidential campaign speech. On the other hand, expressive language sounds like someone giving directions over the phone to a friend or writing out a grocery list. Signs of this intelligence also include dialogue, arguments, whispers, laughter, handwritten invitations, letters of correspondence, and poems and essays.

Development

Youngsters or novices imitate the sounds, rhythms, and tones of the language they hear, stringing words together into decipherable fragments and then into fully discernible sentences of proper syntax and sense. Oral language is most often followed by written language—nonsense or serial writing that eventually becomes phonetically spelled words, simple sentences, and fully developed paragraphs. While this is the developmental journey of a young learner, older learners are often introduced to language in oral and written forms simultaneously. Yet, the developmental sequence is still evidenced in the progress from simple to complex forms.

Vygotsky (1986) says that thinking is embedded in the language we use, and Piaget (1972) uses formal learning stages to signal the development of abstract levels of thinking. These mindful abstractions are communicated through language.

Notables

Of note in the verbal/linguistic intelligence is John Fitzgerald Kennedy and his famous call to action: "And so, my fellow Americans, ask not what your country can do for you; ask what you can do for your country." Martin Luther King, Jr.'s resounding refrain, "I have a dream . . ." or the words of Neil Armstrong, "That's one small step for man, one giant leap for mankind." Words like these become emblazoned in one's memories—not as a written message, but as spoken rhetoric of power and strength and vigor.

Personal Profiles

While the verbal/linguistic intelligence may not be considered a total strength of everyone, most claim success with some aspect of it. For example, a student may have finely developed listening skills, yet may be less adept at speaking and articulating ideas. Or, one may sense a real comfort zone in reading, yet feel somewhat inadequate writing down his or her thoughts. Still, there are obvious connections within the complex tapestry of language as suggested by the idea that writers are readers first.

Implications

What does all this mean? It simply points to one of the critical frames of mind that Gardner postulates—the verbal/linguistic frame. And, implied in the exploration of this frame is the need to recognize, appreciate, and refine the skills attributed to this intelligence: reading fact and fiction; writing memos, notes, invitations, letters, essays, novels, short stories, and news releases; speaking formally (speech, debate, presentation) and informally (conversations and dialogues); and listening to messages, music, and media.

While the verbal/ linguistic intelligence may not be considered a total strength of everyone, most claim success with some aspect of it.

MUSICAL/RHYTHMIC INTELLIGENCE

The musical/rhythmic intelligence is represented by the drum. In primitive times the beat of the drum carried messages through its patterned rhythms to the minds of tribesmen far and wide. And today, too, the power of music cannot be overlooked as a primary channel for learning and knowing, sharing and expressing, and perceiving and creating pitch and patterns for the human mind.

Looks and Sounds Like

In a June 1982 article in *Psychology Today* titled "The Music of the Hemispheres," Gardner stated that musical ability is packaged in the brain in more varied ways than verbal or spatial skills. So, too, is the intelligence, which can be seen by strolling through the halls of a school that integrates the curriculum with multiple intelligences.

In one classroom, students memorize their multiplication facts by using a steady rhythm and beat: "3 x 3 = 9, 3 x 4 = 12, 3 x 5 = 15. . . ." Rote memorization of rules of grammar, spelling, or even arithmetic seems to be easier for some through singsong phrases such as the following:

"Conjunction is a junction."
"'I' before 'e' except after 'c'."
"Yours is not to reason why, just invert and multiply."

In the music classroom, students learn melodic sequences that eventually form songs. In the kindergarten room, children find their spots on the rug when transitional music is played by the teacher. Music is played in the gym as part of the PE department's "strive to be fit" aerobics program. A steady rhythm is tapped out by students learning to type in the computer room. And in the the English-as-a-second-language (ESL) room, students learn folk songs as their model for language development.

Development

The musical/rhythmic intelligence, often regarded as innate talent, is nurtured and developed in many ways. Typically, youngsters are exposed informally to music in their home environments through a variety of media. At some point, they may begin taking private lessons to learn a musical instrument, and they may join the school band or orchestra. This is how students develop lifetime skills to support their musical/rhythmic intelligence.

Notables

One of the most globally recognized and enduring musicians is Mozart. He describes his relationship to music and its composition in this way:

> When I am . . . completely by myself, entirely alone . . . or during the night when I cannot sleep, it is on such occasions that my ideas flow best and most abundantly. Whence and how these come I know not nor can I force them . . . . Nor do I hear in my imagination the parts successively, but I hear them *gleich alles zusammen* [at the same time, all together]. (Peter, 1977, p. 123)

Among those renowned in the musical/rhythmic intelligence are Italian operatic tenor Luciano Pavarotti and violinist Isaac Perlman.

Personal Profile

It is clear that the profile of human potential is incomplete without the musical/rhythmic intelligence, and everyone possesses some degree of aptitude. Gardner is careful to point out that this intelligence meets the rigorous criteria he has set, which therefore qualifies it as an intelligence. While some prefer to consider musical ability a talent rather than an intelligence, it is, however, easily trained and developed.

While some prefer to consider musical ability a talent rather than an intelligence, it is, however, easily trained and developed.

Implications

Since music, rhythm, and beat are regarded as the elements of one of the seven intelligences, it behooves us as educators to include them as an integral part of the curriculum. Youngsters need to give this intelligence the exercise and reinforcement it needs in order to develop and blossom. School districts that embrace Gardner's theory of seven intelligences must also embrace music and the other arts, for they are undeniably interconnected. J. David Bowick, superintendent of the Oakland Unified School District, explains:

> During my school days, music was the reason to learn, the access to learning, the joy in learning. For other ghetto kids with whom I grew up and for those whom I later taught, music, art, dance, drama, and other "frills" were the inspiration that led many of them up and out of poverty (Bowick, 1984).

BODILY/KINESTHETIC INTELLIGENCE

The bodily/kinesthetic intelligence is symbolized by a clapboard—the director's call for action. Action is the key to this intelligence. The body is the conduit for the mind, and muscle memory obtained from experiences is what defines the bodily/kinesthetic intelligence.

Looks and Sounds Like

To envision the bodily/kinesthetic intelligence, imagine the precision of high-flying acrobats in a circus ring or pirouettes performed by a prima ballerina; think of the strength and timing of a prize fighter or the massive, symmetrical, fully toned body of a weightlifter. Hear the sounds of the bodily/kinesthetic intelligence as a typist beats out a rapid and steady rhythm, a pianist's fingers fly across a piano's keys, or a symphony performs a crescendo in dynamic, earth-shattering brilliance.

Development

Perhaps the easiest way to describe the development of this bodily/kinesthetic intelligence is to compare it to Posner and Keele's (1973) accepted stages of skill development—novice, advanced beginner, competent user, proficient performer, and expert. These stages are best illustrated by describing the different stages of learning to snow ski.

Novices process pieces, but not necessarily in order. For example, they often learn to go down a hill before they know how to stop or control their downhill run. *Advanced beginners* put together various pieces and practice in sequence. They don't really care about the results; they just want to know if they are doing it right. As learners become more competent, they care about the relationship of skill to the whole experience. *Competent* skiers are able to put together strings of turns and eventually master the hill. They're in a comfort zone and it's fun. *Proficient performers* have forgotten exactly *how* they ski. Their performance is automatic. *Experts* have also forgotten everything about the step-by-step progression of skiing and often can't explain it to someone else. Instead, they *show* the person how to ski, oftentimes glossing over difficult points.

The stages of learning, while more noticeable in gross motor activities, also apply to fine motor developments such as writing, computing, auto repairing, and playing the trombone. In essence, the bodily/kinesthetic intelligence, whether used with gross motor or fine motor skills, grows and develops in fairly predictable ways.

Notables

The notables in this intelligence span myriad fields, one of which is dancing. A familiar name from this field is Mikhail Baryshnikov. His fantastic leaps across the stage seem to defy gravity, and his exquisite technique astounds audiences. Just as

Baryshnikov's image is known to the world of dance, Michael Jordan's gravity-defying image is legendary in the world of sports. Other notables with a strong bodily/kinesthetic intelligence include Kristy Yamaguchi, Walter Payton, and Bo Jackson.

Personal Profiles

The frame of mind described in Gardner's concept of the bodily/kinesthetic intelligence is evidenced early on in the fine and gross motor skills of youngsters. In fact, a major focus of exemplary early childhood programs is in this kinesthetic arena. Yet, just as with the other intelligences, personal profiles for the bodily/kinesthetic intelligence run the gamut from naturally skilled and proficient learners to the poorly coordinated and obtuse performers.

The bodily/kinesthetic intelligence, whether used with gross motor skills or fine motor skills, grows and develops in fairly predictable ways.

There are those who can type quite proficiently and there are those who prefer to peck along with two index fingers. There are those who excel in a number of sports and those who choose not to participate in physically oriented activities. Some can play a musical instrument with no problem, while others claim to be "all thumbs." Of course, many people fall somewhere between the two extremes and learn to type competently, play a fair game of tennis, and pick away at their guitars.

Implications

The overriding implications for the full development of the bodily/kinesthetic intelligence lies in a rich classroom that invites hands-on investigations, immersion in experiential learning situations, and long-term, authentic projects that require manipulation and maneuvering. This intelligence flourishes beyond the classroom walls in outdoor educational trips, field trips, and excursions. Gardner suggests (1983) that through the bodily/kinesthetic intelligence students experience and learn in children's museums, which invite sensory exploration and discovery learning.

Much like Dewey's (1938) seminal piece, *Education and Experience*, the bodily/kinesthetic intelligence requires fertile territory for growth and development. With this intelligence, needed environmental richness extends naturally from the gym, playground, and track into various playing fields, stadiums, and sports complexes.

INTERPERSONAL INTELLIGENCE

Represented by the dialogue bubbles of cartoons, the interpersonal intelligence embodies people's interactions. The bubbles illustrate the give-and-take of communication and the punctuation marks symbolize the goal of not only understanding others and their motivations, but also of effectively empathizing with their feelings. Also embedded within the symbol is the idea that we inquire about our world through our interactions with others, and in the process we learn from one another.

Looks and Sounds Like

Interpersonal intelligence looks like a charismatic leader surrounded by an adoring crowd; a glib salesman spinning his or her pitch; a football team's trust, camaraderie, and synchronized play on the field; a teacher coaching a child in language skills; and a doctor holding the hand of a suffering patient.

Sounds of interpersonal intelligence include intimate conversations, arousing evangelic praises, lively debates, Socratic dialogues, structured articulations, phone conversations, shared secrets, political rallies, heated arguments, and cries of "surprise!" The sound of this intelligence is the sound of socialization.

Development

Interpersonal skills develop on a sliding scale ranging from isolation to skillful social interactions. Youngsters learn social behavior as they come in contact with others, first in their immediate family circle, then in peer situations, and then in public encounters. It seems, however, that the socialization process is dependent not only on the frequency of the interactions, but also on the context and intensity of those interactions. For

Figure 1
Social Development

Young Child	Self-Centered Me/Mine
Adolescent	Peer Centered Me/Them
Adult	Team Centered Me/We

example, youngsters who attend nursery schools and have opportunities to interact with other children seem to adjust more easily to traditional schooling because they are more likely to know how to converse, share, and get along with their peers.

It's interesting to track the socialization process of young children as they develop into fully functioning adults. Their development begins with the "me/mine" mentality of very young children, whose self-centered worlds revolve only around themselves. They then move into an adolescent phase and assume a deposture of "me/them." Their lives become ruled by peer pressure and peer approval. As maturing adults, a "me/we" attitude prevails, and they pragmatically embrace a team-centered approach (see Figure 1). There are, of course, many variations to this picture of social development, but, as Gardner states, "the child can come to know himself . . . only through coming to know other individuals" (Gardner, 1983, p. 247).

Notables

Among the notables with obviously high interpersonal intelligences are missionaries who devote their lives to others, such as Mother Teresa, or religious leaders, such as Mahatma Gandhi. Also often noted in this category of interpersonal intelligence are the charismatic leaders in the political arena, including John F. Kennedy, Martin Luther King, Jr., and Bill Clinton. Other personalities who qualify as examples of strong interpersonal intelligences are the interviewers Phil Donahue, Barbara Walters, and Larry King, who all have a talent for getting others to open up.

Personal Profiles

Personalities are typically categorized as introverted or extroverted. Introverts are more comfortable turning inward and are often seen as asocial. Extroverts, on the other hand, seem to thrive on the company of others and are viewed as social butterflies. In reality, of course, most people fall somewhere in-between the two extremes. As with the other intelligences, the spectrum of personal attributes and preferences regarding interpersonal skills is extensive. Yet each has the potential to develop this intelligence to its fullest and call on it when needed.

Implications

Schools fostering the interpersonal intelligence are not didactic, behavioristic models of schooling in which teachers traditionally cover the content and information they want students to know; instead, these schools exemplify a constructivist model of schooling in which students are expected to make meaning in their minds of the subject matter. In this constructivist philosophy, interaction between the students and the teacher is enhanced and extended to include interactions among the students themselves. In essence, this intelligence thrives on active learning within the social context of the classroom.

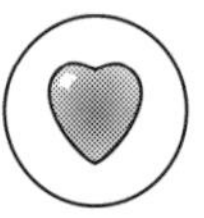

INTRAPERSONAL INTELLIGENCE

Metaphorically, the intrapersonal or introspective intelligence is a valentine invisibly inscribed with the message, "Be Mine." This intelligence also carries the message, "know thyself." Pragmatically, the intrapersonal intelligence represents a frame of mind in which learners internalize learning through thoughtful connections and then transfer it to novel situations through reflective application. It is with the intrapersonal intelligence that one has the ability to become acquainted with him- or herself.

Looks and Sounds Like

The manifestation of the intrapersonal intelligence is seen most vividly in personal diaries, daily journals, thinking logs, sketch pads, and notebooks. Self-reflection, self-awareness, and self-evaluation are often evidenced in these written formats, which evolve over time. Personal growth, acquisition of knowledge, and development of skills such as drawing and sketching are systematically traced through the pages of these continual personal records. They provide fertile ground for meaningful reflection and powerful self-analysis and evaluation.

In another modality, the intrapersonal intelligence sounds like self-editing, such as, "No, I think I'm better at this," or the metacognitive monologue, "I must remember to talk more slowly and enunciate my words." As Dr. Art Costa, professor emeritus at Sacramento State University of California, has been heard to say that when you catch yourself talking aloud—to yourself—that's metacognitive. Metacognition is the act of planning, monitoring, or evaluating one's own behavior. Metacognition embodies the frame of mind Gardner labels as the intrapersonal intelligence.

Metacognition is the act of planning, monitoring, or evaluating one's own behavior. Metacognition embodies . . . the intrapersonal intelligence.

Development

The intrapersonal intelligence develops, according to Swartz and Perkins (1987), in four incremental stages: tacit, aware, strategic, and reflective. *Tacit* behavior refers to using a skill or idea in an oblivious state. For example, young students may be able to read, but they seem totally unaware of the strategies they use—or even that they have an exceptional ability in this area. When students enter the next stage, *awareness*, they become cognizant of their strategies and/or their levels of performance. They are able to step back from the action and "freeze frame" their behavior. Subsequently, as they become more introspective, they advance to the *strategic* phase. In this phase, they consciously select particular models of behavior. For example, our readers might deliberately plan to skim or scan an essay for needed information because they know it is an efficient strategy for certain tasks. In turn, the *reflective stage* occurs when a student is able to reflect upon the degree of success or failure of the strategic method they used.

While the concept of intrapersonal intelligence seems to embody various stages or levels of proficiency, these stages are not locked into a chronological map. On the contrary, individuals embrace this introspective intelligence in similar patterns as Gardner's other intelligences. Although these patterns of occurrence are individually programmed to some extent, they are also dependent upon stimuli from the surrounding environment. If a culture values intrapersonal reflection, as many Eastern countries do, the intrapersonal intelligence is more likely to attract the attention and exercise it needs to develop and flourish.

Notables

Naturally, notables in the intrapersonal arena often include people in the field of psychology such as Freud and Jung; writers such as Emerson and Thoreau; artists such as Leonardo da Vinci; and philosophers such as Socrates, Plato, or Confucius.

Personal Profiles

The intrapersonal intelligence is present in varying degrees for each of us. There are those who seem totally unaware of their own behavior or how that behavior affects the people around them. Who among us has not been at a party, in the midst of a "braggart" or "blow hard," who drones on incessantly, unaware of a cool reception, total boredom, or a shrinking audience? On the other hand, there are those who are deeply reflective and acutely aware of their actions and words. Remember Dale Carnegie's message in *How to Win Friends and Influence People?* To paraphrase his intent—find out what the other party wants, then with that as your goal, proceed with the interaction.

Implications

The intrapersonal intelligence must be fostered and developed if real, significant, and long-lasting transfer of learning is to take place. For it is in the awareness, the strategic planning, and the reflective evaluation that students capture information and apply it in purposeful ways. Journals, logs, and portfolios for self-evaluation and dialogue with others help students articulate their strengths and weaknesses. They are necessary components of schooling that guide the development of the intrapersonal intelligence.

Being aware of the seven intelligences and understanding the significance of "jagged" personal profiles are the first steps toward embracing Gardner's theory as a viable tool in the classroom. When multiple intelligences and personal profiles are recognized, teachers discover valuable concepts for planning more holistic, varied, and integrated.

REFERENCES

Ausubel, D. (1978). *Ed. Psych: A cognitive view* (2nd ed.). New York: Holt, Rinehart, & Winston.

Bowick, J. D. (1984, Summer). Crowded back-to-basics bandwagon is off, veering crazily. *Music Educators Journal.*

Dewey, J. (1938). *Education and experience.* New York: Macmillan.

Gardner, H. (1993). *Multiple intelligences: The theory in practice.* New York: Harper Collins.

Gardner, H. (1989). *To open minds.* New York: Basic Books.

Gardner, H. (1983). *Frames of mind: The theory of multiple intelligences.* New York: Basic Books.

Peter, L. S. (1977). *Peter's quotations: Ideas for our time.* New York: Morrow.

Piaget, J. (1972). *The epistemology of interdisciplinary relationships.* Paris: Organization for Economic Cooperation and Development.

Polya, G. (1945). *How to solve it: A new aspect of mathematical method.* Princeton, NJ: Princeton University Press.

Posner, M. I., & Keele, S. W. (1973). Skill learning. In R. M. W. Travers (Ed.), *Second handbook of research on teaching.* Chicago: Rand McNally.

Swartz, R., & Perkins, D. (1987). *Teaching thinking skills: Theory and practice.* New York: Freeman.

Vygotsky, L. S. (1986). *Thought and language* (Rev. ed.). Cambridge, MA: MIT Press.

Vignettes: Teaching Thinking

by Robin Fogarty

The following scenarios are observations of actual classroom teachers. The scenarios focus on four areas of the instructional process that include teaching for, of, with, and about thinking. To elaborate briefly: 1) Setting the climate for thinking encompasses physical room arrangement, teacher mobility, question and response strategies, and teacher expectations. 2) Teaching the skills of thinking involves explicit instruction in both critical and creative mental processes such as prioritizing, inferring, and generalizing. 3) Structuring the interaction with thinking focuses on student-to-student interactions as well as students interacting with the materials and information with advanced organizers. 4) Metacognitive processing about thinking stresses processing that requires student awareness and control over their own thinking and learning. These four areas correspond with the four elements of classroom instruction highlighted during the staff development inservices that served as the catalysts to a study of teacher transfer.

SCENARIO ONE: THE GUIDE

Setting the Climate for Thinking

As one enters through the doors of the French class, it's as if one just stepped onto a touring bus along the streets of gay "Paree!" The excitement of the adventure that's about to begin is signaled in the animated voice of the petite, energetic tour guide.

Vacillating, staccato style, between French and English, she greets the various student passengers with personal remarks and grand, sweeping motions to accompany her facial expressions and excited tone of voice.

Adapted from *Training to Transfer: The Role of Creativity in the Adult Learner.* Doctoral Dissertation, Loyola University of Chicago. © 1989 by Robin Fogarty.

"Bonjour"
"Yea! Yea!"
"Merci"
"Mon amie"
"Oui"
"N'est ce pas?"
"Parlez-vous Français?"

Amidst this settling-in process, fellow passengers cluster together and exchange greetings and remarks. Gingerly, yet briskly, le guide de tour makes her way about the "bus." Varied points of interest are previewed for the group; some are traditional, historical or relevant "musts," while others are deliciously cultural and festive in nature.

"Today, we must review the book for the test on verbs and verb tenses."

"Did you see the piece on Jean Paul Sartre?"

"We'll be ordering croissants—chocolate or plain—one each . . . mmmm."

"Notice the photo of the Mardi Gras."

Teaching the Skills of Thinking

As the formal "tour" begins, the vibrant narration of the guide seems to increase in volume and momentum in expectancy of what's ahead. Yet as the bus proceeds and makes its first stop, her voice settles into a more rehearsed, more reserved style, with occasional bursts of enthusiasm as an idea strikes her.

"N'est ce pas? Isn't that so? Isn't that right? Doesn't she? Isn't it?"

"Mon—masculine!"

"Let's zip through endings."

Some points on the tour seem only to be endured for their traditional value. The excitement is missing from this formerly lively voice as the guide quiets down and instructs the passengers to read in the guidebook.

"Review separately; by yourself; independently."

After some time has elapsed, she looks up from her official seat.

"Fini?" she asks, and proceeds to review the book answers with the whole group.

This guidebook capsulizes the basic information that the passengers need. She uses the book to cover the basics. But to sense the real France and bring it alive for her passengers, she transmits the essence of the country through the cultural, festive elements so familiar to her from her own extensive experiences.

Pantomime and acting come naturally to this guide as she communicates with these inexperienced visitors to France.

Pantomime and acting come naturally to this guide as she communicates with these inexperienced visitors to France.

"Lunettes: glasses; little moon" (She circles her eyes with her fingers in exaggerated gestures and makes an aside.) "lunatic: looks at the moon"

"la neige" (She draws a snowman on the board and pretends to shiver uncontrollably.)

"faire du vent" (She whistles like the wind.)

Thinking skills are interjected to help the passengers grasp the numerous things that they glimpse through the window as the bus streaks by.

"Encore. Visualize. Close your eyes. See it. Type it in."

"Look for terms and relationships."

"Vous ne savez pas? You don't know? Try to describe it."

The guide's immersion in French and love for the real France and the memories she holds surface throughout her talk. Yet, the flow is abbreviated, stopped, over and over again, much like the intermittent motion of the starts and stops of the tour bus itself. The undercurrent of excitement, evident in the voice, is the one continuous thread tying the journey together.

Structuring the Interaction with Thinking

As the bus begins its last leg, she keeps the audience tuned in through a variety of games and activities that vary the pace and tempo of the ride.

"Bingo—Team one, team two, call out a number. Go for a square. You can coach each other."

"Memory game—you must act out all previous words (angry, search, shrug...) and add your word to the progressive memory game. Now, chant these four times: e, es, e. Encore! Visualize; see it; type it in your brain:

-e -es -e -ons -ez -ent"

"Find your partner. Do exercises one and two. En Francais! Ensemble; review; finish the book for the test."

"Review for culture test. Team one, team two, get close together."

"Interview your partner in French. Ask three questions; the rest will guess who you interviewed. En Francais!"

Metacognitive Processing About Thinking

Hoping to get them to internalize, to question, to become involved in a personal way, the guide leads the passengers in some reflective processing.

Hoping to get them to internalize, to question . . . the guide leads the passengers in some reflective processing.

"Does everyone have this? Don't be shy. Scream! Yell!"

"There'll be lots of details on the test tomorrow. Go slowly."

"Look at the list. Choose carefully."

"We need your brain power."

"Reflect on the questions. Write a few words."

Winding down and nearing the end of this brief tour, the students begin to shuffle their belongings and prepare for the exodus off the bus. France, in a flash, then onto the next tour.

SCENARIO TWO: THE WIZARD

Setting the Climate for Thinking

Bounding about the room as if he had springs in his shoes, the wizard teases his student audience/participants with puzzles, riddles, and reasoning.

"Chris, give it a shot. He chooses door number four. Now, tell us the answer you've selected and why."

"Process of elimination? Good technique. Fantastic! Why?"

"Another one. He chooses door number three. Ratio. Why?"

"Great. We did just finish talking about ratio the day

before. Talking about what we did the day before helps us get to today."

The wizard lets his audience/participants know that they are part of the show. He tells them that he teaches, they teach others, and they teach themselves. But, he also provides a constant pattern of feedback and reinforcement that, even in a playful manner, seems to honor and dignify every answer.

The wizard knows his students well, and he uses clever humor throughout his class that signals he is right on target with what's going on.

"This group is hot."

"Hear some good talking here."

"Holy Smokes! You got this! How?"

"No idea? Remember you can go to other groups."

"Is this all? Check with others. Talk to teammates."

"I'll tell you. That's the right one. Now, you tell me why."

"Bingo, Linda's ready."

The audience knows that the wizard is the "wise one"; yet his uses of "magic" as he searches among them for evidence of thinking intrigues them. He challenges them in such an entertaining manner that they are almost caught in wonder as he captures their interest and catches them thinking.

"What is the geometric mean?"

"Oh, listen I feel a theorem coming on," he says a student carefully states her idea.

"Ever play the Pyramid game? What do these have in common? Say one word: sewer pipe, mountain, ski hill."

"Slope! Silly. You've already figured out that this is leading to something."

The wizard knows his students well, and he uses clever humor throughout his class that signals he is right on target with what's going on.

"He has it in his head. That's why he's not writing it down."

"I thought I had to dust the cobwebs—but I need a snow shovel!"

"David, this is the easiest one (question) in America."

"He doesn't believe it. Convince him."

"I can help you with it, but I can't reteach the whole course."

"I thought about inventing graph paper Kleenex. Why is that a good idea?"

The wizard signals expectations that will transfer the learning beyond the classroom and into future academic or life situations.

"If you're going to be successful quizzer—when you hit the door—you must learn it for life, not just for the test."

Teaching the Skills of Thinking

This wizardry continues throughout the session as he entices students into entertainingly complex problem-solving situations. His pacing is fast as he poses question upon question. Expectations are there for students to respond and justify.

"Door number four—linear equation? Want to change your idea?"

"What do you think?"

"Why only consider positive values?"

"Have you see this one before? Yep, it was on the test. How many wrote four, not negative four?"

The wizard relishes in his games and exhibits a contagious energy and enthusiasm for his art. He believes that kids are used to being entertained and uses that knowledge to work for him in the classroom.

"Now you might like this one."

"Why is Jeopardy the best game show? Yes—they give the answer. You ask the question."

"In the relay race, there will be five rounds. And remember goose egg gets double points. That, keeps us all in the race."

His energetic quizzing forces students to hypothesize, analyze, verify, and evaluate.

Forced Hypothesis Question: "What was the name of the last chapter? How does it connect?"

Forced Analysis Question: "What makes number four different?"

Forced Verification Question: "Algebra I, Algebra II, Trig. Right, Jeff. Why is trig like geometry? How did you get it?"

Forced Evaluation Question: "Did we accomplish it?"

Structuring the Interaction with Thinking

His lightning speed and unpredictable targeting keep students alert and involved, yet support is always evident and feedback is specific and pointed.

"Anyone need help?"

"Tests—very fine, twenty-three out of thirty was the average score."

The wizard varies the interactions depending on the purpose.

"We'll need partners for this one."

"Girls take odd rows. Boys take even."

"Teams by rows."

Metacognitive Processing About Thinking

Above all, as the wizard works his spell on the captive audience, he spins a constant tale of why they are doing what they are doing. His modeling of explanations and reasons overrides every aspect of the interaction. The students leave with an understanding of not only what and how, but also a sense of why.

The students leave with an understanding of not only what and how, but also a sense of why.

"Why do I make you memorize theorems and definitions? Because in mathematics, the system is built from scratch. If pieces are missing, the pyramid tumbles. You must memorize certain things."

"Don't let your algebra get in the way of trig."

"What are some memory tricks? Learn part now; before school ends, learn another section; before tomorrow, learn the rest; or tape record it and play it in your sleep."

"Bring a calculator. I will make sure you know how to use it." The wizard sums up his feelings when he says, "I don't come to work. I come to school. I have fun, too."

SCENARIO THREE: THE COACH

Setting the Climate for Thinking

The climate is informal, with student performers funneling into the tiered choral room. Activity swirls around the grand piano placed strategically in the center of the semi-circular tiers.

Students handle the management of materials and equipment with efficient procedures, set at some time earlier in the year. Attendance, announcements, money collections for the full agenda of extracurricular events, as well as books and sheet music are all systematically managed by various students. They appear responsibly in charge and seem to tend to the tasks with pride and care.

"Management."

"Symphony tickets, up front." (Another student collects money.)

"Bus, after 1:00 p.m."

"I have an announcement."

Her demeanor suggests enthusiasm for this role that requires much of her time and energy, both in and out of the school setting.

Students stop by the piano area in a steady stream, making requests or excuses, or just to say hello in passing as they make their way to designated spots on the rows of tiered risers. The coach reacts personally to each, fielding the multitude of decisions in a friendly, (sometimes even nonverbal) expedient manner.

The warmest of smiles lights her face, just as her demeanor suggests enthusiasm for this role that requires much of her time and energy, both in and out of the school setting.

All this commotion is abruptly halted as her coaching posture is assumed and a chord is sounded on the piano to signal attention and readiness for the work at hand.

"Warm-ups, first."

"Jeff, turn around."

"Sit tall."

"Quiet."

"Breathe."

"Jeffrey!"

Modeling, smiling, she waits expectantly for their full attention.

The energy level is incredible, the pacing brisk, the content heavy. A sense of purpose pervades the atmosphere as the group prepares for their many performance dates. Just as in any performing art, the show is the goal. Preparations for upcoming events keep interest piqued and pressure high.

"Madrigals. Methodist Church." (An aside to the unknowing visitor, she says, "We've been selected as one of six groups to go to Allerton in March.")

"Sunrise service."

"Madrigals—concert in hall before Band and Orchestra."

Throughout the rehearsal, the music coach takes the lead in accompanying each piece both vocally and technically. With fingers flying across the keys, she grandly mouths the lyrics, sets the tempo, plays the melody, and interjects cues to signal direction, style, and intent of the music.

"Let's run this section."

"Stay with me."

"Watch the pitch."

"Yes. Better!"

"Do we look motivated?"

All in the room are immersed in this world of music and performing. Yet, time is allotted for special interests of students, aside from the traditional high school repertoire, as individual interests and talents are showcased.

"Extra credit performances. Who's first?"

"West Side Story."

"Next? Beth."

"Friends, by M. W. Smith."

Yet, as these young people perform, they instinctively rely on the inherent talents of the coach. Their appreciation (and awe) of her talents is seen in the requests for accompaniment. Regardless of the selection, they expect her to know it and she rarely disappoints them in their expectations.

"West Side Story. Will you play for me?"

"Play with me? I'm having trouble with the rhythm."

"One voice lesson. Will you run through it with me?"

Expectations are high. The school has a reputation to uphold and the students are aware of this. They are motivated to excel.

"Sectionals. Last chance to fix up. One week from Thursday."

"You have one minute to review text. Then, we'll do it from memory."

"Okay, you know what you have to do."

Teaching the Skills of Thinking

This experienced coach models the behaviors of direct instruction of a skill. Directions are clear, concise, and crisp. Monitoring is ongoing as she laces the practices with pointed feedback that is both positive and critical, as the students strive for perfection in their performance.

This experienced coach models the behaviors of direct instruction of a skill. Directions are clear, concise, and crisp.

"Class. We'll take the alto section."

"Sopranos, do you see where you are?"

"Good. Chopped."

"I need a tenor."

"We're starting."

"Bravo."

"Tenors. Sing with them. Then cut out and let them do the refrain."

"Phrase ending. Not too fast."

To clarify her directions, this coach relies on vivid analogies to make her instructions concrete and explicit. These mental pictures are often accompanied with the gestures and pantomime noted earlier.

"Swell, like an organ opening the pedal."

"Tune it . . . hold on . . . like an oxygen tank on your back."

"Shh—spit it out like pulling taffy. Look!" (She demonstrates.)

". . . swimming a little bit in that section."

". . . like an orange peel inside out in back of your throat."

Structuring the Interaction with Thinking

Throughout the intense, fast-paced classes, the coach is interacting intensely with the whole group, while intervening with specific cues and feedback for the different sections and for individual performers.

"Listen! Listen! Balance the chord; space back here, in tune."

"Shape it, Carol!"

"Altos! Flat!"

"Space it back. Drop out altos."

Modeling images through pantomime and stressing posture, facial expression, tongue position, and the set of the jaw, the skillful performance of the experienced coach is mirrored by the students. Reflective imaging in this vocal music class epitomizes the same metaphorical mirroring behavior used in the coaching of athletic champions.

"Sit tall." (She models.)

"Shape your mouth. Pucker! Pucker!" (She exaggerates a pucker and deadpans, as students dissolve in laughter.)

"Lips barely touching." (She shows them.)

"Sit tall. Breathe!" (She demonstrates the breathing.)

Aware of the need to move and restructure to keep the intensity and focus, the coach arranges the class accordingly or gives instructions for students to change stance at their places.

"Quickly. Form a big circle."

"Five around the piano."

"Stand in a circle. Mix up."

"All cluster around piano for this part."

"Stand in formation."

Metacognitive Processing About Thinking

Metacognition, how to sing it and why, is built into this instructor's repertoire. Instinctively understanding the value for monitoring and evaluating one's own behavior, this coach models an ongoing, talk-aloud strategy that students tend to internalize over time. Her ear for mistakes is uncanny as she targets problem spots in the group, adjusts immediately, and carries the group through the piece.

"What's happening to pitch?"

"Last two measures. Right. See the connection."

"Whatever happens, stay with me."

"That's better, sopranos; better vowel on 'a'."
"... takes too much concentration. Sections are mixed up."
"Keep tapping quarter notes."

Evaluation is requested as well as given, as this coach guides her players toward improvement, synchronization, and pride in doing their best.

"What will make this phrase better?"
"What about vowels?"
"Altos. What are you doing? Look at the notes."
"Compare this to the performance last night." (A student answers, "More balanced"—with his explanation of what he meant.)

SCENARIO FOUR: THE WEAVER

Setting the Climate for Thinking

With patience and precision, this master weaves the threads of his discipline into an intricate pattern of exquisite design as he instructs his student apprentices. The pattern begins with a skillful approach to questioning students as he asks and probes and extends:

"Why?"
"Explain?"
"Then? ... Then? ... Then?"
"What else?"
"Who agrees? Disagrees? Why?"

The artistry of the questioning pattern is elaborated as he intentionally introduces each point by weaving the name of the student and the student's response into a spiraling question and response design.

"Dave says..."
"Katie might be on to something..."
"Ken shakes his head..."
"Tatiana thinks..."
"Let's build on Scott's comment..."
"Victor, right on the money..."

He shares his enthusiasm for his craft with students as he delights in the wonders of science.

"Isn't it amazing that every single inherited characteristic is determined by five elements?"

"Imagine, red hair, blue eyes, each dictated into every single cell."

"We're talking plants, right? So how does the water get all the way to the top of the redwood tree?"

"Let's solve the mystery. Why are some groups seeing change in the water color and others are not?"

And his expectations for student thinking and for cooperative interactions are signaled both verbally and nonverbally with humor and warmth as he weaves his way throughout the openings in the rows of desks.

"Scott, draw some parameters on this."

"Victor, what about..."

"Steve needs help. Who's gonna bail him out?"

"Tim, are you catching some dreams?"

He laces the lecture with questions that lead students to hypothesize, predict, evaluate, compare, and conclude.

Teaching the Skills of Thinking

The complexity of his weaving technique is further illustrated as he masterfully integrates lecture information and textbook references into this already complex verbal interchange. He laces the lecture with questions that lead students to hypothesize, predict, evaluate, compare, and conclude.

"Replication, rather than duplication—half new molecules, half old. Do you buy that?"

"Isotope, another form of an element."

"Notice the question in Watson."

"There are a lot of appendices. Turn to the back of your books."

But the design of the weaver begins to reveal several more layers of intricate, deliberate patterns. The master weaver delicately manipulates the cloth of this classroom as he introduces the threads of higher-level thinking.

"Looking at the data, what conclusions can you draw?"

"What evidence supports your statement?"

"I suggest you compare RNA and DNA."

"Let's hypothesize ... one more possible theory ..."

"Predict what you think will happen."

"Can we capture the key concept? Can we generalize what we've said?"

As the students are drawn into this beautifully designed web of intrigue, the weaver illustrates the conceptual information with colorful and relevant analogies. By describing these concrete examples that are familiar to students, he anchors the new learning throughout the patterned interaction with carefully selected mental images.

"...pairing replication, like a zipper with teeth on one side."

"How many have worked a jigsaw? Anyone else start on the outside, the boundary? Why?"

"Just like Indianapolis. They don't just turn a key. A guy stands behind the car and ignites the turbo charger."

"It's similar to a squeeze coin purse..."

"You've seen the paratroopers come out of the door like a chain reaction..."

"...like a Slinky, stretched out."

Structuring the Interaction with Thinking

Using his skill, the master weaver integrates the patterns of interpersonal interaction into the encompassing design. Taking advantage of the lab in the back of the room, he frequently organizes small groups of students around the lab tables that have been carefully equipped and set up with the necessary materials.

"Use the dice rolls to determine the number."

"Illustrate the final creature you've created showing all the critical attributes."

"With your lab partners, make a classification key for another group's creature."

"Determine in your groups the roles for each member."

"Kids who finish first, act as consultants to other groups."

Paralleling the interpersonal interactions of cooperative groups, the weaver also incorporates interactions with the concepts and materials. Both pencil-and-paper advance organizers and hands-on laboratory experiments are interspersed into the instructional strategies.

"Using the morphological grid, or matrix,..."

"Before the session begins, mingle (using the question sheet) and see how many can answer these questions. For example, find someone who can compare a plant cell to a jail cell."

Metacognitive Processing About Thinking

Adding the final touches to his intricate pattern of classroom interactions, the weaver knits the metacognitive element into the finished fabrics of his teaching. His structured processing and discussions help students stand back from the lesson at hand and look at it as a strategy or skill for future use. This is the thread he uses to tie the learnings together. Through this metacognitive element he helps students extrapolate the essence of an idea and apply the concepts across curricular disciplines and into life situations.

Paralleling the interpersonal interactions of cooperative groups, the weaver also incorporates interactions with the concepts and materials.

"Did anyone find out from the math teacher about the double helix we were talking about in here (science)?"

"You should be writing notes in your thinking log throughout—about the theory of evolution."

"A practical application: the pipes in your home all have calcium deposits . . . more pressure . . . dribble . . ."

The weaver further illustrates his mastery and understanding of the learning process with a subtle, but powerful, metacognitive strategy at the end of the period.

"Take the last five minutes to get organized for your next class."

Not surprisingly, he continues to weave the threads of his own learning into various applications in his life outside the biology lab.

"I'm going to use the web strategy with my real estate class tomorrow night."

"I can't wait to teach the gifted summer school (third graders) so I can try these ideas out there."

"I presented at the Illinois Science Teachers Association, and I used the create-a-creature classification lesson."

"I'll be presenting again in Chicago in November. I'm going to use the people search, again."

SCENARIO FIVE: THE COUNSELOR

Setting the Climate for Thinking

The focus is on fashion, food, and family as students in the Home Economics sections learn to "Celebrate Life." The settings vary with activities planned for typical classrooms, the day care center, kitchen units, sewing rooms, and even video recording studios. The diversity of programs depicts the diversity of life itself, as this caring teacher assumes the role of counselor and sets the climate for learning.

She quietly monitors the discussion . . . dignifying every answer and placing a focus on individual worth.

"Let's get together in a circle."

"We've changed the desks from rows to a circle so we can see and hear each other."

"Let's go around the circle."

As she quietly monitors the discussion, she questions from a counseling or psychological perspective, dignifying every answer and placing a focus on individual worth.

"So you're saying…" (She paraphrases.)

"I've gotten a new insight." (She honors the contributer.)

"What would a compromise approach be?"

"Yes. That seems basic to good mental health, doesn't it?"

"What did you discover?"

"What else?"

"Dave, how do you feel?"

Teaching the Skills of Thinking

Always in a warm, yet dignified manner, she smiles and reflects on the student response, then pushes the class toward analysis, synthesis, and evaluation.

"What are you hearing? Can you summarize?"

"As you review, find the questions you think you know the answers to. Then ask those questions of others to verify."

"Prepare selected readings. Be ready to compare."

"Watch a friend's presentation (of a children's book) and give feedback for improvement."

The diversity of skills necessary for the many areas of learning is evidenced in the topics listed on the Spring program, Celebrate Life:

Nutritional Notes—analyzing the elements of healthy and nutritious meals

Color Highlights—comparing and contrasting color tones for cosmetics and fashion

Childlife and Literature—dramatizing the essence of the story line and analyzing the lessons in the story

Child Development Studies—analyzing the developmental stages and inferring the implications for parents and teachers

Stress—evaluating and problem solving

We Manage—sequencing, prioritizing, organizing, researching

Fashion Display—designing, critiquing

Commercial Foods—decision making

Projects with concrete products provide the perfect setting to integrate skills involved in the creative process.

Projects with concrete products provide the perfect setting to integrate skills involved in the creative process. Students generate ideas, put their ideas together in a novel way, attend to details by analyzing problem areas, revise, enhance, critique, and, finally, celebrate a job well done through various productions targeted to selective audiences.

"Prepare a piece of children's literature. Use puppets, costumes, scenery, props, voice changes . . . whatever you think."

"We'll videotape each presentation so you can see yourself."

"The spring program, Celebrate Life, was a huge success. We have to move to a larger hall."

"The spring program may be the only opportunity some of these kids have to be on stage . . . and they are great. They do a beautiful job."

Structuring the Interaction with Thinking

Taking full advantage of the practical arts format which provides the ideal setting for structuring informal small groups and face-to-face interactions, this teacher is particularly sensitive to the benefits of such structures.

Tailoring each interaction for optimal emotional support, she prepares carefully for the lesson. Sometimes large circles are deemed best for personal sharings.

"Let's use the large circle so we can hear each other."

"The role-playing characters should sit in the center of the semicircle so we can view your faces as you talk."

The counseling perspective is at the root of every interchange as she . . . opts for the solution or action that dignifies and develops each individual.

Other times, the interaction pattern preferred is small teams.

"For the parents' rights scenarios, find two other 'law partners' and form a law firm."

"Build cases for the parents with the law in mind. Each partner in your firm should help support your stand."

"For the dress rehearsals, find a partner who will watch and tell you what it looks like."

"Work in teams for the show. Prepare together."

"I'll meet the teams in the video room."

The counseling perspective is at the root of every interchange as she perceives the underlying problems or circumstances surrounding the student and opts for the solution or action that dignifies and develops each individual. Flexibility is emphasized over and over.

"One girl was very mouthy yesterday, and the kids sensed it and handled it."

"We'll finish the video that _________ brought to share."

"I planned for the parents' rights law teams, but we can start those tomorrow."

"I noticed you were really touched by the film. I almost cried, too."

"I had planned a different lesson, but the slide production *Shades* deals with peer pressure and seems so pertinent. We'll catch up this week."

Metacognitive Processing About Thinking

Although, at times, the kids think they've maneuvered her, this teacher is fully aware of what's going on. Her authorship of several texts in the field provides evidence that she is acutely tuned in to student behavior. In turn, she leads them toward self-awareness or she provides opportunities for self-processing.

"Can we make this work?"

"I think it's important to watch your own videotape so you can see yourself and think about things before you present to the kids."

"Ask yourself if you know it? Then ask yourself if you know it well enough to write about it."

"Isn't it interesting how the weather affects a group?"

"Why do you think we all like the weekends so much?"

"Do an attitude analysis. See how you feel?"

When conflicts arise between cognitive instruction and human needs, this counselor understands that the affective domain rules the cognitive. She opens herself up to peer criticism, perhaps, but one senses a sureness within her that she lives the values she believes as she provides a richness of opportunities for her students.

"A teacher asked me how I could let those kids perform on stage when they were such amateurs. But I believe they need that experience."

Section 3

Active Learning . . . I Teach, but You Must Learn

We learn
10% of what we read,
20% of what we hear,
30% of what we see,
50% of what we see and hear,
70% of what is discussed with others,
80% of what we experience personally, and
95% of what we teach to others.
—William Glasser

Understanding the constructivist's theory of education as opposed to the traditional behavioristic view is paramount to embracing the concept of active learning. Believing that the mind constructs meaning and makes sense of the world by connecting new input to prior knowledge and past experiences is quite different from the formerly held view of education as a "pour and store" process in which the teacher teaches and the kids repeat the same information on a test or quiz.

It is natural for those who embrace the cognitive or constructivist view to value cooperative learning as a primary student channel for learning and internalizing new ideas. The tag line, "I teach, but you must learn," is the essence of this active learning philosophy. The teacher is the resource expert, the facilitator, and the coach, active in presenting information and structuring opportunities to learn. But in the end, it is the student who must take on the more active role of inquirer, investigator, and internalizer, for it is the student who must incorporate the new information into a pre-existing, personally tailored schemata.

Noting Glasser's findings on how one learns, the structures present in fully functioning cooperative learning groups fill the bill. Not only do students see, hear, discuss, and experience learning in cooperative groups, they also are often expected to teach one another.

Undergirding the section, the first article, "Building a Research Synthesis," relays an impressive body of research combined over the past thirty years. A synthesis of the literature features Johnson and Johnson (1989), Kagan (1990), Slavin (1980), and Sharan and Sharan (1976), culminating with a glimpse at the cognitive model of cooperative learning espoused by Bellanca and Fogarty (1991).

Building on the introduction of the cognitive model is the article, "What Does the Ultimate Cooperative Classroom Look Like?," that fully describes the five critical elements of cooperative learning groups. Included in this model are components that align to the acronym, BUILD—Build in higher-order thinking, Unite the teams, Insure individual accountability, Look over and discuss, and Develop social skills.

Targeting the high school and college level instructor, "The New School Lecture: Cooperative Interactions That Encourage Student Thinking" illustrates ten cooperative strategies to make the lecture (or standup teaching) more interactive. Strategies include simple structures such as the rhetorical question and think-pair-share to more intense interactions such as the jigsaw and the human graph.

Appropriately, the active learning section takes its final bow with a set of vignettes in "Vignettes: Multiage Groupings." While all the vignettes depict active learning classrooms, each targets a different age group: a primary classroom, an intermediate multiage group, and a high school cluster.

Building a Research Synthesis

by James Bellanca and Robin Fogarty

Any naysayer who says that cooperative learning is just a fad or another new wrinkle may find the following bit of history interesting. In the earliest settlements, the pioneer families knew the benefits of tutoring their children in groups. Very often, older students paired with the younger to "cipher the slates," read stories, and review their Bible lessons. In the pioneer schools, several families bunched their children into one room. The young teacher, very often one of the oldest students, relied heavily on the children to help each other with lessons. Well into the twentieth century in rural America, the one-room schoolhouse—with cross-age tutors, cooperative learning groups, and group investigations—was the norm. Not until the urban school emerged and the modern factory arrived did schools adopt the assembly line model of teaching and learning. Even at that time, educational leaders such as Francis Parker, superintendent of Quincy Public School (1875–80), John Dewey, Carlton Washborne, and Martin Deutsch were strong advocates of the cooperative learning model. As early as 1897, Triplett was conducting the first formal studies. Today, thanks to the work of Johnson and Johnson, Slavin, and others, numerous studies document the powerful effects of cooperative learning as well as the specific elements needed to make cooperation work in the classroom. No other instructional method used today can claim the quantity or quality of research highlighting its success.

From *If Minds Matter: A Foreword to the Future, Vol. II*, pp. 189–200.

In the 1970s, two major school issues gave birth to a concentrated focus on cooperative learning. The first was the mainstreaming issue; the second was the integration challenge. When Public Law 94-142 was passed by Congress in the 1970s, schools had to restructure classrooms to include the handicapped. Many students previously separated from regular classroom life were mainstreamed. Regular teachers, not knowing how to deal with students who had physical disabilities or learning or behavioral problems, were concerned. The first concern focused on how the "regular" and the "special" students would get along. Many of the mainstreamed students lacked social skills and could easily antagonize their peers; many regular students, who were equally lacking in these social skills, estranged their new classmates.

Following the integration directions established by the Supreme Court in Brown vs. the Board of Education, 1954, schools across the nation were challenged to restructure student assignment patterns. "Separate but equal" schools were out. As students from different racial groups were mixed into unsegregated schools and classrooms, the concerns focused on how these young people would get along.

Roger and David Johnson, two brothers at the University of Minnesota, proposed a solution that applied to both challenges—direct instruction of social skills with guided classroom practice. They theorized that students who were taught to work cooperatively in small groups would develop positive social skills. This in turn, they speculated, would speed the integration of students who saw each other as different.

To everyone's pleasant surprise, the data gathered in these early programs not only showed that their methods worked as planned for improving student-to-student interaction, but also had two unpredicted side effects—dramatic increases in the academic achievement of students and improvement in students' self-esteem.

From these early studies sprang more than five hundred studies by Johnson and Johnson and other researchers. Over and over, with a consistency and reliability remarkable for a school methodology, the studies have demonstrated how and why cooperative learning is one of the most powerful teaching and learning tools available. In a research article on the various models of teaching, Joyce, Showers, and Rolheiser-Bennett (1987) wrote: "Research on cooperative learning is overwhelmingly positive, and the cooperative approaches are appropriate for all curriculum areas. The more complex the outcomes (higher-order processing of information, problem solving, social skills, and attitudes), the greater are the effects."

The results of the research on cooperative learning hold true regardless of factors such as age, subject matter, race, nationality, and sex.

No instructional tool has held researchers' attention more than the cooperative model has. Johnson and Johnson, perhaps the most prolific researchers of cooperative learning, claim we know more about cooperative learning than any other instructional methodology. They further point out that the results of the research on cooperative learning hold true regardless of factors such as age, subject matter, race, nationality, and sex.

THE MAJOR FINDINGS

- Students who learn in the cooperative model perform better academically than students who learn in the individualistic or competitive models. Johnson et al.'s 1981 meta-analysis of 122 studies shows that cooperative learning tended to give higher achievement results than the other two methods, especially with such higher-level tasks as problem solving, concept attainment, and prediction. Further studies indicate why this superior success occurs.
- Because of the amount of cognitive rehearsal, all students at all ability levels in cooperative learning groups enhance their short- and long-term memory as well as their critical thinking skills (Johnson and Johnson, 1983).
- Because cooperative experiences promote positive self-acceptance, students improve their learning, self-esteem, liking for school, and motivation to participate (Johnson and Johnson, 1983).
- Because cooperative learning leads to positive interaction between students, intrinsic learning motivation and emotional involvement in learning are developed to a high degree (Johnson and Johnson, 1989).

- Because cooperative learning nurtures positive peer relationships and structures positive interactions, students in cooperative learning classrooms develop stronger scholastic aspirations, more positive social behavior, and more positive peer relationships (Johnson, 1979).

There are a variety of successful approaches to cooperative learning. Although it is clear to the researchers that classrooms organized for cooperative learning produce superior academic, social, and personal results, they do debate which is the best approach—at least as measured by research standards. Because few practitioners have the luxury of isolating classroom practice to the purity desired by the researchers, most classroom teachers adopt a single approach or a combination of approaches that works best with their own teaching style and their students. Ironically, the research on staff development tells us that the most effective practitioners are more likely to pull the best from each approach and create their own approaches.

Students in cooperative learning classrooms develop stronger scholastic aspirations, more positive social behavior, and more positive peer relationships.

THE FIVE APPROACHES

A brief look at the major approaches will help teachers clarify the pluses and minuses of each and understand the tremendous wealth of successful cooperative tools that have been developed (see Figure 1).

Model One: The Conceptual Approach

Roger Johnson, a science educator, and his brother, David Johnson, a social psychology researcher, use their early studies of cooperative learning to frame the conceptual approach. The Johnsons argue that all effective cooperative learning is marked by five critical characteristics. If all five characteristics are present, there is cooperative learning; however, if any one attribute is missing, there may be group work, but not cooperative learning.

Figure 1
Cooperative Learning: Five Models

MODEL	CREATOR	DESCRIPTION	PLUSES	MINUSES
CONCEPTUAL	Johnson and Johnson	Theories of cooperation, competition, and expectation	+ creative teachers create + can easily enhance what experienced teacher already does	- extra planning time - not step-by-step - limits gifted children - full commitment - used as a filler - time away from content
CURRICULUM	Slavin	Curriculum packages that have cooperative learning structured into the materials	+ easy to train + daily lessons + pretested strategies + instructional variety + higher-order thinking approach	- no direct teaching of social skills - discourages transfer - not a lot of curriculum packages available
STRUCTURAL	Kagan	A repertoire of interactive strategies	+ simplicity in structures + easy to use + builds repertoire of strategies	- cutesy - assumes transfer if restricted to low-level tasks - limited use
GROUP INVESTIGATION	Sharan and Sharan	The ultimate classroom jigsaw	+ promotes inquiry + builds social skills + encourages creative problem solving + gives depth to content	- not good for curriculum coverage - lack of order and recall
COGNITIVE	Bellanca and Fogarty	A synthesis of the four cooperative learning approaches with higher-order thinking focus	+ synthesis + creative application + transfer + blend graphic organizers + macro-thinking processes	- needs training - needs commitment from school and district - takes time

Johnsons' Five Elements of Cooperative Groups

1. *Face-to-Face Interaction.* The physical arrangement of students in small, heterogeneous groups encourages students to help, share, and support each other's learning.

2. *Individual Accountability.* Each student is responsible for the success and collaboration of the group and for mastering the assigned task.

3. *Cooperative Social Skills.* Students are taught, coached, and monitored in the use of cooperative social skills, which enhance the group work.

4. *Positive Interdependence.* A structure that includes a common goal, group rewards, and role assignments is used to encourage students to assist each other in completing the learning task.

5. *Group Processing.* Students reflect on how well they work as a group to complete the task and how they can improve their teamwork.

In any cooperative lesson, these characteristics overlap. They are identified to reinforce the notion that all groups are not cooperative groups. As mental "coat hooks," the characteristics provide a framework for designing strong and effective cooperative learning tasks. They also provide an umbrella under which a large variety of cooperative strategies, structures, and activities may be gathered. As the teacher designs a cooperative lesson, these characteristics are the checklist to ensure the greatest success.

As mental "coat hooks," the characteristics provide a framework for designing strong and effective cooperative learning tasks.

Pluses and Minuses

For teachers who dislike recipe and workbook teaching, the conceptual model is a delight. In effect, the Johnsons' research acts as a touchstone against which the experienced teacher can measure what he or she already does with groups and make quick, positive adjustments that result in greater student-to-student teamwork. For the teacher who has never used groups, the approach provides standards that point out some sure ways to start. The Johnsons recognize—as do adult learning researchers such as Fullan, Knowles, and Krupp—that a teacher is most likely to add to a repertoire of skills and strategies when there are street lights to guide the progress.

There are several minuses to the conceptual model. First, it requires extra time for planning lessons. Even when used only as guided lesson practice, this approach requires time to restructure lesson plans. When the teacher is taking a bolder step to prepare an inquiry or group investigation, even more time is needed.

Second, the conceptual approach doesn't work well for teachers who want a workbook, ditto masters for step-by-step procedure manuals, absolute quiet, or straight rows of desks. This approach requires a teacher who is most comfortable creating lessons in and around required concepts and skills. The teacher who cannot tolerate ambiguity and the chance that a lesson might go flat without a step-by-step procedure manual, workbooks, or blackline masters shouldn't start here.

Third, the conceptual model may end up as poison for the bright child. When a teacher restricts most of the cooperative learning to low-level recall tasks (vocabulary review, computational practice, etc.), the gifted child never gets the chance to soar. Instead, he or she ends up as a substitute teacher, doing work for the other children, never reaping any of the social or intellectual benefits.

The conceptual approach . . . requires a teacher who is most comfortable creating lessons in and around required concepts and skills.

Fourth, the conceptual model requires a full commitment to learning and transfer. The teacher needs time to learn the model, to develop the skills, strategies, and structures and to redesign the classroom. As Bruce Joyce (1986) has pointed out, this instructional change process requires not only well-taught demonstrations, but also a solid peer coaching program and administrative support for implementing the changes.

Fifth, because there is no prepared day-to-day cooperative learning curriculum, the conceptual model sometimes is used only as a filler for "What do we do on Friday afternoons?" and "Let's play a cooperative game."

Finally, the conceptual approach bumps against the "coverage" curriculum. It takes more time in the crowded day to teach lessons in the conceptual model of cooperative learning. Where does the social skill instruction fit in? Where is the time for group processing? The conceptual approach demands time away from content coverage to ensure successful learning by all students.

Model Two: The Curriculum Approach

Slavin's research (1980), conducted with colleagues at the Johns Hopkins University Center for Research on Elementary and Middle Schools, focuses on cooperative learning and basic skill instruction. Slavin and his colleagues have developed a series of cooperative curriculum programs in math and language arts. They have prescribed specific cooperative strategies that teachers can easily learn as they promote heterogeneous cooperation. Because they desire workable alternatives to tracking and ability grouping practices, especially where those practices are detrimental to poor and minority children, they stress packages that all teachers can easily use. Slavin's curriculum packages include:

- Team Accelerated Instruction (TAI)
- Cooperative Integrated Reading and Composition (CIRC)
- Teams, Games, Tournaments (TGT)
- Student Teams, Achievement Division (STAD)

Team Accelerated Instruction (TAI). This mathematics program combines cooperative learning with individualized instruction in a heterogeneous classroom. Designed for grades three to six, TAI utilizes the students to tutor each other, to encourage accurate work, to produce positive social effects, and to handle the record-keeping logistics of individualized instruction or programmed learning. Every eight weeks, teams of high, middle, and low achievers take achievement tests for placement in the individualized program. In the teams, students help each other through the material. Each day, the teacher pulls students from the heterogeneous groups for focused instruction. Students work in teams and across teams to progress through the material. Each week, progress scores are established for each team. Criteria are established in advance for the degrees of recognition each team receives.

TAI is most notable for dispelling the myth that math instruction must be done by track or ability group. One look at the results clearly shows how TAI students of all abilities do better at computation in concepts and at applications with supportive effects in math self-concept, math liking, behavior, relations, and acceptance of differences (Slavin, 1980).

Cooperative Integrated Reading and Composition (CIRC). In preparing a cooperative curriculum for language arts, grades three and four, Slavin's group used cooperative methods for reading groups (eight to fifteen students) and reading teams (two or three students). As students work in their teams, they earn points for their groups. Points based on scores from quizzes, essays, and book reports allow students to earn certificates. As some teams use a variety of strategies, the teacher monitors progress or instructs other teams in comprehension strategies (e.g., predicting, comparing, drawing conclusions). Included in the strategies are partner reading, story prediction, words-aloud practice, spelling review, partner checking, and team comprehension games. At times, students work individually doing independent reading, basal work, or book reports.

CIRC research results are most notable for showing the benefits of cooperative learning with mainstreamed handicapped students, without detriment to the highest-performing students.

CIRC research results are most notable for showing the benefits of cooperative learning with mainstreamed handicapped students, without detriment to the highest-performing students. In the studies, high, medium, and low performers showed equal gains, although the mainstreamed handicapped gains were most impressive.

Teams, Games, Tournaments (TGT). This may be the most widely known of Slavin's curricular approaches and is adaptable to any curricular area, K–12. In this format, students work in groups to master content provided by the teacher. After practicing on worksheets, students demonstrate mastery of the content in weekly tournaments. Students compete in teams against other teams of equal ability (e.g., top achievers vs. top achievers).

Student Teams, Achievement Division (STAD). STAD was designed by Slavin and the Johns Hopkins Group in 1982. In these heterogeneous groups, four or five students of mixed ability, ethnicity, and gender work on worksheets that already have the answers provided. The common goal is to understand the answers, not fill in the blanks. The teams quiz each other until all members understand the answers. The task is completed when the teacher gives an individual quiz to each member. The team score is the sum of the improvement points earned by each individual. Special recognition is given to the teams with the greatest improvement.

Pluses and Minuses

There are seven pluses for the curriculum approach to cooperative learning: (1) It is easy to train teachers. The lessons and strategies are preset for a beginning level training program and show how to use the set curriculum. (2) The approach builds in daily cooperative learning that needs little pre-planning on the teacher's part. By setting out daily lessons, there is higher probability that they will be used. (3) The strategies are pretested as appropriate to each content. The teacher can worry less about "doing the right thing." (4) The curriculum has built-in instructional variety. Small-group, large-group, and individual activities are balanced with direct instruction by the teacher. (5) The programs take a higher-order thinking approach to direct instruction and guided practice of content. (6) Most of the critical attributes of cooperative learning outlined by the Johnsons are inherent within each curriculum. And, (7) it gets results in self-esteem as well as in academic achievement.

Most of the critical attributes of cooperative learning outlined by the Johnsons are inherent within each curriculum.

The minuses most frequently discussed regarding the curriculum approach center on social skill instruction. In the model, social skills are developed indirectly. There is no room given for direct instruction to students on how to work cooperatively. While the approach works very well with skilled classroom managers and with students who are well-behaved, many teachers report that it breaks down when competition (as in TGT or CIRC) between groups becomes too intense, the teacher lacks strong management skills, or the students have little experience or valuing of cooperative learning.

The second minus derives from the first curriculum thrust. The detailed, step-by-step procedure for implementing cooperative learning within a set curriculum discourages transfer of the approach to other curricular areas. For instance, if the teacher is using CIRC for math, he or she may not see any way to use cooperative learning elements in reading social studies.

The third minus is the very small number of developed cooperative curricula available for the classroom. Although some major educational publishers are suggesting some cooperative activities within science and language arts texts, the scope of well-developed cooperative curricula is limited.

Model Three: The Structural Approach

Since 1967, Spencer Kagan has focused his research on the structural approach to cooperative learning. This approach is based on the creation, analysis, and application of content-free structures that cause students to interact in positive ways in the classrooms. Content-free structures, usable with any content, enable the teacher to make multiple applications of a single structure in a variety of subjects. (The debate about content-free structures and content-specific structures is heard, it seems, whenever skill theorists get together. Their debates on study skills, thinking skills, social skills, and reading skills have very similar dialogues. While there is clear evidence that both content-free and content-specific structures produce positive effects, there is little proof that one method is superior to the other.)

Content-free structures, usable with any content, enable the teacher to make multiple applications of a single structure in a variety of subjects.

Kagan's structures fall into three groups:

- **In Turn.** The teacher structures a task in which individuals take a turn in a prescribed order. Included among these are round robin or response in turn, round table, four corners, and three-step interview.
- **Jigsaw.** The teacher structures the task so that each student in the group has part of the information to study. When all members teach each other their material, the whole is greater than the parts. Level I jigsaw, level II jigsaw, co-op—co-op, and think-pair-share all follow this format.
- **Match-Ups.** The teacher structures student-to-student tasks, which formally and informally create cooperative situations. Included here are match mine, numbered heads together, co-op cards, and partners.

Pluses and Minuses

The pluses of the structural approach begin with its simplicity. Each structure is easy to use. This means it takes less than an hour of staff development time to master a single structure and to develop a variety of appropriate activities. The new structures blend quickly with a lecture format and provide practical ways to develop quick, informal student interactions and well-structured discussions.

Because of the number of structure options, a teacher can introduce more variety into the daily regimen and thus boost motivation.

Just as teachers easily switch to cooperative structures from more traditional classroom methods, students also easily adapt to the new methods. Because of the number of structure options, a teacher can introduce more variety into the daily regimen and thus boost motivation.

As the teacher builds a more extensive repertoire of cooperative structures, it is possible to find a number of ways to create multidimensional lessons. For example:

Anticipatory Set. The teacher calls a student to the front of the class and interviews the student. "Who are you? What is your age? Where were you born? When did you start school here? Why do you think I am asking you these questions?" The answer to the why question would be to model an interview that uses the basic five questions of who, what, when, where, and why.

Objective. The teacher shows the lesson objective on the overhead: "To develop interview questions in preparation for a news article."

Input. The teacher shows the newspaper model on the overhead, explains the key questions, and demonstrates how the parts of the graphic are used. She or he uses the questions asked in the anticipatory set to demonstrate.

Checking for Understanding. The teacher tells the students to turn to a neighbor. Next, one student in each pair explains to the partner how to use the newspaper model to generate the questions. After three minutes, the groups stop. Several different listeners from the pairs describe what they heard. Other students give corrective feedback as needed.

Guided Practice. The teacher distributes one copy of the model to each pair. A recorder and a checker are assigned. The pairs review roles and cooperative guidelines as the teacher monitors and assists the pairs as needed. After this round, several pairs describe the questions they asked and explain why they made each selection. Again, corrective feedback is encouraged. A second round of models is given out for additional practice.

Unguided Practice. For homework, all students are given a sheet of instructions for interviewing a household member of their choice.

Closure. On the next day, each pair joins a second pair and they review and critique each other's interview questions. This is followed by an all-class discussion about interview questions. Which questions are most important? Why? What benefits the writer?

Another plus is that the structures readily lend themselves to problem solving and the application of thinking tasks. For example, partner structures can work at any level of thinking (see Figure 2).

Figure 2
Three Thinking Levels

Thinking Level I: Gathering Information

1. Assign each pair in a team a list of vocabulary words. Have the pairs coach and quiz each other on the meanings of assigned words. If any pair is unsure of a definition, have it check with another pair for advice.
2. When all pairs are ready, have a final check for mastery in each team. Follow this with a quiz in which teams compete against each other.

Thinking Level II: Processing Information

1. Have each pair use the vocabulary words to create a story about the current season of the year. If any pair gets stuck, let it travel for help to another pair.
2. Have each pair share its story with the team. Encourage the team to explain why each story was done well.

Thinking Level III: Applying Information

1. Have each pair hypothesize changes that might occur to the current season of the year if global warming increases in the next decade.
2. Have pairs share their hypotheses in a team. Assign one person in a team to list the hypotheses on a sheet of newsprint. Encourage the teams to discuss and rank their hypotheses based on which effect would be most disastrous.

The simplicity of the structural approach is a double-edged sword. Because the structures look fun and cute, a teacher may save the structures for Friday afternoon fillers. Consequently, the students get the message that these are play activities, and they reap little value from the potential richness of the cooperative structure.

The second minus is that the structural approach assumes a great deal about student transfer of the cooperative ethic, cooperative skills, and cooperative behaviors. Much is left to the teacher's enthusiasm, assertiveness, and ability to design a variety of lessons for each content area—that is, if the teacher's classroom management skills and enthusiasm are to hook students into cooperative tasks. However, because the structural approach works best as a hook, the cooperative skills are transferred more by osmosis than by formal instruction. As with the curriculum approach, the lack of formal group processing and social skill instruction limits the transfer of cooperative skills beyond the specific task to the super learners.

The third minus of the structural approach occurs when the teacher restricts the use of cooperative structures to low-level and routine classroom tasks (spelling words, worksheets, computation drill and practice, etc.). Students quickly perceive such limited use as a gambit to manipulate quick interest.

Model Four: The Group Investigation Approach

One classroom teacher who used both the conceptual approach and the structural approach called group investigation the ultimate jigsaw. "For my classes," she says, "group investigation is the most powerful and empowering of the cooperative methods." In group investigation, students work together to plan how they will find answers to key questions about a topic of mutual interest. The group breaks the work down into individual or pair investigation tasks. Each person gathers the assigned information and brings it to the group for discussion, synthesis, and reporting to the class. The teacher plays the major facilitating role through each stage of this inquiry process (see Figure 3).

Figure 3
Sharan and Sharan's Group Investigation Model

Stage One: Posing the Big Question and Forming Groups by Interest. The teacher frames the broad topic, which the students investigate as a big question.

- What do you think will happen if the U.S. produces twice as much nuclear waste per year each year for the next decade?
- How would American society be different today if we had lost World War II?
- What can we learn from a study of plant life?

After the big question, students are encouraged to brainstorm what they want to know about the topic. If they need stimulation, the teacher provides a potpourri of print or video materials, a guest lecturer, or a field trip. Generated questions are reviewed in teams, and then classified and synthesized into subtopics for small-group investigation.

Stage Two: Identifying the Inquiry Problem and Planning How to Research. Each student selects a subtopic to investigate. The subtopic teams formulate the problem statement and help each other discuss and plan the search process.

Stage Three: Dividing Up the Work and Gathering Information. The groups divide up the research. Members research their information, analyze it, and draw initial conclusions.

Stage Four: Preparing the Report. The groups translate their results into a class report. The teacher schedules the reports.

Stage Five: Presenting and Evaluating the Report. As the groups make formal presentations, the teacher guides discussions on their results. Finally, students evaluate their work.

Pluses and Minuses

If the teacher wants the optimum structure for encouraging inquiry, student-to-student interaction, cooperative social skill development, creative problem solving, and communication skills, this approach provides it. If the teacher wants the maximum opportunity to use his or her facilitation skills with students, group investigation provides it. If the teacher wants students to delve deeply into a concept in the curriculum, then he or she will find no better motivator.

On the other hand, if the teacher is concerned about curriculum coverage or a supervisor who expects quiet students seated in rows or needs to know what each student is doing every moment, then group investigation will not work. If students are not well prepared for positive interaction, question asking, problem solving, and consensus seeking, or if they cannot handle the open-ended tasks, the group investigation will fall flat. And if parents expect uniform assignments, daily quizzes, and grades, grades, grades, don't even think about group investigation. In short, the minuses of this approach focus on lack of order and recall; its pluses focus on abundant cognitive rehearsal.

Model Five: The Cognitive Approach

A study of these various approaches shows that no one approach is sufficient or superior. Cooperative learning in some form is a necessary tool for use in every effective classroom. It serves the practical teacher to use a design that borrows the best from each approach and builds a foundation for thoughtfulness.

It serves the practical teacher to use a design that borrows the best from each approach and builds a foundation for thoughtfulness.

As we have listened and worked with teachers in their classrooms, it has become more and more clear that a synthesized model that ties cooperative learning with a critical and creative thinking context of learning for transfer is needed. We look at cooperative learning as an essential ingredient for developing students who are better able to think critically and creatively. We sometimes sketch the picture of cooperative learning as a jet engine with critical and creative thinking skills being the fuel. When put together, they produce the power needed for soaring to new frontiers of discovery and adventure.

The Essential Concepts Plus One

The Johnson and Johnson model outlines the five essential ingredients that distinguish cooperative learning from other forms of group work and that are necessary for making cooperative learning succeed in the classroom. When combined with cognitive processing (lessons focus on higher-order thinking tasks), the additional element of thinking for transfer is also added. And when each and every lesson is structured from this transfer perspective, even more dynamic changes occur in the classroom.

What the Kagan (1990) model calls cooperative structures, trainers in other fields, such as Blanchard et al. (business training and development), Canfield and Wells (self-esteem), Raths (values clarification), and Goodman (creative problem solving), have called strategies. Whichever name is used, the common element is that the strategies approach to staff development encourages the quickest transfer and use without falling into the workbook mentality. In Bellanca and Fogarty's cognitive model, an inductive approach is used. First, teacher trainees begin with basic strategies that are easy to apply and use. This is the practical element. The integrated staff development program begins with participants working together to plan how to weave these basic strategies into the classroom. After the trainees have experienced strategies both as students and as teachers, they explore the conceptual framework; the concepts prevent the strategies from being isolated games. Later, in an advanced program, after intensive classroom application, the trainees focus on the more sophisticated strategies. These require students with higher-level social skills and concentration on inert cognition, problem solving, and reasoning in a variety of contents (e.g., math reasoning, language arts, science). In the final stage, trainees concentrate on two leaders for mentor coaching and curriculum renewal. Both extend the use of cooperative learning and cognitive instruction to teamwork and problem solving as key components for effective transfer.

Pluses and Minuses

The cognitive model asks for a long-term and intense commitment to staff development. Moreover, it expects that what happens in the training program, as well as what happens in the classroom, will be used. With this synthesis, teachers can begin switching from a focus on recall and quick-answer tests to a focus on transferring knowledge and skills across the curriculum and into life outside the school walls.

This model takes time. In an already crowded curriculum, with more and more coverage being required, where is the time for group processing, metacognition, or social skills? To do these functions well, content coverage must give way.

The teacher who uses this model needs a high tolerance for ambiguity. If the classroom is a world of one right answer, the first precondition for developing intelligent behaviors and social skills is lacking. In this model, greater emphasis is placed on helping youngsters process and apply information than on having students memorize great quantities of detailed information. The teacher most often is asked to challenge and extend thinking and less often to inoculate students with information.

Thinking and cooperating require more time for in-depth exploration of concepts and practice of skills and an emphasis on inquiry rather than answers.

Teachers using the cognitive model also need strong planning skills and a creative beat. There is no page-by-page recipe or lock-step teacher's guide. Teachers must feel comfortable with their own ability to design lessons that incorporate not only cooperative learning, but also intelligent behavior and reasoning skills.

This model requires intense and supportive staff development for most implementors. This means the district will need to spend money not only for intensive training days, but also for coaching teams, administrative inservice, and opportunities to restructure curriculum.

The cognitive model is difficult to test with standardized instruments. This is especially true when trying to measure students' transfer of concepts, their ability to reason, and their acquisition of knowledge. To succeed, assessments other than scantron tests are needed. The cognitive model asks students to strive for intelligent behavior, not test results. This is well outside the norms imposed by the current interest in quick tests of isolated facts and skills.

The cognitive model will push a school on essential curricular change. Thinking and cooperating require more time for in-depth exploration of concepts and practice of skills and an emphasis on inquiry rather than answers. When the coverage of curriculum is the norm and isolated facts are king, there is no time for quality thinking or intense cooperation. Unless the school district is ready to challenge the restrictive time limits and coverage of materials, and unless it is ready to redesign curricula with transfer in mind, teachers can expect students to have a more difficult time with transfer.

The cognitive model does not necessitate total curricular changeover. But it does facilitate change by encouraging teachers to set new priorities in their curricula—i.e., "What are the most important concepts to establish firmly, and what are the facts to cover more quickly?"

It also encourages teachers to think about thinking skills as tools for unifying and integrating their curriculum. For instance, they can teach prediction in depth with language arts lessons and use science, math, and social studies materials for students to practice thinking skills in cooperative groups.

In effect, the combination of cooperative learning and cognitive development is not just equal to a math computation in addition (cooperation plus thinking is not the same as 3+3=6), but rather a multiplication of components (3x3=9) in the classroom. Add still another factor, a transfer-based staff-development program with structured coaching and support, and a powerful, exponential change process that produces effective, multidimensional results (3x3x3=27) is engaged.

REFERENCES

Bellanca, J., & Fogarty, R. (1991). *Blueprints for thinking in the cooperative classroom.* Palatine, IL: IRI/Skylight Publishing.

Canfield, J., & Wells, H. (1976). *100 ways to enhance self-concept in the classroom: A handbook for teachers and parents.* Englewood Cliffs, NJ: Prentice-Hall.

Deutsch, M. (1949). An experimental study of the effects of cooperation and competition upon group processes. *Human Relations, 2*, 199–232.

Fullan, M. (1982). *The meaning of educational change.* New York: Teachers College Press.

Johnson, D. W. (1979). *Educational psychology.* Englewood Cliffs, NJ: Prentice-Hall.

Johnson, D. W., & Johnson, R. (1989). *Cooperation and competition: Theory and research.* Edina, MN: Interaction Book Company.

Johnson, D. W., & Johnson, R. (1983). The socialization and achievement crises: Are cooperative learning experiences the solution? In L. Bickman

(Ed.), *Applied social psychology annual 4.* Beverly Hills, CA: Sage Publications.

Johnson, D. W., Maruyama, G., Johnson, R., Nelson, D., & Skon, L. (1981). Effects of cooperative, competitive, and individualistic goal structures on achievement: A meta-analysis. *Psychological Bulletin, 89,* 47–62.

Joyce, B. (1986). *Improving America's schools.* White Plains, NY: Longman.

Joyce, B., Showers, B., & Rolheiser-Bennett, C. (1987). Staff development and student learning: A synthesis of research on models of teaching. *Educational Leadership, 45*(2).

Kagan, S. (1990). *Cooperative learning resources for teachers.* San Juan Capistrano, CA: Resources for Teachers.

Sharan, S., & Sharan, Y. (1976). *Small group teaching.* Englewood Cliffs, NJ: Educational Technology Publications.

Slavin, R. E. (1980). *Using student team learning.* Baltimore, MD: Center for Social Organization of Schools, Johns Hopkins University.

Slavin, R., Leavey, M., & Madden, N. (1982). *Team-assisted individualization: Mathematics teachers' manual.* Baltimore, MD: Center for Social Organization of Schools, Johns Hopkins University.

Triplett, N. (1987). The dynamic factors in peacemaking and competition. *American Journal of Psychology, 9,* 507–533.

What Does the Ultimate Cooperative Classroom Look Like?

by Robin Fogarty and James Bellanca

Progress through the various phases of the small-group process is usually punctuated by intermittent setbacks. The ebb and flow of movement toward and away from a smoothly functioning, high-challenge environment is the usual pattern. Although there are setbacks, forward progress is still being made. Over time, the unmistakable signs of maturing group behavior become apparent.

The ebb and flow of movement toward and away from a smoothly functioning, high-challenge environment is the usual pattern.

To visualize what a high-performance, high-challenge cooperative classroom looks like, a blueprint design for thinking and cooperating is presented. This high-functioning instructional design strikes a delicate balance between student-to-student interactions in cooperative learning models and student-to-material interactions in information-processing models.

Elaborating on the dual interactions of student-to-student collaborations and student-to-information processing, Figure 1 illustrates the ultimate high-performance instruction model. This model dictates intense involvement by all students. The intensity of this student involvement is determined by certain critical elements.

Figure 1
The IRI/Skylight Model for Cooperative Learning

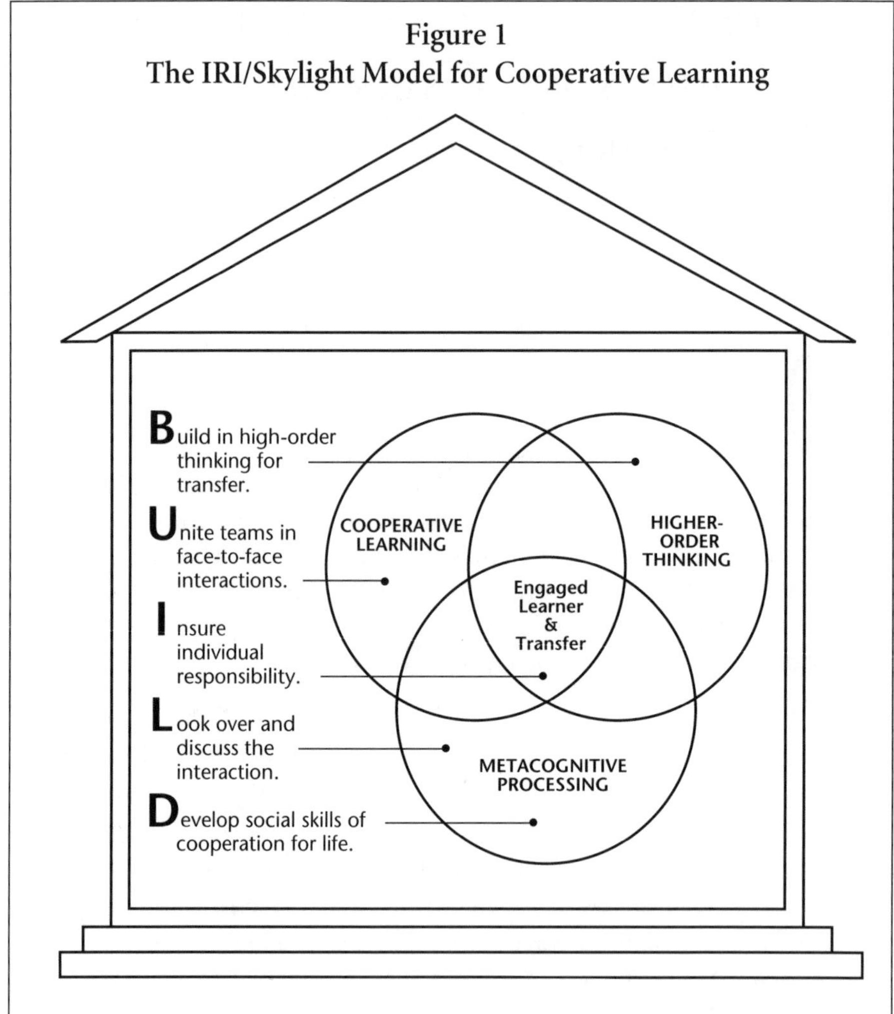

STUDENT-TO-STUDENT INTERACTION

The cooperative learning model of student-to-student interaction requires one to BUILD in certain elements to achieve the researched outcomes. The acronym BUILD (Marcus & McDonald, 1990) represents five key components that comprise the effective cooperative model (see Figure 2).

In Figure 3, the critical elements of BUILD are used as the organizing headings, and myriad cooperative skills and strategies are charted. For example, strategies for "L"—to look over

Figure 2
The Elements of BUILD

B To achieve effective cooperative groups in which student learning, achievement, and self-esteem are all increased significantly, the teacher-facilitator must build higher-level thinking into the tasks. By creating high challenges within the group assignment, cooperation automatically gets a boost because the members sense that they need the group to meet the challenge. In turn, the higher-level metacognitive discussion will promote transfer.

U A united group—a group with a "sink or swim together" posture—is formed by the members. When students know that they either all make it together or none of them makes it alone, the motivation to cooperate is naturally sparked. Helping create interdependence in the groups to accomplish individual as well as group goals is a key to the high-performance classroom.

I Another critical element is helping individual students learn in highly personal and relevant ways—ways that hold each group member accountable for achieving the task and learning the material. Often, students new to cooperative models are unskilled at learning *and* being accountable. High-performing classrooms take deliberate, visible, and more sophisticated steps to insure individual learning. These steps range from quick, individual quizzes to more elaborate, independent applications.

L Taking time to look over what the group has done—to plan, monitor, and evaluate both the academic task and the cooperative task—is another critical element in the high-performing classroom. The metacognitive model, which promotes further application and transfer of the lesson, also fosters critiquing among the group members. Without the group processing time, little, if any, transfer is likely to take place. Yet, by simply addressing the group behaviors and task results, students exhibit noticeable tendencies toward meaningful transfer.

D A final element for high-functioning cooperative learning teams is the explicit attention to developing social skills, which are needed for communicating, building trust, promoting leadership, and resolving conflicts. The structured cooperative learning models target specific social skills that help students develop into valuable, contributing, and empathetic members of groups. Targeted social skills might include the active listening behaviors of paraphrasing, affirming, and clarifying; the leadership skill of encouraging others; and the conflict resolution skills of disagreeing with ideas and not people, listening to others' points of view, and seeking consensus.

Figure 3
Quick Reference: Cooperative Learning Lesson Plan

	B	U	I	L	D	
	Build in High-Order Thinking	**Unite Teams**	**Insure Individual Responsibility**	**Look Over and Discuss**	**Develop Social Skills**	
	Problem Solving Decision Making Creative Ideation	*Build Trust and Teamwork*	*Insure Individual Learning and Responsibility*	*Plan, Monitor, and Evaluate*	*Communication Leadership Conflict Resolution*	
1	Critical and creative thinking	Bonding and group identity	Assigned roles	Goal setting	Paraphrase	I hear . . . . I see . . . .
2	3-to-1 technique	Shared materials	Quiz	PMI	Affirm	That's a good idea.
3	Problem solving	Single product	Random responses	Human graph	Clarify	Tell me more!
4	Decision making	Jigsaw	Individual application	Teacher observation sheet	Test options	What else?
5	Fat & skinny questions	Lottery	Individual grades	Student observer feedback	Sense tone	That feels ___
6	Application	Bonus points	Signatures. I agree! I understand!	Success award	Encourage others	No put-downs!
7	Transfer within/across/into	Group grade	Round robin (Wraparound)	Thinking log entry	Accept others' ideas	Set DOVE guidelines
8	Graphic organizers	Group reward	Homework	Individual transfer or application	T-Chart	Looks like Sounds like
9	Metacognitive exercises	Consensus	Bonus points	Team ad	Disagree with ideas, not people	Other points of view
10	Making metaphors	Extended projects	Expert jigsaw	Mrs. Potter's Questions	Reach consensus	5 to fist

and discuss—include Mrs. Potter's Questions, a thinking log, an observation sheet, and a PMI chart. Methods for "U"—unite teams—include a single product, shared materials, a jigsaw approach, and bonus points. As the teacher of the high-performance classroom plans ongoing lessons, this quick reference serves as a guide to ensure that the critical elements of high-challenge cooperative group lessons are included. By plotting a lesson that has an element from each column, the teacher readily puts together a success-oriented, high-contact, high-content cooperative lesson.

For instance, plotting one element in each column might look like this:

B	U	I	L	D
Creative thinking				
	Shared materials			
		Quiz		
			Mrs. Potter's Questions	
				DOVE guidelines

In working with a math class on problem solving, this teacher might use the elements designated above to design the following lesson:

Building in higher-order thinking: The students will predict or estimate a reasonable answer (using creative thinking).

Uniting the group: Students will solve their problems on large poster paper and list their strategies using the same materials.

Insuring individual responsibility: One student will be selected from each group for a quiz on the problem type.

Looking over and discussing what was done: Students will review Mrs. Potter's Questions in their small groups and samples will be reported to the class. Mrs. Potter's Questions are standard metacognitive questions that promote reflective thinking and foster future applications. These questions need to be used repeatedly to process student thinking during cooperative learning tasks in the classroom.

- What were we supposed to do?
- What did we do well?
- What would we do differently?
- Do we need any help?

Developing a social skill: The DOVE guidelines will be part of the instructional input before the group approaches the task.

Defer judgment on ideas.

Opt for original ideas.

Vast numbers of ideas.

Expand by piggybacking on another's idea.

STUDENT-TO-INFORMATION INTERACTION

The student-to-student interaction that results in intense learner involvement is only half of the interaction model for the high-performance classroom. The other part of the interactive model includes student-to-information interactions.

When processing information in an interactive classroom, the student becomes intensely involved with the information being studied.

To promote student interaction with information, couple every cooperative task in the classroom with a complex cognitive task. Explicitly build higher-order thinking processes into high-challenge lessons. Target specific microskills for thinking or string several thinking skills together into a macroprocess approach to complex thinking (see Figures 4 and 5). Using BUILD and the thinking skills and thinking processes ensures a high-challenge activity.

ELEMENTARY LESSON EXAMPLE: MAMMAL MANIA

Using a completed BUILD chart of the cooperative learning elements, scan and select key elements for the envisioned lesson "Mammal Mania." By using the BUILD chart, you can easily include the critical elements of a higher-order thinking cooperative lesson in your plan. For example, you might create the BUILD chart in Figure 6 and choose the circled items for use in a cooperative lesson.

Figure 4
Microskills

Critical Thinking Skills

1. Attributing
2. Comparing/Contrasting
3. Classifying
4. Sequencing
5. Prioritizing
6. Drawing Conclusions
7. Determining Cause/Effect
8. Analyzing for Bias
9. Analyzing for Assumptions
10. Solving for Analogies
11. Evaluating
12. Decision Making

Creative Thinking Skills

1. Brainstorming
2. Visualizing
3. Personifying
4. Inventing
5. Associating Relationships
6. Inferring
7. Generalizing
8. Predicting
9. Hypothesizing
10. Making Analogies
11. Dealing with Ambiguity and Paradox
12. Problem Solving

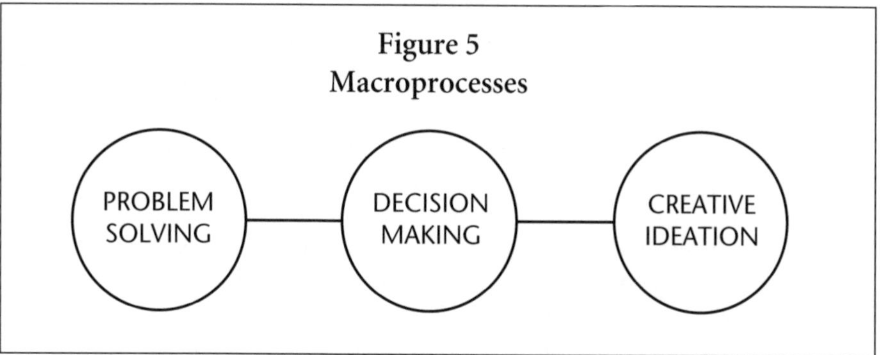

Figure 5
Macroprocesses

- B - Critical and creative thinking (brainstorming, inventing, performing) stretch the mind.
- U - Establishing a group identity unites each team.
- I - Assigned roles keep members accountable for tasks and learning.
- L - Mrs. Potter's Questions structure quality review.
- D - Setting guidelines for students to accept others' ideas reinforces social skills.

Figure 6
Sample Cooperative Lesson Planner: Elementary Example

	B	U	I	L	D	
	Build in High-Order Thinking	**U**nite Teams	**I**nsure Individual Responsibility	**L**ook Over and Discuss	**D**evelop Social Skills	
	Problem Solving Decision Making Creative Ideation	*Build Trust and Teamwork*	*Insure Individual Learning and Responsibility*	*Plan, Monitor, and Evaluate*	*Communication Leadership Conflict Resolution*	
1	Critical and creative thinking	Bonding and group identity	Assigned roles	Goal setting	Paraphrase	I hear . . . . I see . . . .
2	3-to-1 technique	Shared materials	Quiz	PMI	Affirm	That's a good idea.
3	Problem solving	Single product	Random responses	Human graph	Clarify	Tell me more!
4	Decision making	Jigsaw	Individual application	Teacher observation sheet	Test options	What else?
5	Fat & skinny questions	Lottery	Individual grades	Student observer feedback	Sense tone	That feels ____
6	Application	Bonus points	Signatures. I agree! I understand!	Success award	Encourage others	No put-downs!
7	Transfer within/across/into	Group grade	Round robin (Wraparound)	Thinking log entry	Accept others' ideas	Set DOVE guidelines
8	Graphic organizers	Group reward	Homework	Individual transfer or application	T-Chart	Looks like Sounds like
9	Metacognitive exercises	Consensus	Bonus points	Team ad	Disagree with ideas, not people	Other points of view
10	Making metaphors	Extended projects	Expert jigsaw	Mrs. Potter's Questions	Reach consensus	5 to fist

Next, using the list of microskills for thinking in Figure 7 as a reference, select an appropriate thinking skill(s) for the lesson.

Using all of the chosen elements as a guide for designing the lesson, incorporate the specific components into the plan. For example, in preparation for a spring field trip to the zoo, which is a culminating activity for the mammal unit in science, the following lesson has been created using the selected elements.

Have students brainstorm, as a class, a web of mammals (see Figure 8).

Ask students to turn to a partner and recall the critical attributes of mammals. Instruct them to check that all listed animals fit the definition.

Next, arrange students into groups of three and assign roles of recorder/illustrator, animal trainer, and actor.

Figure 7
Microskills for Elementary Lesson

Critical Thinking Skills

1. Attributing
2. Comparing/Contrasting
3. Classifying
4. Sequencing
5. Prioritizing
6. Drawing Conclusions
7. Determining Cause/Effect
8. Analyzing for Bias
9. Analyzing for Assumptions
10. Solving for Analogies
11. Evaluating
12. Decision Making

Creative Thinking Skills

1. Brainstorming
2. Visualizing
3. Personifying
4. Inventing
5. Associating Relationships
6. Inferring
7. Generalizing
8. Predicting
9. Hypothesizing
10. Making Analogies
11. Dealing with Ambiguity and Paradox
12. Problem Solving

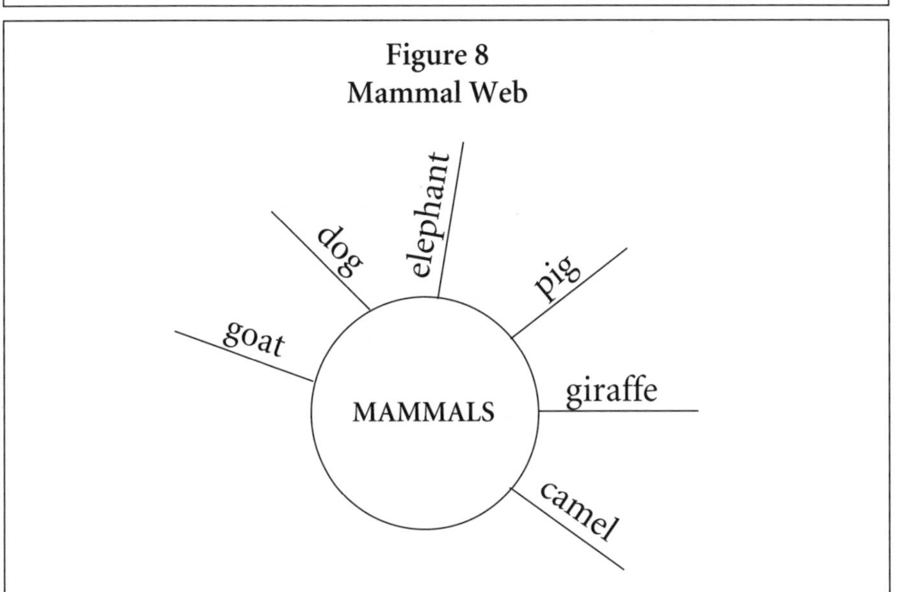

Figure 8
Mammal Web

Explain to the groups that their first task is to select an animal from the unit and to invent a name for their team that signifies their mammal selections. A group name creates a group identity. For example, their group name might be the Elephant Explorers.

Instruct students that they are going to use a strategy called That's A Good Idea (cooperative skill: accepting others' ideas) to create an animal that can talk and behave like a person (creative thinking skill: personifying). Begin by having students list human characteristics and behaviors for a mammal.

For example, the first person gives a human trait to the elephant ("He can ride a bike.").

The second person tells why that trait is a good idea ("That's a good idea because he can get around faster.") and then gives another trait to the elephant ("He can also talk.").

The third person tells why the last trait given is a good idea ("That's a good idea because he can communicate with others.") and then gives another idea ("He can fly kites too.").

Continue around the group until all members have praised another's idea *and* added a trait to the animal. (Let students know they may pass but they cannot repeat another's idea.) As the traits and praises are stated, have the recorder write them on a group chart.

Tell students the goal is to create a fictional character (an animal) out of their mammal that can behave in human ways. They must brainstorm at least six improvements to add to their mammal. Once the recorder/illustrator has listed everyone's improvements on a large sheet, have him or her draw the animal in a way that shows the personified characteristics (see Figure 9).

The final task requires the animal trainer and the animal actor to perform a brief skit incorporating the various human characteristics. These performances can be done for another small group or for the whole class.

For affective processing, ask students to "become the animal." Ask them to imagine the actions and feelings of the mammal. Then, in their groups of three, have them finish this statement:

I want to be more like ____________________ because . . . .
(animal)

Figure 9
An Elephant Who's Like a Person

Trait	That's a Good Idea Because . . .
1. He can ride a bike.	1. He can get around faster.
2. He can talk.	2. He can communicate with others.
3. He can fly kites.	3.

For social processing, have students discuss why it is important to add ideas to the group and to accept others' ideas.

For cognitive processing, have students talk about the thinking skill of personifying and answer these questions:

- What was difficult about trying to change the animal into a human-like character?
- Why is using That's A Good Idea (responses in turn) a good idea?

For metacognitive processing, have the groups talk through Mrs. Potter's Questions:

- What were we supposed to do?
- What did we do well?
- What should we do differently?
- Do we need any help?

MIDDLE SCHOOL LESSON EXAMPLE: METRIC MATTERS
Using a completed BUILD chart of the cooperative learning elements, scan and select key elements for the envisioned lesson "Metric Matters."

For example, thinking about the purpose of the lesson, which is to force application of the metric model into various subjects, you could select the elements in Figure 10 to create a cooperative lesson.

- B - A graphic organizer creates a higher-order thinking lesson.
- U - Bonus points in groups unite the teams.
- I - A wraparound ensures the individual learning process.
- L - A thinking log entry forces students to look back and reflect on the lesson.
- D - Encouragement is targeted for social skill building.

Figure 10
Sample Cooperative Lesson Planner: Middle School Example

	B	U	I	L	D	
	Build in High-Order Thinking	Unite Teams	Insure Individual Responsibility	Look Over and Discuss	Develop Social Skills	
	Problem Solving Decision Making Creative Ideation	*Build Trust and Teamwork*	*Insure Individual Learning and Responsibility*	*Plan, Monitor, and Evaluate*	*Communication Leadership Conflict Resolution*	
1	Critical and creative thinking	Bonding and group identity	Assigned roles	Goal setting	Paraphrase	I hear . . . . I see . . . .
2	3-to-1 technique	Shared materials	Quiz	PMI	Affirm	That's a good idea.
3	Problem solving	Single product	Random responses	Human graph	Clarify	Tell me more!
4	Decision making	Jigsaw	Individual application	Teacher observation sheet	Test options	What else?
5	Fat & skinny questions	Lottery	Individual grades	Student observer feedback	Sense tone	That feels ___
6	Application	Bonus points	Signatures. I agree! I understand!	Success award	Encourage others	No put-downs!
7	Transfer within/across/into	Group grade	Round robin (Wraparound)	Thinking log entry	Accept others' ideas	Set DOVE guidelines
8	Graphic organizers	Group reward	Homework	Individual transfer or application	T-Chart	Looks like Sounds like
9	Metacognitive exercises	Consensus	Bonus points	Team ad	Disagree with ideas, not people	Other points of view
10	Making metaphors	Extended projects	Expert jigsaw	Mrs. Potter's Questions	Reach consensus	5 to fist

Figure 11
Microskills for Middle School Lesson

Critical Thinking Skills	Creative Thinking Skills
1. Attributing	1. Brainstorming (circled)
2. Comparing/Contrasting	2. Visualizing
3. Classifying	3. Personifying
4. Sequencing	4. Inventing
5. Prioritizing (circled)	5. Associating Relationships
6. Drawing Conclusions	6. Inferring
7. Determining Cause/Effect	7. Generalizing
8. Analyzing for Bias	8. Predicting
9. Analyzing for Assumptions	9. Hypothesizing
10. Solving for Analogies	10. Making Analogies
11. Evaluating	11. Dealing with Ambiguity and Paradox
12. Decision Making	12. Problem Solving (circled)

Figure 12
Sharan & Sharan Group Investigation Model

Step 1: Pose the big question and form groups by interest.
Step 2: Identify the inquiry problem and plan how to research.
Step 3: Divide up the work and gather information.
Step 4: Synthesize, summarize, and write the report.
Step 5: Present by groups and evaluate.

Next, select appropriate microskills for thinking from the list, as shown in Figure 11.

The following lesson is described—using the selected elements—as it might occur based on the Sharan and Sharan (1976) group investigation model (see Figure 12).

Figure 13
Metric Matters Mind Map

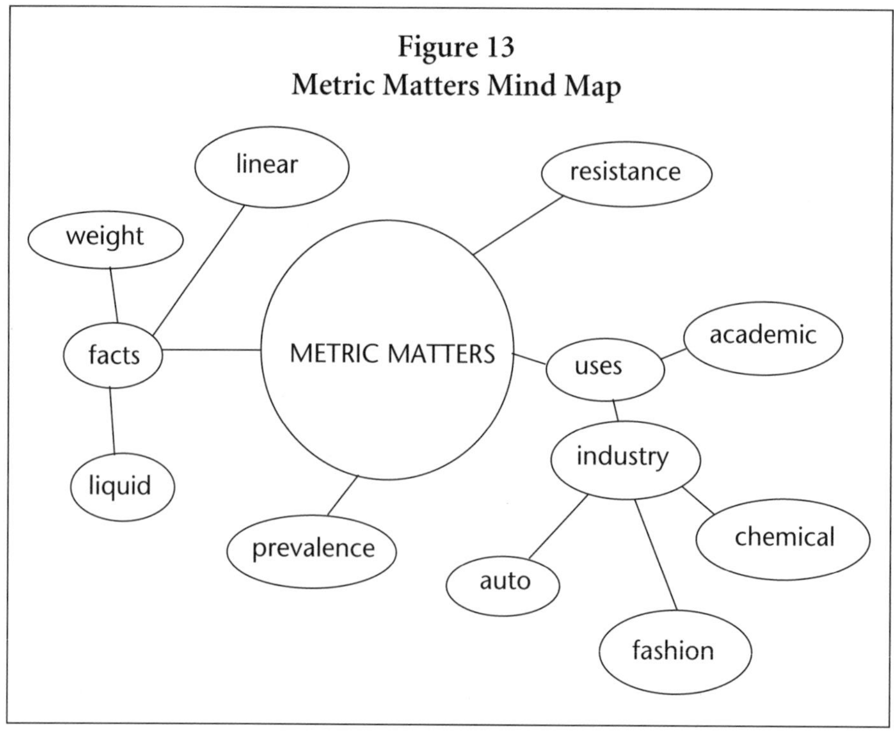

First, give the following input:

Academic Task Focus:	Using the metric system in two subject areas
Cooperative Task Focus:	Encouraging others
Thinking Task Focus:	Brainstorming, prioritizing, problem solving, transferring

Then, through discussion with the class, fill in a graphic organizer (such as the mind map in Figure 13) with various aspects of metric matters that groups may want to investigate. Allow students to brainstorm many ideas.

Group Investigation Step One: Pose the Big Question and Form Groups by Topics of Interest

Once the general topic has been properly explored, ask students to rearrange themselves according to their specific topics of interest. Require no more than three students to a group in the early attempts of the group investigation model.

Group Investigation Step Two: Identify the Inquiry Problem and Plan How to Research

Instruct groups to discuss ways to gather information for the initial research needed. Suggest library resources, primary resources such as interviews, and other media possibilities. Also, suggest the librarian as a quick resource.

Group Investigation Step Three: Divide Up the Work and Gather Information

a. Specify the jigsaw model in which each member is responsible for a piece of the completed puzzle.

b. Have groups set a time and date to reconvene with their completed parts.

c. Choose a checker to see that all members contribute.

Group Investigation Step Four: Synthesize, Summarize, and Prepare the Presentation

Instruct students in the refinements of the jigsaw model. That is, as each member contributes to the whole, the members must have definite ways to teach each other about their particular parts as they prioritize, share, synthesize, and summarize information (see Figure 14). Without a thorough understanding of each separate piece, the synthesis will be fragmented and superficial. When group investigation is working well with a high-performing group, a synergy occurs in which the final piece is far richer than any work done by a single student.

Group Investigation Step Five: a) Present the Information

The groups problem solve a final presentation that fulfills the task requirements. Student teams demonstrate how the metric matters they investigated can be applied across at least two content lessons. This demonstration can be presented to another group or to the whole class. Bonus points are given to each group member who actually applies the idea in another class. Proof from the other teacher is required.

Figure 14
Ways to Teach Another

Tell

Model

Demonstrate

Draw

Give Examples

Use Visuals

Make Analogies

Quiz

Group Investigation Step Five: b) Evaluate

For affective processing, ask students to discuss their feelings about the group investigation jigsaw. Do a quick wraparound with the stem "I felt . . . ."

For social skill processing, have students talk about how they encouraged each other.

For cognitive processing, have students discuss the pros and cons of the group investigation process that they just used.

For metacognitive processing, ask students to discuss the "So what?" aspects of group investigation. How can they parlay this model into other situations—"Now what?"

HIGH SCHOOL LESSON EXAMPLE: IN DEFENSE OF HUMAN RIGHTS

Using a completed BUILD chart of the cooperative learning elements, scan and select key elements for the envisioned lesson "In Defense of Human Rights" (see Figure 15).

- B - Application of the group investigation information builds in higher-order thinking.
- U - The jigsaw unites the members as they rely on each other to help complete the assignment.

Figure 15
Sample Cooperative Lesson Planner: High School Example

	B	U	I	L	D	
	Build in High-Order Thinking	Unite Teams	Insure Individual Responsibility	Look Over and Discuss	Develop Social Skills	
	Problem Solving Decision Making Creative Ideation	*Build Trust and Teamwork*	*Insure Individual Learning and Responsibility*	*Plan, Monitor, and Evaluate*	*Communication Leadership Conflict Resolution*	
1	Critical and creative thinking	Bonding and group identity	Assigned roles	Goal setting	Paraphrase	I hear . . . . I see . . . .
2	3-to-1 technique	Shared materials	Quiz	PMI	Affirm	That's a good idea.
3	Problem solving	Single product	Random responses	Human graph	Clarify	Tell me more!
4	Decision making	Jigsaw	Individual application	Teacher observation sheet	Test options	What else?
5	Fat & skinny questions	Lottery	Individual grades	Student observer feedback	Sense tone	That feels ____
6	Application	Bonus points	Signatures. I agree! I understand!	Success award	Encourage others	No put-downs!
7	Transfer within/across/into	Group grade	Round robin (Wraparound)	Thinking log entry	Accept others' ideas	Set DOVE guidelines
8	Graphic organizers	Group reward	Homework	Individual transfer or application	T-Chart	Looks like Sounds like
9	Metacognitive exercises	Consensus	Bonus points	Team ad	Disagree with ideas, not people	Other points of view
10	Making metaphors	Extended projects	Expert jigsaw	Mrs. Potter's Questions	Reach consensus	5 to fist

I - Individual criteria insures individual learning by forcing students to state their reasoning.

L - PMI allows time to look over and discuss all aspects of the lesson.

D - Reaching consensus gives students practice in using their social skills.

Next, select appropriate strategies from the list of microskills for thinking, as shown in Figure 16.

With the cooperative elements in mind, explain the project to the students. Through small-group investigation students will explore the topic "In Defense of Human Rights." With their groups they will present a five-minute report to the class. The purpose of each presentation is to delineate a particular right of

Figure 16
Microskills in High School Lesson

Critical Thinking Skills	Creative Thinking Skills
1. Attributing	1. Brainstorming
2. Comparing/Contrasting	2. Visualizing
3. Classifying	3. Personifying
4. Sequencing	4. Inventing
5. Prioritizing	5. Associating Relationships
6. Drawing Conclusions	6. Inferring
7. Determining Cause/Effect	7. Generalizing
8. Analyzing for Bias	8. Predicting
9. Analyzing for Assumptions	9. Hypothesizing
10. Solving for Analogies	10. Making Analogies
11. Evaluating	11. Dealing with Ambiguity and Paradox
12. Decision Making	12. Problem Solving

human beings that has been abused throughout history. The reports should project an empathetic viewpoint. Humor may be used. Good taste and appropriateness should be part of the grading criteria.

After the presentations, each student is responsible for applying information presented in a paper that takes a human rights position other than the one researched by his or her group. In other words, each must gather information from the other groups' presentations in order to formulate their individual positions on human rights issues.

As a class, brainstorm a number of human rights issues (e.g., our own bill of rights, right to bear children, right to choose own spouse, hostages, treatment of mentally ill, censorship, POWs, homelessness, free speech, citizenship, assembly, discrimination, free elections).

Group Investigation Step One: Pose the Big Question and Form Groups by Topics of Interest

Instruct students to form their small groups according to topics of interest. Limit the groups to three or four students each. Suggest that each team create a group name to designate its topic.

Group Investigation Step Two: Identify the Inquiry Problem and Plan How to Research

Using the jigsaw model for group investigation, the teams should discuss and plan their research procedures. Be sure the groups include a variety of sources for gathering information about past abuses of human rights.

Group Investigation Step Three: Divide Up the Work and Gather Information

Have group members take individual responsibility for specific pieces of the whole project. Have group checkers collect completed assignments and data from the various members. Have groups set a date, time, and place to share their various segments.

Group Investigation Step Four: Synthesize, Summarize, and Prepare a Report

Have student teams reassemble with their respective pieces of information. In the jigsaw format, as each person shares his or her piece, care is taken in *how* that sharing is done. This is really the teachable moment, when each member teaches the other members of the group. Remind students that each member is responsible for learning *all* the pieces of information as they fit them together into a total picture—their presentations.

Group Investigation Step Five: a) Present by Groups

After reaching consensus on a presentation format, student groups should present their "In Defense of Human Rights" reports to the class.

Require students to fill in observation sheets to use as reference prompters when evaluating the information and writing their papers. Or, you may want to videotape the presentations.

Group Investigation Step Five: b) Evaluate

For affective processing, discuss the following question within the small groups: How did your feelings influence your performance?

For social skill processing, have students describe an instance when their behavior infringed on someone else's rights.

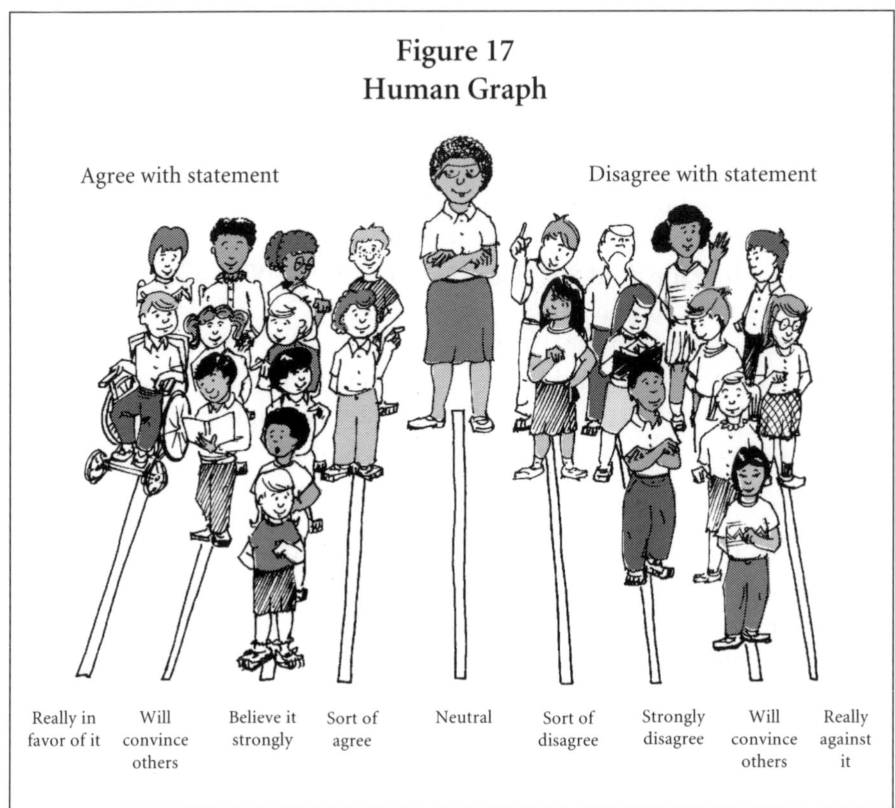

Figure 17
Human Graph

Figure 18
Group Investigation

Plus (+)	
Minus (+)	
Interesting (?)	

For cognitive processing, use the human graph to take readings on the issues discussed in this lesson. Have students display their intensity of feelings using the ratings in Figure 17 and evaluate their thinking by stating the criteria for their decision. For metacognitive processing, use a PMI chart (deBono, 1970) to evaluate Sharan and Sharan's group investigation model (see Figure 18).

REFERENCES

Bellanca, J. (1991). *Building a caring, cooperative classroom.* Palatine, IL: IRI/Skylight Publishing.

Bellanca, J., & Fogarty, R. (1991). *Blueprints for thinking in the cooperative classroom.* Palatine, IL: IRI/Skylight Publishing.

deBono, E. (1970). *Lateral thinking.* New York: Harper & Row.

Fogarty, R. (1990). *Designs for cooperative interactions.* Palatine, IL: IRI/Skylight Publishing.

Kohn, A. (1993). *Punished by rewards.* New York: Houghton-Mifflin.

Glasser, W. (1986). *Control theory in the classroom.* New York: Harper.

Johnson, D. W., & Johnson, R. (1978). Cooperative, competitive, and individualistic learning. *Journal of Research and Development in Education, 12,* 3–15.

Joyce, B. R. (1986). *Improving America's schools.* White Plains, NY: Longman.

Joyce, B. R. & Showers, B. (1983). *Power in staff development through research and training.* Alexandria, VA: Association for Supervision and Curriculum Development.

Marcus, S. A., & McDonald, P. (1990). *Tools for the cooperative classroom.* Palatine, IL: IRI/Skylight Publishing.

McCabe, M., & Rhoades, J. (1988). *The nurturing classroom.* Willits, CA: ITA Publications.

Scearce, C. (1993). *100 ways to build teams.* Palatine, IL: IRI/Skylight Publishing.

Sharan, S. & Sharan, Y. (1976). *Small-group teaching.* Englewood Cliffs, NJ: Educational Technology Publications.

Slavin, R. E. (1983). When does cooperative learning increase student achievement? *Psychology Bulletin, 94,* 429–445.

The New School "Lecture": Cooperative Interactions That Engage Student Thinking

by Robin Fogarty and James Bellanca

The new "lecture" does not resemble the old lecture very much; in fact, the new "lecture" is really a myriad of interaction patterns. These authentic interaction models take the focus off the lecturer and put it squarely on the learner. From kindergarten classrooms to college lecture halls, educators are moving toward more involving models of instruction. The emergence of the new school "lecture" is unmistakable.

From kindergarten classrooms to college lecture halls, educators are moving toward more involving models of instruction.

At one end of the spectrum of possibilities for cooperative interactions is the traditional stand-up teaching model. In this model the learner is viewed as a vessel to be filled. At the other end of the spectrum is a total group involvement model called the Human Graph, in which the learners actually move to spots on an imaginary graph that symbolize their position on an issue.

The shift from the most didactic teaching models to more intensely involving models is no easy task for teachers. Just as in any paradigm shift, major philosophical underpinnings are

---

shaken. Yet, the move toward the new school "lecture," with its accent on student interactions, is made easier if seen as a gradual change. Student involvement is designed so that strategies increase student participation by degrees. In this way, teachers and students are able to adjust and adapt to the new model over time.

Surprisingly and almost unfailingly, once the philosophical shift begins, once teachers begin implementing cooperative interactions, the evidence of student motivation becomes so overwhelmingly visible that teachers are encouraged to try more. The momentum builds for both teachers and students, and before long "the new school lecture" becomes the norm in the classroom. By then, the novelty of the models is no longer the challenge. The challenge becomes choosing the most appropriate interactive designs for the target lesson; it is choosing a design in which the final focus rests on the learner, not on the lecturer.

The challenge becomes . . . choosing a design in which the final focus rests on the learner, not on the lecturer.

AN OVERVIEW OF TWELVE COOPERATIVE INTERACTIONS

The many variables that come into play as one is selecting the most appropriate interactive strategy include time, space and facilities, level and behavior of students, number of students, purpose of the lesson, background and experiences of the students, support materials, and teacher expertise.

In the high-content, high-support, high-challenge classroom (see Figure 1), the overriding goal is intense student involvement and the subsequent transfer of learning across subject areas and into life situations. High content refers to rigorous disciplines such as the sciences, the humanities, and the arts; high support cites the expectation for cooperative interactions; and high challenge dictates the need for meaningful and thoughtful learner activities. By accumulating a repertoire of interactive strategies and coupling student involvement with information-processing models, the skillful teacher moves learning for all students to new depths. As one surveys the various

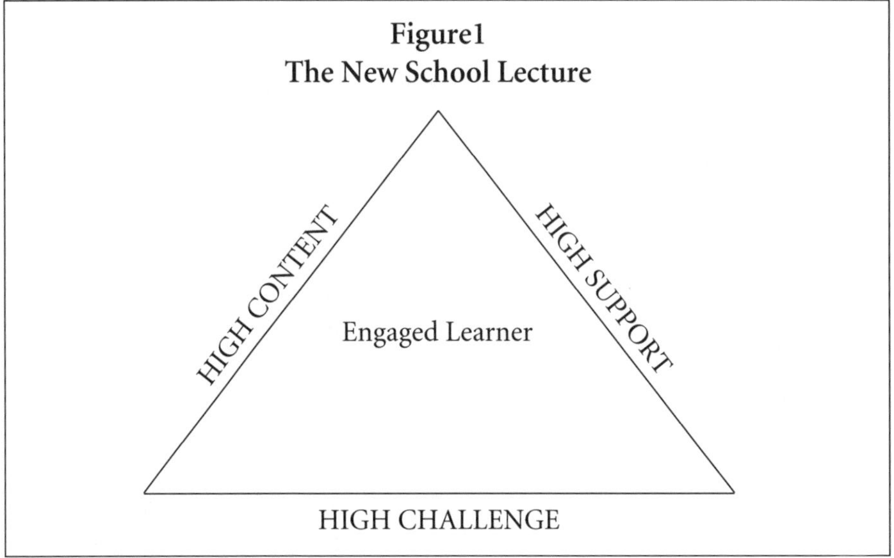

interactive strategies, it becomes apparent that different strategies are appropriate for different classroom situations.

Twelve basic cooperative interactive models are presented at the end of this chapter. These models can be adapted to meet less-involving to more-involving teaching goals. For example, the strategies in Model 1, Lecture/Rhetorical Questioning, require minimal learner participation, while Model 8, Cooperative Learning: Groups, or Model 10, Forced Response: Wrap Around, engage the learner intensely due to the very nature and structure of the strategies.

The skillful teacher introduces increasingly engaging interactive models over time. As students become more adept in their social skills, the models are selected strictly for appropriateness. Initially, however, the models are subtly slotted into the lessons to familiarize students with the different interactions and to lead them toward involvement in the learning situation.

Each model included at the end of the chapter indicates the type of interaction, a source, and a lesson description. The prescription suggests when this particular model might be appropriate. A classroom *vignette* provides brief illustrations of the interactions that define the model. The brief *notes* are metacognitive cues or labels that explain the example under scrutiny.

Interactive models work with all levels—elementary, middle, high school, and college. Each of these particular examples features just one of the levels. Adjustments by the instructor are needed to tailor the examples for age, grade, and content appropriateness.

CONCLUSION

Based on current research and practice, the cooperative interaction designs that distinguish the new school lecture from the traditional seem to offer a positive and optimistic prognosis for future use in our nation's classrooms. By their very nature, cooperative learning strategies create a bubbling-up effect among both students and teachers. They somehow produce an energy that is at once contagious and self-propelling.

Teachers using cooperative interactions in the classroom say the positive effects on student motivation, achievement, and self-concept are so immediately visible and so astonishingly dramatic that the incentives are there for novices to do more. That's why cooperative learning has taken root in schools at the grass-roots level.

The designs for thoughtful interactions presented in this chapter provide a vigorous repertoire of instructional strategies. The seasoned practitioner will appropriately select from these strategies as opportunities occur in the instructional arena.

By varying the types of interactions and creating designs or variations on the themes presented, teachers provide a myriad of social and cognitive learning experiences for students. In turn, students reveal both their social skills and their thinking paradigms as they become involved in and responsible for their own learning.

The old lecture, according to John Gould, is "an occasion when you numb one end to benefit the other" (Peter, 1977, p. 101). The new school lecture, however, is more like a conversation. In a conversation, as Richard Armour suggests, "it is all right to *hold* the conversation for a time, but you should *let go of* it now and then" (p. 119). The new school lecture sees the teacher skillfully holding student attention and letting go of center stage, thus inviting thoughtful and engaging student conversations.

Model 1

Source	Type of Interaction
Perhaps "Professor Kingsfield" from *The Paper Chase*	**Lecture/Rhetorical Questioning** 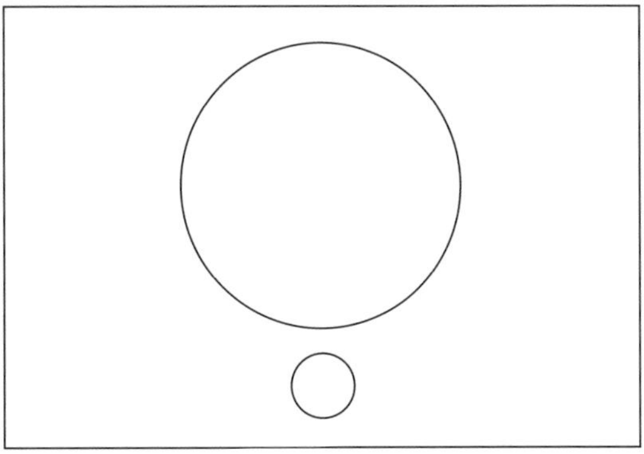
Description	
Traditional lecture or standup teaching in which interaction is a one-way broadcast, punctuated with occasional rhetorical questioning.	
(Suggested) Prescription	**Lesson: Ethics of Medical Technology** **Level: College**
Use with large groups and/or lots of information; punctuate with rhetorical questions throughout.	Methodology class at a university level in which 200 students attend an hour lecture twice a week as part of a required premed course.
Notes	**Vignette: Lecture/Rhetorical Questioning**
Lecture Input (or Teacher Talk)	*With the breakthroughs in medical technology, the options for life support systems are increasing at a rapid rate.*
Rhetorical Question	*How do you think that affects us?*
Lecture Input (or Teacher Talk)	*It seems quite straightforward to make a technical decision. But one must consider all the implications of that decision.*
Rhetorical Question	*Haven't we all faced a dilemma such as this?*

Model 2

Source	Type of Interaction
Hunter, 1993	**Signaling and Direct Questioning: Surveying**
Description	
Traditional lecture format interrupted every five to seven minutes; a posed question that requires a physical signal from students (raised hands) or a single student response that may require some elaboration.	
(Suggested) Prescription	**Lesson: Biology/DNA** **Level: Grade 10**
Use to make lecture slightly more interactive (á la interactive video model) so students are hooked momentarily—at least interacting with a physical response or a one-student in-depth answer.	As the high school biology teacher punctuates his DNA lecture with signaling questions, he deliberately weaves direct questions into the lecture for occasional in-depth student responses.
Notes	**Vignette: Signaling and Direct Questioning**
Signaling	*How many agree? Disagree?*
Direct question	*David, tell us why you agree with the text, why you believe the assumptions are true.*
Student response	*Well, I'm not sure, but I was connecting this idea to . . .*

Model 3

Source	Type of Interaction
Weaver & Cotrell, 1986	**Turn To Your Partner And . . . (TTYPA)**
Description	
An informal strategy used throughout an input sequence in which two students discuss ideas from in the lecture.	
(Suggested) Prescription	**Lesson: Down Memory Lane Level: Grade 8**
Use to punctuate a lecture, a film, or a reading. After 7–8 minutes of straight talk, students need to be actively cued and engaged.	This informal, quick interaction, in which students turn to a partner and dialogue briefly on a specifically directed task, is used effectively as students are guided to model both cognition and metacognition in a lesson on thinking.
Notes	**Vignette: TTYPA**
Lecturer	*Metacognition is thinking about your thinking. Let me demonstrate.* *Turn to your partner and recite a piece you know by memory. Then, switch roles and listen to your partner's memorized piece.*
Student 1 response	*Four score and seven years ago . . .*
Student 2 response	*We the people of the United States . . .*
Lecturer	*That's called cognition.* *Now, turn to your partner and tell each other how you learned that piece by heart so well that you could say it today.*
Student 1 response	*I learned by repeating . . .*
Lecturer	*Thinking about how you learned is called metacognition.*

Model 4

Source	Type of Interaction
Bloom & Broder, 1950 Whimbey, 1975	**Paired Partners: Thinking Aloud**
Description	
A problem solver talks his way strategically through a problem. A partner monitors his progress with cues and questions. Both reflect on problem-solving patterns.	
(Suggested) Prescription	**Lesson: Math Problem Solving** **Level: Grade 6**
Use over time to develop metacognitive, think-aloud tracking of student behaviors.	One partner thinks aloud as he or she solves a problem. The monitor cues the thinking with appropriate questions as the problem solver works systematically through the math calculations.
Notes	**Vignette: Paired Partners**
Teacher	*With partners, solve this story problem using the think-aloud strategy.*
Problem solver (Thinks aloud and says everything that occurs to him or her in a systematic procedure.)	*I'm going to add these two numbers. Then, I'll . . .*
Monitor (Asks leading questions to elicit the inner reasoning.)	*Why are you doing that? Are you expecting a larger number or a smaller number than the original?*
Problem solver (Elaborates and catches another thought for a new strategy.)	*Because the question calls for a total, I'm thinking the number, of course, will be larger and therefore I will add or multiply. Hmm, could I multiply here?*

Model 5

Source	Type of Interaction
Lyman & McTighe, 1988	**Dyads: Think/Pair/Share** 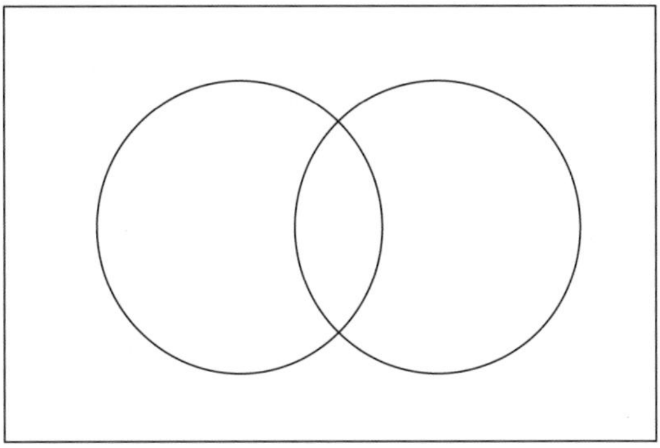
Description	
Partners are cued to think first with the use of wait time. Then pairs of students share their thoughts with each other. After pairing, students may share in the whole class.	
(Suggested) Prescription	**Lesson: The Non-Listening Game** **Level: Grade 3**
Use when formal wait time is needed for student internalization and connection making; use any time thoughtful articulation will help students understand.	To teach the social skill of active listening needed for cooperative interactions, the non-listening game is used. By exaggerating the opposite behavior, students more readily focus on the desired behavior.
Notes	**Vignette: Dyads**
Initial activity	Following a partner interaction for which a "listener" is asked to exhibit *non*-listening behaviors to the "speaker," the teacher instructs students:
Think alone	*Think about the things the listener did that signaled no listening.* (Wait 3-10 seconds.)
Pair/share	Listener: *I looked away.* Speaker: *You interrupted me.* Listener: *I felt bad because I knew I wasn't paying attention. It was rude.* Speaker: *I wanted to quit talking to you.*

Model 6

<table>
<tr><th>Source</th><th>Type of Interaction</th></tr>
<tr><td>Rowe, 1969
Costa, 1986</td><td rowspan="3">Triads: Observer Feedback</td></tr>
<tr><td>Description</td></tr>
<tr><td>Partners practice a designated interaction while a third-party observer records and reports feedback data.</td></tr>
<tr><td>(Suggested) Prescription</td><td>Lesson: Fat and Skinny Questions   Level: Grade 11</td></tr>
<tr><td>Use when partner interactions can be extended or elaborated by objective observer feedback.</td><td>To teach students to use higher-order questions, the teacher introduces the concept of fat and skinny questions and then asks student trios to practice their question asking.</td></tr>
<tr><td>Notes</td><td>Vignette: Triads</td></tr>
<tr><td>Teacher targets behavior to look for.</td><td>Observers, I will be noting FAT and Skinny questions. FAT questions will be those that elicit elaborate answers with examples and details. Skinny questions will be those that get "Yes, No, Maybe So" answers.</td></tr>
<tr><td>Question asked (Recorded as a FAT question.)</td><td>Interviewer: How do you compare and contrast democracy to socialism?
Interviewee: Similarities might include _____ while differences include _____.</td></tr>
<tr><td>Question asked (Recorded as a Skinny question.)</td><td>Interviewer: Which do you prefer?
Interviewee: The former!</td></tr>
<tr><td>Question asked (Recorded as a FAT question.)</td><td>Interviewer: Imagine justifying your choice. What might you say?</td></tr>
</table>

Model 7

Source	Type of Interaction
Fogarty & Opeka, 1988	**2–4–8: Tell/Retell**
Description	
Partners tell their own stories. Then they retell a partner's story. The pairs double—2–4–8.	
(Suggested) Prescription	**Lesson: Show and Tell** **Level: Grade 1**
Use to structure active listening in a partner sharing or for a quick gathering of lots of ideas.	In a typical primary classroom, "show and tell" time is structured carefully for both speaking and listening skills.
Notes	**Vignette: 2–4–8**
2 Partners share show and tell items. Ⓐ Ⓑ	A: *This is my skin from a snake. I found it on the hiking path. It was there in the sunshine. I think the snake wiggled out of it while he was getting a suntan.* B: *I brought my favorite Transformer. My dad couldn't figure it out. I had to help him. It's pretty tricky if you don't know much about them.*
4 A tells B's, B tells A's C tells D's, D tells C's Ⓐ Ⓑ Ⓒ Ⓓ	A: *"B" brought the Transformer that his dad couldn't figure out.* B: *"A" found a snake's skin while he was hiking.* C: *"D" brought photographs of his birthday party at the pizza place.* D. *"C" forgot her show and tell but she told me about her ride in the rowboat.*
8 Each tells a new story.	A: *"C" forgot hers but she rode in a rowboat.* B: *"D" has pictures of the pizza place.* C: *"B" can transform his Transformer.* D: *"A" has the skin of a snake.*

Model 8

<table>
<tr><th>Source</th><th>Type of Interaction</th></tr>
<tr><td>Johnsons, 1986
Slavin, 1983
Kagan, 1988</td><td rowspan="3">Cooperative Learning: Groups 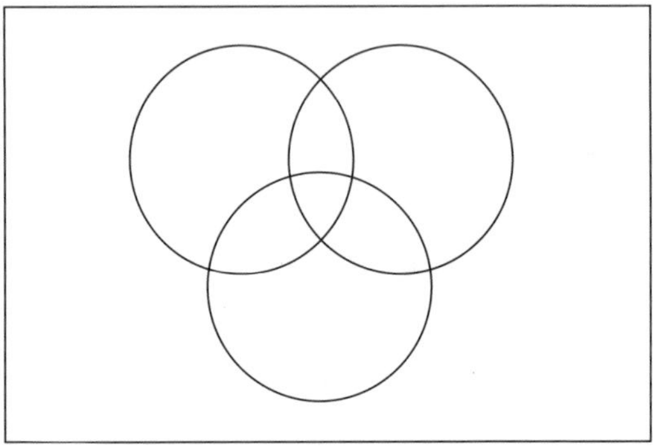</td></tr>
<tr><td>Description</td></tr>
<tr><td>Three to five learners, heterogeneously grouped for an academic task. Key elements for formal cooperative groups include positive interdependence, individual accountability, group processing, social skills, and face-to-face interactions.</td></tr>
<tr><th>(Suggested) Prescription</th><th>Lesson: Prediction (BET) Level: Grade 7</th></tr>
<tr><td>Use to engage students intensely in the processing activities needed for learning for transfer.</td><td>Cooperative groups are used in a Directed Reading Thinking Activity (DRTA) to predict and justify what students think will happen next in a story.</td></tr>
<tr><th>Notes</th><th>Vignette: Cooperative Learning</th></tr>
<tr><td>Checker checks for understanding
(Teacher monitors)</td><td>Does everyone understand? We will use BET.

Base on facts
Express possibilities
Tender a bet on what we think will happen next in the story entitled "The Dinner Party"</td></tr>
<tr><td>Encourager
(Teacher monitors)</td><td>Encourages response in turn:
• I think it's a murder mystery because of the title.
• I think it's about cannibals. There will be a twist.
• Maybe it's about animals having a tea party. This is from school, you know.</td></tr>
<tr><td>Encourager
(Group consensus)</td><td>Let's write down the cannibal idea because it's so different. What do the rest of you think?</td></tr>
<tr><td>Recorder</td><td>Writes down group answer.</td></tr>
</table>

Model 9

Source	Type of Interaction
Fogarty & Bellanca, 1987	**Traveling Clusters: People Search** 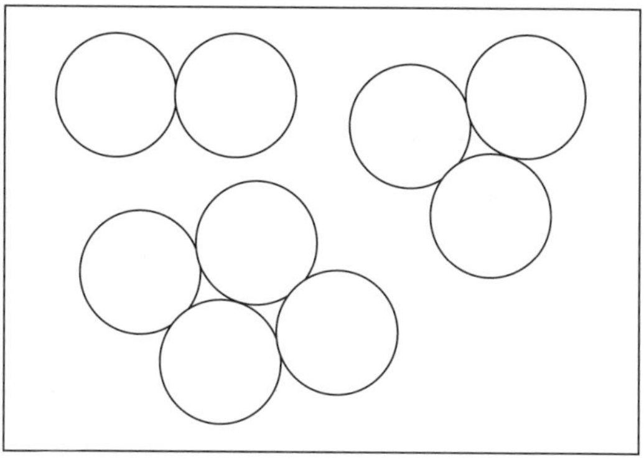
Description	
Students are prompted with questions to move about and find someone who . . . . Informal clusters form as students select new partners in their search for answers to the questions.	
(Suggested) Prescription	**Lesson: People Search** **Level: Grade 12**
Use as ice-breaker, as pre-learning strategy to activate prior knowledge or as a review of important concepts prior to a test.	A lesson used as a pre-learning strategy to "stir up" prior knowledge about thinking skills. The cue sheet starts the student interaction.
Notes	**Vignette: Traveling Clusters**
Prompted by sheet	Using: Find Someone Who . . . 1. Can classify friends 2. Can name problem-solving steps 3. 4. 5.
Students move about and talk to each other.	Student A: *I think I can classify friends into four groups.* Student B: *Great. Go ahead.* Student A: *The good, the bad, the ugly, and best friend.* Student B: *Super. Maybe, I can help you with the steps to problem solving. First, decide on the real problem . . .*
Students move on to newly forming clusters of 2, 3, or 4 students.	Student A: *Thanks. Talk to you later.*

Model 10

Source	Type of Interaction
Howe & Howe, 1975	**Forced Response: Wrap Around** 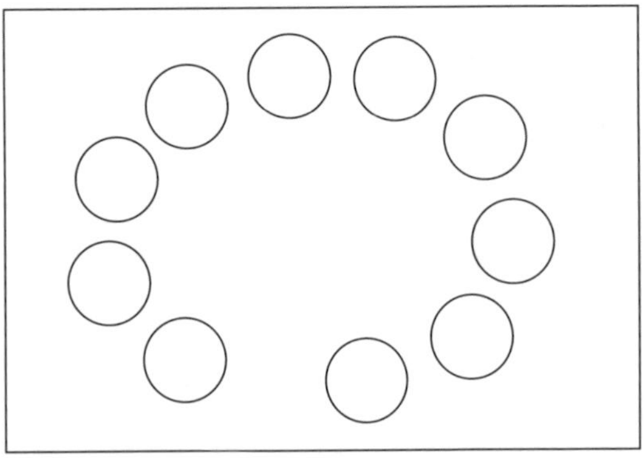
Description	
Round-robin style, students respond in turn to a lead-in statement cued by the teacher.	
(Suggested) Prescription	**Lesson: Analogies** **Level: Grade 5**
Use to anchor individual thoughts or give a quick reading of the group.	At the close of the lesson, students are asked to compare thinking to an animal. After jotting down some ideas, a verbal wrap around the room is used to share the ideas.
Notes	**Vignette: Forced Response**
	Wrapping around the room, each student responds in turn . . .
Response of student #1	*Thinking is like a frog because it hops around in your mind.*
Teacher	[Signals next student without judging each response.]
Student #2	*Thinking is like an elephant because it's heavy on your mind.*
Teacher	[Nods.]
Student #3	*Thinking is like a horse because both can throw you.*
Student #4	*Thinking is like the cat family because it helps to be in a group.*
Student #5	*Thinking is like a monkey because you can fool around with both.*
Student #6	*Thinking is like a chicken because both can lay an egg!*

Model 11

Source	Type of Interaction
Fogarty & Bellanca, 1987	**Total Group Response: Human Graph**
Description	
Students advocate an opinion by standing at designated spots on an imaginary axis. This human graph is a living, breathing graph that can change as students change positions.	
(Suggested) Prescription	**Lesson: Equity** **Level: Grade 9**
Use to take a quick but highly visible reading of the group members' feelings on an issue, idea, or concept.	Used to introduce a unit on Equity Issues, the teacher structures an agree/disagree statement for sampling "public opinion."
Notes	**Vignette: Total Group Response**
Present graph format	Disagree — Neutral — Agree D Die for it, C Convince others, B Believe, A Disagree | A Agree, B Believe, C Convince others, D Die for it
Teacher cues for graphing interaction	*Indicate how strongly you agree or disagree:* Women are stronger than men.
Students move on graph	D C B A A B C D
Sample reasons from students	*I agree strongly. Think about the pioneer women and the hardships they had to overcome.*

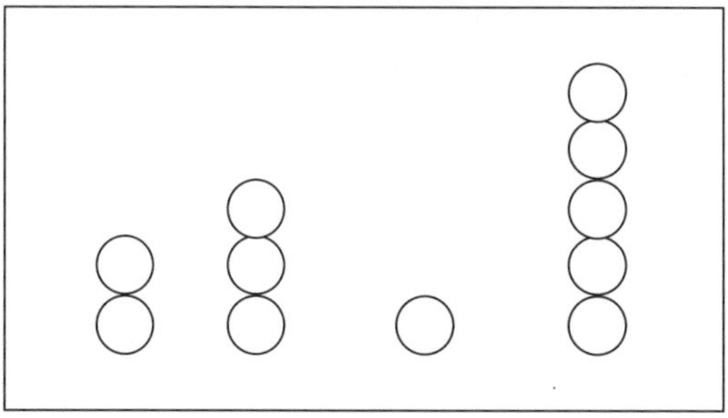

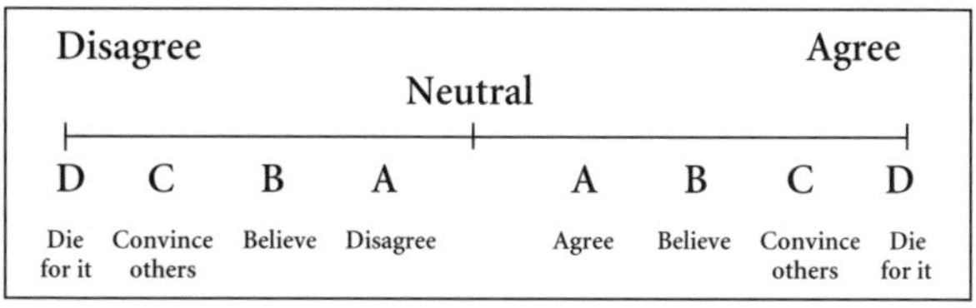

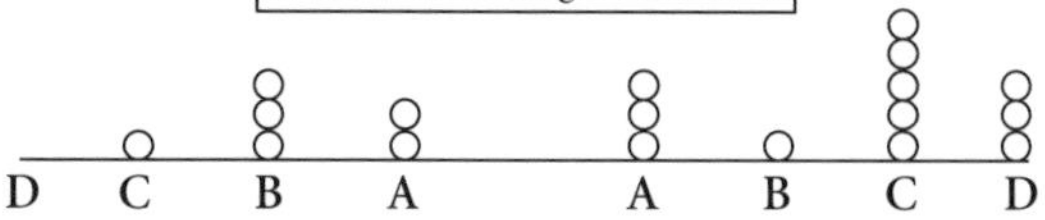

Model 12

Source	Type of Interaction
Aronson, 1978 Sharan and Sharan, 1976	**Group Investigation: The Ultimate Jigsaw**
Description	
Each member has a piece of the puzzle; responsibility is divided; to get the whole picture, or all the information, the separate pieces must be reassembled or synthesized into the completed puzzle by the various group members.	
(Suggested) Prescription	**Lesson: Geographic Regions Level: Grade 4**
Use when groups are socially sophisticated or to build individual responsibility within the team.	In a fourth grade classroom, groups of three students are given regions of the United States to investigate and research. The group is ultimately responsible to know all three regions and will "teach each other." Students with the same topic help each other master it before presenting it to their groups.
Notes	**Vignette: Group Investigation**
Teacher	*Ones, take the Eastern seaboard. Twos, research the mid-section of the country. Threes, gather information about the western portion of the United States.*
Student #1	*I'm going to start in the library.*
Student #2	*I need to define my area.*
Student #3	*This is great. I love the West.*

REFERENCES

Aronson, E. (1978). *The jigsaw classroom.* Beverly Hills, CA: Sage Publications.

Bloom, B., & Broder, L. (1950). *Problem solving process of college students.* Chicago: University of Chicago Press.

Clarke, J., Wideman, R., & Eadie, S. (1990). *Together we learn.* Toronto: Prentice-Hall.

Costa, A. (1986). *Teaching for intelligent behavior.* Unpublished syllabus (3rd ed.).

Dalton, J. (1985). *Adventures in thinking.* Melbourne, Australia: Thomas Nelson Australia.

Fogarty, R., & Bellanca, J. (1987). *Patterns for thinking: Patterns for transfer.* Palatine, IL: IRI/Skylight Publishing.

Fogarty, R., & Opeka, K. (1988). *Start them thinking.* Palatine, IL: IRI/Skylight Publishing.

Howe, L., & Howe, M. (1975). *Personalizing education: Values clarification and beyond.* New York: Hart.

Hunter, M. (1983). *Reinforcement.* El Segundo, CA: Tip Publications.

Johnson, R., & Johnson, D. (1986). *Circles of learning: Cooperation in the classroom.* Alexandria, VA: Association for Supervision and Curriculum Development.

Kagan, S. (1988). *Cooperative learning: Resources for teachers.* San Juan Capistrano, CA: Resources for Teachers.

Lyman, F., & McTighe, J. (1988, April). Cueing thinking in the classroom: The promise of theory-embedded tools. *Educational Leadership,* p. 7.

Peter, L. J. (1977). *Peter's quotations: Ideas for our time.* New York: Bantam Books.

Reid, J., Forrestal, P., & Cook, J. (1989). *Small group learning in the classroom.* Scarborough, Australia: Chalkface Press.

Rowe, M. B. (1969). Science, silence and sanctions. *Science and Children, 6,* 11–13.

Sharan, S., & Sharan, Y. (1976). *Small group teaching.* Englewood Cliffs, NJ: Educational Testing Publications.

Slavin, R. E. (1983). *Cooperative learning.* New York: Longman.

Weaver, R., & Cotrell, H. (1986, Summer). Using interactive images in the lecture hall. *Educational Horizons, 64*(4), 180–185.

Whimbey, A., & Whimbey, L. (1975). *Intelligence can be taught.* New York: Innovative Science.

Vignettes: Multiage Groupings

by Robin Fogarty

A painted rainbow, a historic cemetery, and cowards turned heroes are the stuff these schools are made of. Envision the vignettes and experience three alternative programs that ignite and integrate learning for all students. Understand how creative educators are "breaking down the barriers" with nongraded, multiage, continuous progress, and developmentally appropriate, untracked models of holistic, interdisciplinary, learner-centered classrooms, reminiscent of the romanticized little red school house of days gone by.

VIGNETTE ONE: SOMEBODIES WHO MAKE THE RAINBOW REAL: ORGANIC LEARNING IN THE PRIMARY CLUSTER

> Orange construction paper strips fully stocked in a coffee can; a large black marker; a round reading table with several little chairs; shoebox "fish" games about the room; and a line formed around the teacher. Words are rehearsed and called out to classmates as they approach the front of the line: Butterfly, the Refrigerator, Raggedy Ann and Andy, Piano, Garden, Girl, Prickly, Whale, and Dumbo.

These words are what Sylvia Ashton-Warner (1963) calls the organic words that comprise the "key vocabulary" of each child learner. Using a whole language approach to reading in the primary classroom, this New Zealander models a fully integrated learning environment that can be anchored by just one word as illustrated in the following poems:

Adapted from *Integrating Curricula with Multiple Intelligences: Teams, Themes, and Threads,* pp. 94–110, 174–175.

Deep Inside of Me

I start with just one word
One special word
Way down deep inside of me.
A word I love
A word I fear
One I can see and touch and hear.
I start with just one word
One special word
Way down deep
Inside of me.

Can do! Can do!

Now, I tell just what
That one word can do.
Popcorn pops,
Jackrabbit hops,
Grass grew.
Birdie flew.
Bluebird sings,
But, bee stings.
Now, I can tell just what
That one word can do.

Add a Few

Hmm, now that I have two
Why not
Add a few.
I tell its color
And shape
And size.
I create a picture of words
For your eyes.
Hmm, now that I have two
Why not add a few.

A Story to Tell

By gosh, by golly, by gee
I've got a whole story
Way down deep
Inside of me.
A story of love, or one about fear,
One I can see
And touch and hear.
By gosh, by golly, by gee
I've got a whole story
Deep down inside of me.

Peacock has lots of feathers. Peacock is in the zoo. People like to see the peacock. Peacock opens its feathers and they are SO PRETTY!

Indeed, Indeed, Indeed

I've got all the words I need.
Words that name and
Words that can do
And words to describe.
Yes, all those words
That are way down deep
In my inside.
Indeed! Indeed! Indeed!
I have all the words I need.

The magician does magic on stage. He did make rabbits come out from his hat. Then he did a bow.

Inside of Me

Believe it or not
All those words that I've got
Can be set free from way down deep
Inside of me.
They can be thought about
Or better yet, said right out
And if I write them down
I'll have a story to say and see
A real story, to really read
From way down deep inside of me.

On t.v. I saw a chimpanzee learning to talk sign language.

He learned and he had to think because it was complicated.

That's why it took so long.

His name is CHARLEY CHIMPANZEE!

Imagine the busy hustle in the classroom as the children nominate their own personal word for the day, a key word in their inner world that helps unlock the mystery of the reading process for each of them and opens the door to myriad related activities that integrate the arts and the academics into meaningful, holistic tasks.

> Emily slowly traces the word *butterfly* with her finger after the teacher has written it on the orange strip. "The easel," she responds to the teacher-initiated question of how she wants to study her word today. "I'm gonna paint my butterfly in beautiful, bright colors," and off she goes to stand on the drippy, sticky butcher paper under the easel in the paint corner.

Erin chooses to "water write" her word on the blackboard, while Matt forms his word out of sea shells on the red mat. Effie uses the dusty pastels to print the word *girl*, and Eric traces the word *Dumbo* in the wet sand.

Following the chatter of the word study time, the children settle down with their handmade orange stapled booklets, which match their word orange cards, and begin their sentence writing:

"Butterfly is beautiful!"	(Emily)
"Piano is magic."	(Erin)
"Garden can grow."	(Matt)
"Girl is pretty."	(Effie)
"Dumbo can fly."	(Eric)

> Some ask the teacher to help them write their sentences, others quiz each other for words they need to fill the page. When the sentences begin to string together and form stories, the children receive sticky dots for punctuating their ideas. The teacher helps the children add headings and titles, and their writing develops. Then, once the sentences are written and crayoned pictures adorn the day's pages, the buzz begins again as partners share their stories with each other.

This scenario repeats each morning until the month ends and the orange word booklets are taken home to parents. The parents know that the goal is for the child to read the sentence booklet to anyone who will listen, including goldfish, grandparents, and the neighbor next door. For every reading, a signature is collected on the inside cover for a Monday morning tally.

Over time, as the year progresses, these youngsters have nine sentence booklets and color coordinated cards for each month of school and a shoebox overflowing with their specially requested words. With the focus on authentic assessment (Burke, 1993), these artifacts provide ongoing evidence of the students' development. In fact, the final assessment tool is a tenth booklet that holds a page from each of the previous ones. The children have quite a time deciding exactly which pages to select for their finished portfolio.

Although the activities in this primary classroom resemble those of many early childhood programs, there are several key elements to silhouette: this is an nongraded class with four-, five-, and six-year-olds included; the curriculum is fully integrated (Fogarty, 1991) through a language arts focus, with music, art, math, science, and social studies creeping into the daily activities through the word boxes and sentence books; and the program provides a platform for genuine investigations and class projects. In addition, the parents are an integral part of the action and the assessment process.

Interestingly, the integration of curriculum permeates every aspect of this classroom as the students learn from each other. For they not only learn their own words, but they're privy to other children's dynamic vocabulary as they interact with these shoebox treasures. They alphabetize, categorize, and prioritize the words as they internalize the learning through reading, writing, listening, and speaking.

> The rainbow is one example of the serendipitous effects of the shoebox curriculum. After Alan paints his "rainbow," lots of children want his word too. In fact, "rainbow" becomes so contagious, a special event is planned and the entire class paints a rainbow so big and so beautiful that they decide to display it over the length of the windowed wall. There is magic as the sunlight filters through the many colors of paint.

Integrated learning and multiage grouping champion this classroom (see Figure 1). Breaking down the barriers is natural with these "somebodies who make the rainbow real."

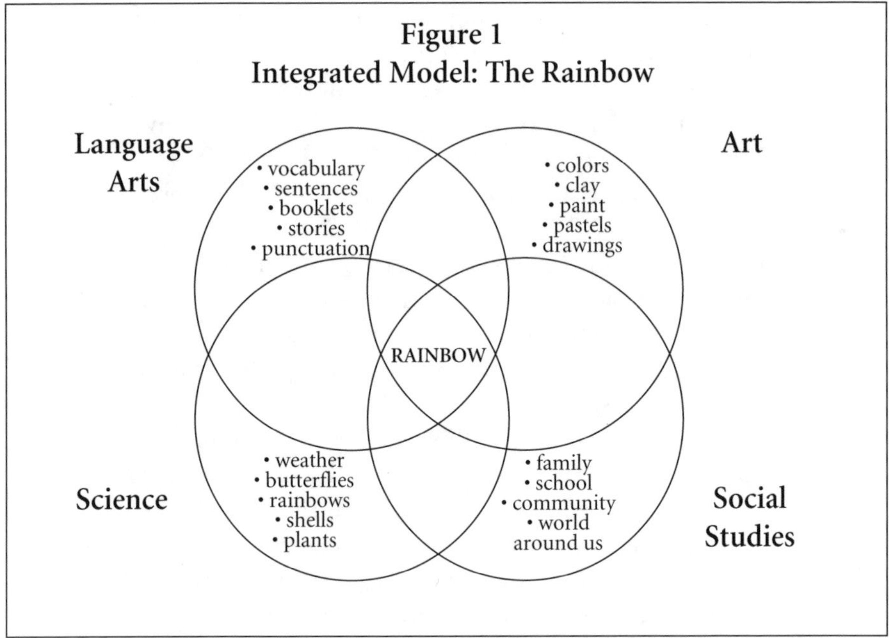

VIGNETTE TWO: KIDS INCORPORATED AND THE CEMETERY STUDY: A MULTIAGE ALTERNATIVE FOR THE INTERMEDIATE CLUSTER

Kinc., the logo for Kids Incorporated, hangs precariously over the doorway that opens into a double classroom with a large folding wall. The shelves that line the windowed wall are packed and stacked with brightly colored, plastic dishpans stuffed with books and papers—some neatly, others randomly, but all punctuated with various writing instruments.

The students are of various sizes, ages, and abilities, and display various levels of industry. Spotted about the room are clusters of students: three girls look at a Beverly Cleary book; two boys are talking about after-school sports; several youngsters, boys and girls, are puzzling over the gerbil cage, while some of the older girls giggle at the boys in the hall.

The side board displays the Track Sheet, a listing of the day's events, but interestingly, only two items carry a time designation: 11:30 a.m.–Lunch and 2:30 p.m.–Safety Assembly. Next to the Track Sheet, two girls check their names off the Homework Due List.

Two teachers talk near the center of the room. Their desks are located in a back-to-back island surrounded by tables of students and learning centers. Near the sink is the science table, completely covered with artifacts that run the gamut from gerbils in training and broken rock specimens, to a jungle of plants and a disorganized assortment of magnets, tools, slides, and the treasured microscope.

Opposite the popular science laboratory is the never-ending activity of what appears to be a simulation of musical chairs. As one child relinquishes a head set, three others scramble for the vacated chair.

Art drips from the walls and hangs from a wire network that crisscrosses the room in a random scrabble design.

Frayed file folders labeled Math Skill Packets are indexed alphabetically in a blue milk crate. A parent-helper checks off assignments at the skill center as a sandy-haired student hands them to her.

This pandemonium quickly diminishes as the 9:00 A.M. bell rings and the younger teacher starts the morning housekeeping chores by taking attendance. With no time to spare, the seasoned teacher holds up the sign Novel Groups and the migration of students begins.

Kids Incorporated is an alternative school *within* a school. It comprises two teachers; fifty-four children, aged eight to twelve; siblings; and parent volunteers. The vision of the two teachers is to create a school setting that embodies the natural elements of the family that nurture authentic learning.

To foster cooperation and a sense of collegiality and team spirit across the various age levels, an extensive outdoor education week is intentionally built into the fall schedule of events. Using the summer and the month of September and part of October to raise money, the teachers plan a mid-October trip to a camp.

Parents have been polled for talent and willingness to participate in small-group sessions scheduled throughout the week. In a backbreaking schedule of events that runs from 7:00 A.M. until 9:00 P.M. are many learning opportunities. Among the featured classes are: (1) Robinson Crusoe, a shelter-building, overnight excursion; (2) The Cemetery Study, a Civil War history lesson that incorporates art and literature; (3) Noodle Mania, a cooking

Figure 2
Threaded Model: Cemetery Study Unit

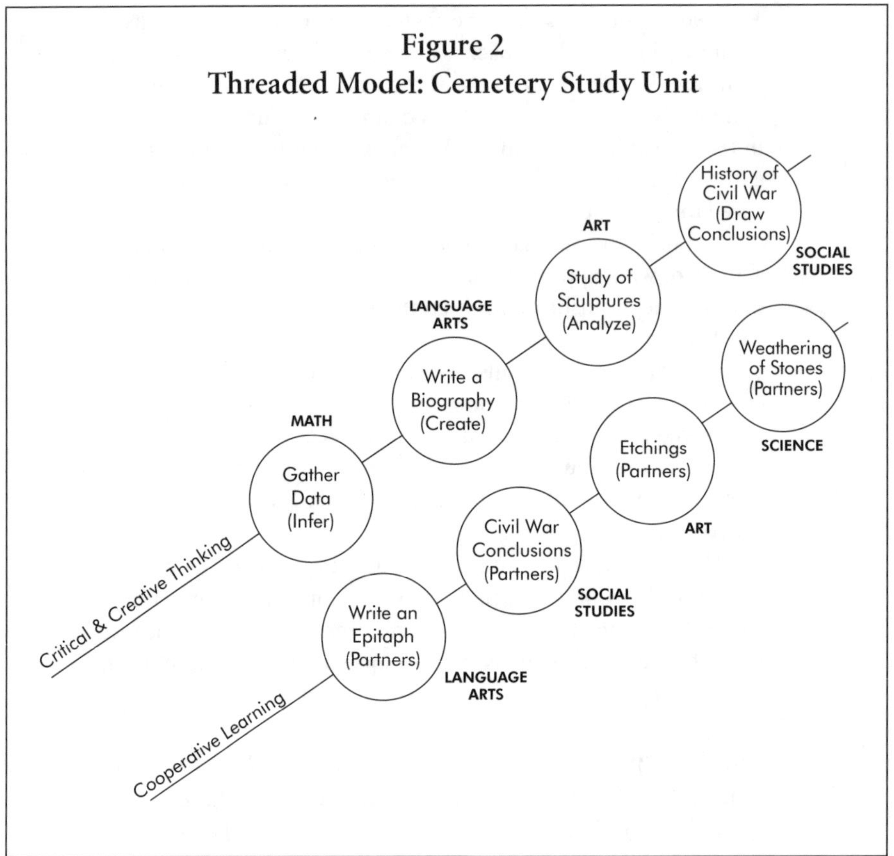

class to prepare noodles and soup for lunch; (4) Bear Hunt, a hiking class where plaster casts of animal tracks are made; and (5) Old McDonald's Farm, a morning of genuine farm chores at the ranch.

Choices are made by students as they fill their schedule from the menu of fifty-plus class offerings. Ghost stories, told around the campfire by a dad who participates in community theater, exemplify a whole-group activity and the diversity of parental involvement.

Integrating curricula is a natural outgrowth of the learning experiences designed for Kinc. To illustrate how significant learning such as cooperation and critical thinking is threaded (Fogarty, 1991) through each camp activity, the Cemetery Study Unit is a good example (see Figure 2).

Working in small archeological dig-type groups, students choose from a list of tasks in their cemetery packet. The suggested activities include:

1. Create five art etchings or rubbings including borders, symbols, lettering, and numerals.
2. Find two epitaphs that appear on the tombstones and write two more.
3. Answer historical questions by viewing various tombstones and gathering pertinent data.
4. Draw a map of the cemetery or a particular part of the cemetery.
5. Gather mathematical information and generate statistical data for generalizations about the Civil War.
6. Investigate the weathering of the tombstones and the conditions of the earth in the cemetery and draw some conclusions.

Learning experiences orchestrated over the week set the stage for activities and interactions for the rest of the year. More importantly, unbreakable bonds are made among the students—young and old, new and familiar. The team building begins with the force of a hurricane. Back at school, the winds always seem gentle by comparison.

VIGNETTE THREE: HOW COURAGE IS LIKE THE RAIN: A PHILOSOPHY STUDY FOR THE SENIOR CLUSTER

> Courage? What does it mean? What comes to mind? Hero. Sudden. Unexpected. Save a child. Train track rescue. *Profiles in Courage.* Inner self. Recognition. War hero. Medals. Purple Heart. Strength. Cowardice. *Catch-22.* Moral courage. *The Wizard of Oz.* Stand up! Stand out! Famous. High dive. Risk. Bungee jump. Untested. Undetected. Under pressure. Surprise, like a summer shower. Rain.
>
> The brainstorm flows through its natural cycle: a burst of ideas, a lull, reignited associations, silliness, novelty, and a final wind down. The teacher pounces on that final word, *rain,* and asks, "How is courage like the rain?"
>
> Heads together, pens poised, the small groups discuss possible comparisons as one team starts to write on the large poster paper: "Courage is like the rain because both . . . hmmm, both

> can happen suddenly; they can come upon you unexpectedly; and . . . .Wait, I've got it . . . they often result in a change for you. If you get caught in the rain and get wet, you change your clothes. If you act in a courageous way it may change how you feel about yourself."

So goes the latest scenario in the senior cluster. Staffed with a teacher team that consists of a guest artist, a visiting attorney, a guidance counselor, and a literature teacher, this philosophy study targets students from the senior cluster levels—incoming freshmen through graduating seniors.

Designed around the age-old discipline of philosophy, students are exposed to an interdisciplinary approach to subject matter. They experience content through the dilemma, paradox, and ambiguity inherent in the universally compelling philosophical issues: truth, justice, equality, authority, wisdom, courage, life, death, and love.

Interwoven in the puzzle are opportunities to explore the issues in myriad domains. For example, in an experiment with authority, students read about historically renowned authority figures, Hitler, Stalin, and McCarthy, and compare them with the authority figures in their own lives. In turn, literature becomes a springboard for historical simulations, real-life role plays, journaling, and depictions of authority through the visual and performing arts.

> "Courage is like the rain . . . isn't that a fresh idea? Let's explore some of the ideas a bit further. For example, what do you mean when you say courage is unexpected? Give us a real illustration."
>
> "Well, when you step on the high dive and you look down, you're really afraid of the fall. Yet, you prepare, just as you've done in practice many times before; you proceed through your ritual of standing at the invisible spot, stepping through the approach, focusing yourself mentally, and performing the precision dive with skill and grace. That's courage, if you ask me."
>
> "I agree. That's certainly a grand display of physical courage. What else?"
>
> "To stand up for what you believe, in front of your friends, when you know you're in the minority. I think that shows courage."

> "Tell us more about that."
>
> "Maybe you like classical music because you've had to learn it and play it in orchestra, but your friends want to listen to hard rock or rap. Even though it's a simple example, we can really pressure each other to the point that it does take some courage to stick to your own ideas."
>
> "That's so true, isn't it? How about one more example of courage?"
>
> "Cowards can be courageous. My grandpa says that a lot of guys in the war ended up as decorated heroes, but they weren't all that heroic in the beginning. Once their plane was shot down or they found themselves in prison camp, their courage got them through."
>
> "Yeah! It's like when someone rescues a kid from a fire or rushes into the street and throws a child free from the path of a car—the courage just happens suddenly, unexpectedly. And someone who seems more like a coward in other situations proves himself a hero with courage."

The integration to the various subjects is evident in this scenario. The fertile themes of courage, trust, and love are transformed into an investigative question and then easily "webbed" out to the various disciplines for appropriate instructional activities and aligned with key goals (Fogarty, 1991).

Figure 3 suggests other subject matter content in a rich web of interdisciplinary activities. This investigation centers around the question: How common is courage? Sparked by that query, investigations in the various disciplines are ignited with activities and accompanying outcomes. Multiple forms of literature are available for student selection. One team studies Hemingway, another compares and contrasts a film to a book, and still another group reads and comments on *Catch-22.* All are focused on the question, "How common is courage?"

To culminate the study of courage, a handout calling for presentations is distributed (see Figure 4). Presentations are as varied as the presenters. Creativity flourishes and debate is lively as students grapple with an unknown. After all, who really knows how common courage is?

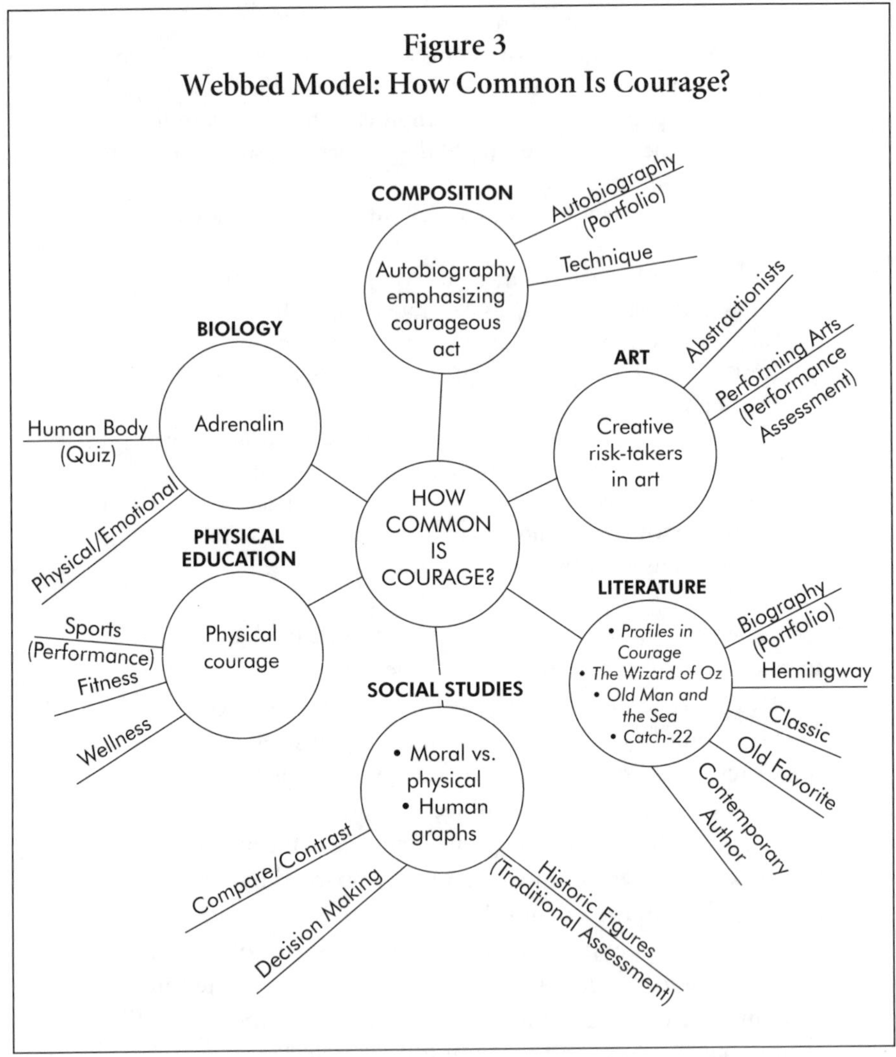

A painted rainbow, a historic cemetery, and cowards turned heroes are the stuff these schools are made of.

Figure 4
Call for Presentations

Please prepare an answer to the essential question: How common is courage? You may use one or any combination of the following expressive forms:

- ❑ Art
- ❑ Music
- ❑ Drama
- ❑ Writing
- ❑ Speaking
- ❑ Other

You may work by yourself or in collaboration with one or two others.

Presentations begin next week. You will have twenty-five minutes to present and five minutes for feedback. Please sign up for a time.

REFERENCES

Anderson, R. H. (1993, January). The return of the nongraded classroom. *Principal*, pp. 9–12.

Anderson, R. H., & Pavan, B. N. (1993). *Nongradedness: Helping it to happen.* Lancaster, PA: Technomic Publishing.

Ashton-Warner, S. (1963). *Teacher.* New York: Simon & Schuster.

Bellanca, J., & Fogarty, R. (1991). *Blueprints for thinking in the cooperative classroom.* Palatine, IL: IRI/Skylight Publishing.

Burke, K. (1994). *The mindful school: How to assess authentic learning.* Palatine, IL: IRI/Skylight Publishing.

Burke, K. (Ed.). (1992). *Authentic assessment: A collection.* Palatine, IL: IRI/Skylight Publishing.

Costa, A. L. (1991). *The school as a home for the mind: A collection of articles.* Palatine, IL: IRI/Skylight Publishing.

Costa, A., Bellanca, J., & Fogarty, R. (Eds.). (1992). *If minds matter: A foreword to the future, Vol. I.* Palatine, IL: IRI/Skylight Publishing.

Costa, A., Bellanca, J., & Fogarty, R. (Eds.). (1992). *If minds matter: A foreword to the future, Vol. II.* Palatine, IL: IRI/Skylight Publishing.

Fogarty, R. (1991). *The mindful school: How to integrate the curricula.* Palatine, IL: IRI/Skylight Publishing.

Fogarty, R. (1990). *Keep them thinking: A handbook of model lessons, level II.* Palatine, IL: IRI/Skylight Publishing.

Fogarty, R., & Bellanca, J. (1987). *Patterns for thinking: Patterns for transfer.* Palatine, IL: IRI/Skylight Publishing.

Fogarty, R., Perkins, D., & Barell, J. (1992). *The mindful school: How to teach for transfer.* Palatine, IL: IRI/Skylight Publishing.

Goodlad, J. I., & Anderson, R. H. (1987). *The nongraded elementary school* (rev. ed.). New York: Teachers College, Columbia University.

Jacobs, H. H. (Ed.). (1989). *Interdisciplinary curriculum: Design and implementation.* Alexandria, VA: Association for Supervision and Curriculum Development.

Pavan, B. N. (1973, March). Good news: Research on the nongraded elementary school. *Elementary School Journal,* pp. 233–242.

Richmond, G. H. (1973). *The micro-society school: A real world in miniature.*

Section 4

Reflective Transfer . . . Teach Them to Fish

Give a man a fish,
and you feed him for a day.
Teach a man to fish,
and you feed him for a lifetime.
—Chinese Proverb

To risk stating the obvious, all teaching is for transfer. What is taught within a particular context is targeted for use in similar contexts and often in dissimilar contexts. For example, when learning to drive a car, the student is expected to be able to drive any car—a stick shift, an automatic, or even a foreign-made car. Likewise, in learning to drive a car, it is assumed that the learner will also be able to drive a jeep, a truck, or even a tractor.

In a more remote context, the student who learns to drive a car is able to transfer much of that learning to piloting a plane. However, within this unique context, additional instruction is naturally needed. Here, transfer of learning from the original context (a car) to the new context (a plane) is not automatic. It requires mindful abstractions as well as more external input.

Exploring the idea of reflective transfer, one must understand the concept of transfer, as illustrated above, and the meaning of metacognition. To explain this mysterious word, an extensive introductory article, "Metacognition," examines its major components: planning, monitoring, and evaluating. Being reflective about one's own thinking and learning processes (or thinking about thinking, as it is often said) is the essence of metacognition. This self-reflection leads naturally to more conscious transfer.

Based on the concept of high-road and low-road transfer (Perkins & Salomon, 1988), the second piece, "Teaching for Transfer," suggests ten shepherding strategies that foster transfer. Five techniques are targeted to "hug" for near or easy transfer, while five additional strategies are developed to "bridge" for far or remote transfer. The article is sprinkled with vignettes that illustrate the "somethings," "somehows," and "somewheres" of transfer.

Paralleling this descriptive article on transfer is a piece delineating the various stages of transfer. In "The Most Significant Outcome," teachers are introduced to a scheme for tracking student transfer. Symbolized by bird metaphors, six distinct levels of transfer are illustrated. These levels describe learners who overlook, duplicate, replicate, integrate, map, and innovate ideas. In addition, strategies for moving students from one level of transfer to the next are suggested.

The encore essay in this section, "Vignettes: Levels of Transfer," offers six brief illustrations of the birds of transfer. Each vignette relates an experience at a specific level of transfer suggested by a corresponding bird image. The intent is that the tales will invoke thoughts of similar personal episodes for the reader.

In four short essays, the complexity of the transfer issue is barely touched. Yet, the ideas presented here open the door to further exploration of the best practices for student-relevant, purposeful transfer of learning.

REFERENCES

Perkins, D., & Salomon, G. (1988, September). Teaching for transfer. *Educational Leadership*, pp. 22–32.

Metacognition

by Robin Fogarty

An intellect is someone whose mind watches itself.—Albert Camus

Metacognition is thinking about thinking; but exactly what does that mean? Metacognition is not even in the dictionary. It sounds pretty esoteric, doesn't it? And if asked to define or describe metacognition, you might feel somewhat inadequate. It's like trying to explain atomic fusion to a five-year-old; you can conceptualize it in your mind, but you don't know how to tell someone else—in simple language—what it is.

In the early '80s when the thinking skills movement was in its infancy, to use the word metacognition in a teacher workshop was risky; people actually became hostile. One time a veteran teacher stood up, red in the face, and demanded, "Why do you have to use words like these? Can't you speak English?" To take some of the mystery (and hostility) out of the word, there are several examples of metacognition that may make it easier to grasp.

A WORKING DEFINITION

Think about a time when you were reading and suddenly you got to the bottom of a page of text and a little voice inside your head said, "I don't know what I just read." With this awareness of knowing what you *don't* know, you employ a recovery strategy and you read the last sentences again, you scan the page of

---

From *The Mindful School: How to Teach for Metacognitive Reflection,* pp. vii–xxi.

paragraphs looking for key words, or you reread the entire page. Whatever you do, you capture the meaning and go on. This awareness—knowing what you know and what you don't know—is called metacognition.

This awareness—knowing what you know and what you don't know—is called metacognition.

A reader who reads and reads and reads and doesn't know that he doesn't know is not using metacognition. The key to metacognitive behavior is this self-awareness of one's own thinking and learning. Once you know, you can't not know; and then you can adjust accordingly. Metacognition is awareness and control over your own thinking behavior.

To have awareness and control over your own thinking, you may plan metacognitively, monitor progress metacognitively, and evaluate metacognitively (Costa, 1991). Thus, the three areas, planning, monitoring, and evaluating, provide the appropriate framework for self-reflection.

PLANNING

Let me give a more specific example of metacognition in the planning stages that might clarify the concept. As a teacher, you plan your lessons prior to class; you take into consideration myriad variables including time, complexity, prior knowledge, student population, etc. This planning phase, the time when you predict, prepare, and plan your day, is a metacognitive time for you.

During this preparation time, it's almost as if you are standing *outside* the situation looking in; you are imagining the actual lesson and the reaction(s) of the class to your plans; you are, in essence, removed from the action. This is metacognitive planning.

MONITORING

Once you begin the actual teaching of the lesson, you move into the cognitive realm. You enter into the context of the subject matter content and execute your lesson plan. You are inputting information for student understanding. However, often in the midst of the teaching act, teachers move out of that cognitive arena and into the metacognitive. Let me illustrate.

Halfway into your explanation of photosynthesis, you notice signs of confusion. One student is rifling through the pages of his science book looking for the part in the text that explains photosynthesis. Another student is doodling a diagram of the process in her notebook, but you can see it is incomplete. Several hands are raised and other students have a glazed look in their eyes.

Noticing all this, in an instantaneous glance up from the blackboard, you immediately shift gears and ask students to turn to their partner and ask a question they have about the process of photosynthesis. After a few minutes—after the partners have tried to answer each other's question—you ask for some sharing so you can clarify the concepts for everyone.

This monitoring of the students' reactions and the resulting adjustment to the instructional input is metacognitive in nature. Whenever we watch student behaviors and log the information for minor adjustments or repairs, we act metacognitively—beyond the cognitive. It's as if we do a "freeze frame" on the teaching in the classroom and take a second look at what's going on. This is metacognition.

Whenever we watch student behaviors and log the information for minor adjustments or repairs, we act metacognitively—beyond the cognitive.

EVALUATING

If you're still confused, or feeling vague about metacognition, let me give you a further example of metacognitive reflection as evaluation.

Think back and try to remember something you memorized as a child, such as a poem, a song, a theorem, or maybe even the multiplication tables: "Four score, and seven years ago . . . ," "ABCDEFG . . . ," "Twas the night before Christmas and all through the house . . . ," "Yours is not to reason why, just invert and multiply." Next, recite that piece from memory, right now. Say it aloud to yourself.

Now, think about how you learned that piece so many years ago that to this very day you can recall it instantly and accurately. Think about the strategies used to learn this so that you can recite it by rote memory. This evaluative thinking—

assessing what you know and how and why you know it—is metacognitive thinking. Thinking about how you learn and being able to generalize those skills and strategies for transfer and use in diverse situations is metacognitive reflection.

WHAT DO THE EXPERTS SAY?

In 1977, John Flavell used the term metacognition to describe "active monitoring and consequent regulation and orchestration of [cognitive] processes, usually in the service of some concrete goal or objective." He went on to identify four elements in metacognitive ability: metacognitive knowledge, experiences, goals, and strategies.

Early work done by Feuerstein (1980) in this area shed light on the emerging concept of metacognition. Through a series of tasks developed over a period of time, Feuerstein's work in cognitive mediation guides students through self-monitoring activities that lead to reflective behavior and transfer. Feuerstein's ground-breaking work in this area and in-depth longitudinal studies in the field provide substantive cognitive theory on which others have built. In fact, Feuerstein's landmark study demonstrates the modifiability of cognitive behavior and changes the view of intelligence as an unchanging entity to a capacity that grows not only in developmentally appropriate ways with age, but also through deliberate interventions or mediated learning experiences.

According to Brown's (1980) research in reading, metacognition is what good readers do when they plan, monitor, and evaluate throughout the process. Brown & Palincsar (1982) believe that we can teach those metacognitive strategies to all children as a way to unlock the reading process for them.

As described earlier, Costa (1981) defines metacognition as our ability to know what we know and what we don't know. It is our ability to plan a strategy for producing needed information, to be conscious of our own steps and strategies during problem solving, and to reflect on and evaluate the productivity of our own thinking. Costa says that when you hear yourself talking to yourself, if you are having an inner dialogue inside your brain and if you evaluate your own decision-making/problem-solving processes, you are experiencing metacognition. He summarizes the research on metacognition as planning, monitoring, and evaluating (1991).

Planning a strategy before embarking on a course of action helps us track the steps. It facilitates making judgments; assessing readiness for different activities; and monitoring our interpretations, perceptions, decisions, and behaviors. An example of this is what superior teachers do daily: develop a teaching strategy for a lesson, keep that strategy in mind throughout the instruction, then reflect upon the strategy to evaluate its effectiveness in producing the desired student outcomes.

Self-Monitoring

Rigney (1980) identified the following self-monitoring skills as necessary for successful performance on intellectual tasks: keeping one's place in a long sequence of operations, knowing that a subgoal has been obtained, and detecting errors and recovering from those errors. In addition, looking ahead and looking back are also important self-monitoring skills. Looking ahead includes learning the structure of a sequence of operations, identifying areas where errors are likely to occur, choosing a strategy that will reduce the possibility of error and provide easy recovery, identifying the kinds of feedback that will be available, and evaluating the usefulness of this feedback. Looking back includes detecting errors previously made, keeping a history of what has been done and what should come next, and assessing the reasonableness of the immediate outcome.

Yet, some believe that not everyone is metacognitive. Whimbey and Whimbey (1976) state that all adults metacognate, while Sternberg and Wagner (1982) say that some people have virtually no idea what they are doing when they perform a task and are often unable to explain their strategies for solving problems.

HOW TO TEACH—NOT DIRECT, BUT INFUSE

Others focus their writing on how to teach for metacognition. If we wish to develop intelligent behavior as a significant outcome of education, instructional strategies purposefully intended to develop children's metacognitive abilities must be infused into our teaching methods, staff development, and supervisory processes (Costa, 1981). Interestingly, *direct* instruction in metacognition may *not* be beneficial. When strategies of problem solving are imposed rather than generated by the students themselves, students' performance may be impaired. Conversely, when students experience the need for problem-solving strategies, induce their own, discuss them, and practice them to the degree that they become spontaneous and unconscious, their metacognition seems to improve (Sternberg and Wagner, 1982). The trick, therefore, is to teach metacognitive skills in a natural, inductive way.

When strategies of problem solving are imposed rather than generated by the students themselves, students' performance may be impaired.

STRATEGIES FOR ENHANCING METACOGNITION

Costa (1991) suggests twelve specific strategies:

Planning Strategy. *Prior* to any learning activity, teachers should develop and discuss strategies and steps for attacking problems, rules to remember, and directions to follow. *During* the activity, teachers can invite students to share their progress, thought processes, and perceptions of their own behavior. *After* the learning activity, teachers can invite students to evaluate how well the rules were obeyed.

Generating Questions. Regardless of the subject area, it is useful for students to pose study questions for themselves prior to and during their reading of textual material. This self-generation of questions facilitates comprehension.

Choosing Consciously. Teachers can promote metacognition by helping students explore the consequences of their choices and decisions prior to and during the act of deciding. Students will then be able to perceive causal relationships between their choice, their actions, and the results they achieved.

Evaluating with Multiple Criteria. Teachers can enhance metacognition by asking students to reflect upon and categorize their actions according to two or more sets of evaluative criteria. An example would be to invite students to distinguish what was done that was helpful or hindering, what they liked or didn't like, and what were pluses and minuses of the activity.

Taking Credit. Teachers may ask students to identify what they have done well and invite them to seek feedback from their peers. The teacher might ask, "What have you done that you're proud of?" and "How would you like to be recognized for doing that?" (name on the board, hug, pat on the back, handshake, applause from the group, and so on). Students will become more conscious of their own behavior and apply a set of internal criteria for those behaviors that they consider good.

Outlawing "I Can't." Students should be asked to identify what information is required, what materials are needed, or what skills are lacking in their ability to perform the desired behavior. This helps students identify the boundaries between what they know and what they need to know.

Paraphrasing or Reflecting Students' Ideas. Some examples of paraphrasing, building upon, extending, and using students' ideas might be to say: "What you're telling me is . . .", "It seems you're saying . . .", or "I think I hear . . . ".

Labeling Students' Behaviors. When teachers place labels on students' cognitive processes, students become conscious of their own actions: "What I see you doing is making out a plan of action for . . ."; "What you are doing is called an experiment"; "You're being very helpful to Mark by sharing your paints. That's an example of cooperation."

Clarifying Students' Terminology. Students often use hollow, vague, and nonspecific terminology. For example, in making value judgments, students might say, "It's not fair," "He's too strict," or "It's no good." Teachers need to clarify these values: What's too strict? What would be more fair?

Role Playing and Simulations. Role playing can promote metacognition because when students assume the roles of other persons, they consciously maintain the attributes and characteristics of that person. Dramatization serves as a hypothesis or prediction of how that person would react in a certain situation. Taking on another role contributes to the reduction of ego-centered perceptions.

Journal Keeping. Writing and illustrating a personal log or a diary throughout an experience causes students to synthesize thoughts and actions and translate them to symbolic form. The record also provides an opportunity to revisit initial perceptions, to compare changes in those perceptions with the addition of more data, to chart the processes of strategic thinking and decision making, to identify the blind alleys and pathways taken, and to recall the successes and tragedies of experimentation. (A variation on writing journals is making video and/or audio tape recordings of actions and performances.)

Modeling. Of all the instructional strategies, modeling the model is by far the most effective. The adage, actions speak louder than words, proves to be true. If students see teachers model behaviors such as delineating a plan and justifying a choice, students are more likely to exhibit those same behaviors.

Beyer (1987) elaborates on a cueing technique to prompt metacognition. Questions Beyer suggests to foster metacognitive behavior are: What am I doing? Why am I doing it? What other way can I do it? How does it work? Can I do it again or another way? How could I help someone else do it?

Current research by Swartz and Perkins (1989) refines the concept of metacognition beyond the accepted, generalized definition of awareness of and control over one's own mind and thinking. They distinguish four levels of metacognitive thought: tacit use, aware use, strategic use, and reflective use.

Tacit use	without thinking about it
Aware use	aware of what and when
Strategic use	conscious strategies
Reflective use	reflects before, during, and after

Tacit use is using a skill or strategy without consciously thinking about the fact that a particular skill or strategy is being employed. For example, little children go into a temper tantrum to get what they want. They automatically revert to this strategy when they're not getting their way. They know that the behavior works. Yet, they are not consciously aware of what they're doing or why they're doing it.

By contrast, aware use of a skill or strategy signals another level of metacognitive behavior. When a child is aware of the reaction a certain behavior gets, the child begins to sense some control over his environment. To follow the temper tantrum example, a child who is becoming aware of how this behavior affects his desired outcome instantly stops crying at the slightest intervention of any sort—being picked up, cooing, a dangled toy, etc. It's almost as if we can see the suspended thinking of the child as he processes what is going on, what results he has gotten from his actions. He is becoming aware of a cause-effect relationship.

In turn, the third level of metacognition delineated by Swartz and Perkins is labeled strategic use. It involves deliberate, conscious, mapped use of that skill or strategy. At this stage, the child in our example consciously maps out a plan. He now knows that if he cries and stomps his feet he will not only get the attention he wants, but he will most likely get *what* he wants because he's tried this strategy before and he knows it works. Therefore, he employs his skills and strategies consciously with a strategic plan in mind.

Only when one can step back beyond the cognitive moment and plan, monitor, and evaluate can he or she begin to under- stand and change.

Finally, the fourth level of metacognition is the most sophisticated, incorporating reflection and self-evaluation. A child displaying this reflective stage of metacognition evaluates a number of viable strategies to get what he wants: throw a temper tantrum, pout, whimper, tease, or joke. After reflecting on his choices and evaluating his chances with each, he selects the one he feels is best.

In the last twenty years of cognitive research, the literature presents an evolving picture of metacognition as a critical component of the intellect. Only when one becomes aware of his or her own behavior, can he or she begin to be self-regulatory about that behavior. Only when one can step back beyond the cognitive moment and plan, monitor, and evaluate can he or she begin to understand and change.

WHY BOTHER TO TEACH FOR METACOGNITION?

As the literature on metacognition expands and the concept of metacognitive reflection unfolds, the practical implication for the classroom becomes clearer. In fact, at first glance, there are three obvious reasons to include metacognitive classroom interactions. The first reason is related to the constructivists' view of learning; the second reason is connected to the prevalent line of cooperative, collaborative models of classroom interactions; and the third reason has to do with fostering transfer of learning to novel situations.

More specifically, constructivists view learning as the process individuals experience as they take in new information and make sense of that information. By making meaning, they are acquiring knowledge. However, individuals who construct knowledge and are aware of the gaps in their understanding of that knowledge are actively using both their cognitive and their metacognitive strategies. In their awareness of what they know and what they don't know, they take the first step in remedying the deficit areas. Thus, both cognition and metacognition are necessary elements in constructing meaning.

As teachers and educators—as architects of the intellect—we can foster and guide the metacognitive behavior of our learners.

Also, in today's classroom the use of cooperative learning and small-group work is considered a cornerstone of the active learning models. As students work together, they have opportunities to articulate their thinking and in the process, internalize learning. As students put ideas into their own words, they learn differently and they learn more substantially. However, the increased use of interactive models dictates an equally increased use personal reflection in which students go inside their own heads and think about their learning. That personal reflection is embedded in metacognitive processing, where students look back and look over their progress.

Still, a third call for metacognitive reflection comes with the ultimate purpose of learning: to transfer and use that learning in other places. To foster meaningful application and transfer of learning, student reflection is key. Again, metacognitive strategies provide the necessary format to promote learning not just for a test, but for a lifetime—not just for recall, but for lifelong logic and reasoning.

METACOGNITION AND THE TEACHER

As teachers and educators—as architects of the intellect—we can foster and guide the metacognitive behavior of our learners. Using the staid and true model of the thoughtful classroom that suggests that we teach for, of, with, and about thinking, an emerging idea begins to make sense of quality instruction (see Figure 1).

Figure 1
Teaching For, Of, With, and About Thinking

Teaching **FOR** Thoughtfulness (Satisfactory)	Teaching **OF** Thoughtfulness (Good)
Teaching **WITH** Thoughtfulness (Excellent)	Teaching **ABOUT** Thoughtfulness (Superior)

Teaching FOR Thoughtfulness
In the classroom, the *satisfactory* teacher sets a warm and caring climate for students to feel good about themselves and to build their self-confidence and faith in their abilities. This teacher is concerned with the affective as well as the cognitive development of her students.

For example, one fifth grade teacher talks to her students about the strategy of "wait time." She explains that after she asks a question, no one is to answer; they are to take three to ten seconds to think. By utilizing this strategy of "silence," she establishes a safe climate and high expectations for all students to think before they answer.

Teaching OF Thoughtfulness
The *good* teacher goes beyond setting the climate for a thoughtful classroom. This teacher addresses the microskills of thinking and explicitly teaches both critical and creative thinking in a direct instructional model to ensure that students know the skills and have the tools for lifelong learning.

For example, one teacher incorporates the microskill of predicting by asking students to generate synonyms for predicting: forecasting, anticipating, etc. She probes for examples of when they use predicting—weather, moods of parents, reaction of friends, etc.—and infuses prediction strategies into the subject matter context—predict reasonable answers in math, predict outcomes of experiments in science, predict story endings in literature, etc.

Teaching WITH Thoughtfulness

The *excellent* teacher not only creates a warm and caring climate for thinking and employs a direct instruction in the skills of thinking, but also incorporates the strategies of a truly interactive classroom to teach with thinking. Cooperative learning strategies become an integral part of the learning environment as students become actively involved in their learning experiences. Graphic organizers are used extensively in all group work so student thinking is both visible and audible as they cooperatively solve problems and complete assigned tasks.

For example, using graphic organizers such as webs and mind maps to depict their thinking about a science unit and using cooperative learning groups to jigsaw a social studies chapter in the text are typical instructional activities that foster active learning and intense student involvement.

Teaching ABOUT Thoughtfulness

Finally, in this ideal scenario, the *superior* teacher goes beyond the cognitive and into the metacognitive. The superior teacher knows that setting the climate for thinking and teaching explicit skills through cooperative learning must be accompanied by reflective discussion strategies to make meaning of the learning. Through reflective discussion, students learn to think about the how and why of what they're doing. This reflection allows them to process their thinking and behavior and, in turn, foster transfer and application of their learning.

For example, after a learning activity, the teacher asks students to complete a stem for their log entry: After working with fractions today, I'm wondering.... Or the teacher may require students to reflect on their strategies in the cooperative groups: "Talk about what you did well today as a group and what you can improve upon."

FOUR ELEMENTS: IN SUMMARY

By including the four distinct areas of teaching for, of, with, and about thinking, the skillful teacher teaches not only for the moment, but for the long run. The superior teacher naturally causes students to be aware of their own learning and to be strategic and reflective about that learning. This thoughtful student reflection, in turn, fosters creative application and transfer of ideas as students bridge learning into their everyday lives.

THE METACOGNITIVE MIRRORS

Once we understand the concept of metacognition and the value it has in deep understanding for learning, we are ready to explore the various tools and strategies that foster metacognition. In the broadest sense, these techniques fall into three distinct categories as suggested by Costa and others. The three categories are planning, monitoring, and evaluating.

Let me create an image of these three processes that may help illuminate these ideas. The concept of metacognition is like a mirror, because both illuminate flaws as well as positive attributes, both change with time, and both provide not only first glimpses but second looks.

To carry the mirror metaphor even further, there are various kinds of mirrors that seem respectively appropriate to the various types of metacognitive reflection. The mirrors for *reflective planning* are the full-length, three-way mirrors found in the dressing rooms of large department stores. These triple mirrors provide full exposure to all angles—a necessary view as one lays out plans, trying to anticipate the many facets of an idea.

Yet, the mirrors for *reflective monitoring* are the rear view and side view mirrors found on cars, trucks, and vans, allowing a clear view as one proceeds along a chosen path. These personally positioned mirrors provide the needed perspective to guide progress, signal the need for adjustments, and allow for margins of error in each particular situation.

Finally, the magnifying mirror of a compact seems most appropriate for *reflective evaluation.* This hand-held mirror enlarges the selected image for careful scrutiny and close evaluation. With this larger-than-life view, reflections are easily inspected for subtle flaws or positive enhancements.

And, just as each mirror is used for different purposes, so too are the metacognitive tools used for different purposes: to look ahead and plan, to look over and monitor, or to look back and evaluate.

REFERENCES

Beyer, B. K. (1987). *Practical strategies for the teaching of thinking.* Boston: Allyn & Bacon.

Brown, A. L. (1980). Metacognitive development and reading. In Bruce, B. C., & Brewer, W. F., *Theoretical issues in reading comprehension.* Hillsdale, NJ: Lawrence Erlbaum.

Brown, A. L., & Palincsar, A. S. (1982, September). Inducing strategic learning from texts by means of informed, self-control training. (Technical Report No. 262). Cambridge, MA: Bolt, Beranek, and Newman.

Costa, A. L. (1991). *The school as a home for the mind.* Palatine, IL: IRI/Skylight Publishing.

Costa, A. L. (1984, November). Mediating the metacognitive. *Educational Leadership,* pp. 57–62.

Costa, A. L. (1981, October). Teaching for intelligent behavior. *Educational Leadership,* pp. 29–32.

Feuerstein, R. (1980). *Instrumental enrichment: An intervention program for cognitive modifiability.* In collaboration with Y. Rand, M. B. Hoffman, & R. Miller. Baltimore: University Park Press.

Flavell, J. (1979). *Cognitive Development.* Englewood Cliffs, NJ: Prentice-Hall.

Rigney, J. W. (1980). Cognitive learning strategies and qualities in information processing. In R. Snow, P. Federico, & W. Montague (Eds.), *Aptitudes, learning, and instruction,* Volume 1. Hillsdale, NJ: Lawrence Erlbaum.

Sternberg, R., & Wagner, R. (1982, July). Understanding intelligence: What's in it for educators? Paper submitted to the National Commission on Excellence in Education, Washington, DC.

Swartz, R. J. & Perkins, D. N. (1991). Structured teaching for critical thinking and reasoning in standard subject area instruction. In Perkins, D., Segal, J., & Voss, J. F. (Eds.), *Informal reasoning and education.* Hillsdale, NJ: Lawrence Erlbaum.

Whimbey, A. (1975). *Intelligence can be taught.* New York: Innovative Science.

Teaching for Transfer

by Robin Fogarty

All teaching is for transfer. All learning is for transfer. The mission of the thinking classrooms, then, is to extend learning, to bridge the old to the new, and to lead students toward relevant transfer and use across academic content and into life situations.

In our work with teachers in the area of teaching for transfer (Fogarty, Perkins, & Barell, 1991), we have found a simple framework to be helpful. As we explore such questions as "Why am I teaching this?" and "Where is the transfer?" with teachers, we introduce this notion:

> There are SOMETHINGS that we SOMEHOW want to use SOMEWHERE.

To clarify this esoteric statement of transfer, the diagram in Figure 1 illustrates the somethings, somehows, and somewheres inherent in the transfer of learning.

Basically, the diagram illustrates that there are somethings that we want to transfer. These include the more obvious things such as content, knowledge, and skills as well as the more universal things such as principles, concepts, attitudes and dispositions. As we plan lessons, the identified somethings determine the shape of those lessons. For example, if a targeted something is the attitude of cooperation and teamwork, the lesson will need activity components that require collaboration.

Figure 1

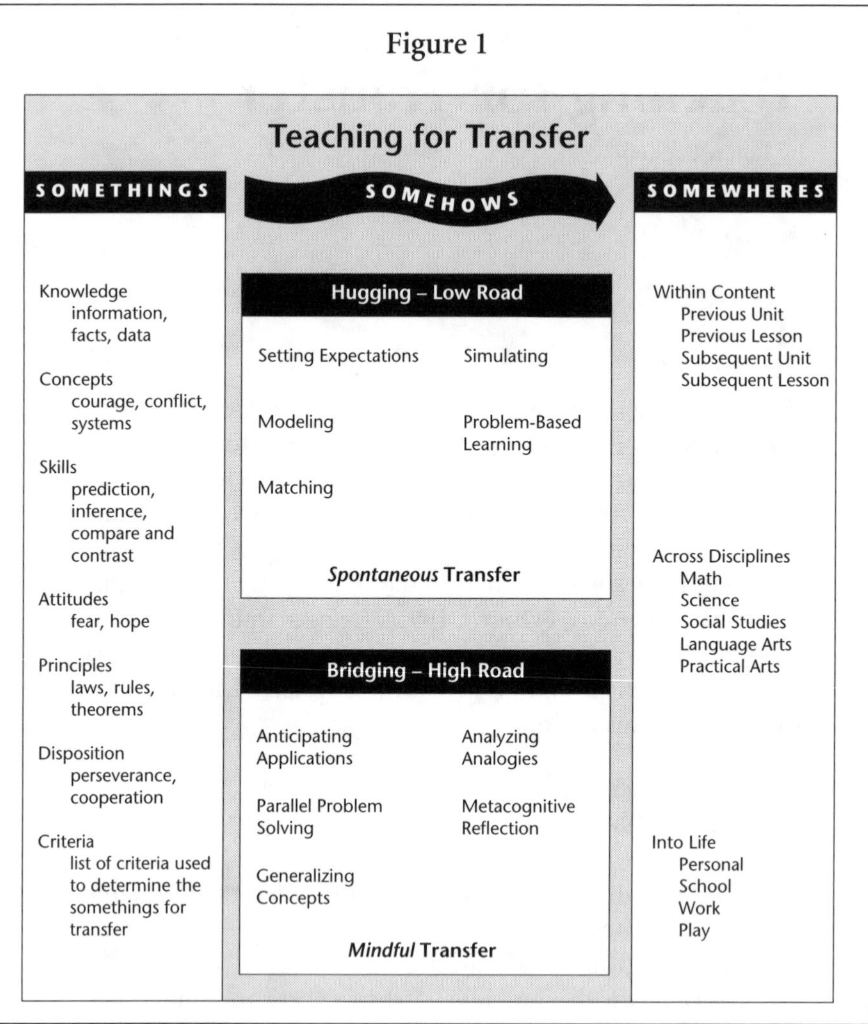

Paralleling this attention to the somethings of a lesson, another consideration illustrated in Figure 1 is the somewhere. Exactly where might this something transfer? Within the content? Across other subject matter lessons? Into life situations? Determining the somewheres ahead of time or anticipating future applications also has an impact on the shape of the lesson.

However, once the somethings are sifted out and the somewheres consciously targeted, the somehows of transfer are the next consideration. The center of the diagram in Figure 1 illustrates the somehows, or transfer options, that are available.

These options include both low-road mediation strategies that hug the lesson closely or high-road bridging techniques that require thoughtful application. Either way, through simple hugging strategies, such as setting expectations, modeling, matching, simulating, and using problem-based learning, or through more complex bridging strategies, such as anticipating applications, parallel problem solving, generalizing concepts, analyzing analogies, and cultivating metacognition, explicit mediation fosters the transfer of learning.

The primary focus of this chapter is to describe and illustrate the practical aspects of how to teach for transfer. Therefore, the emphasis is on the somehows or mediation strategies of transfer. However, in order to present a truly practical model of teaching for transfer, some attention must be given to ways of finding the somethings worth teaching and ways to target the somewheres.

THE SOMETHINGS OF TRANSFER

[Scenario One: Prior to a lesson introducing the Periodic Table of Elements, the teacher deliberately looks for the somethings worth teaching to make the relevance explicit to students for later transfer.]

PHYSICS TEACHER: (He points to a dilapidated and yellowed Periodic Table of Elements hanging above the black lab table. The chart is framed along the bottom with an uneven fringe of frayed threads.) *You will be responsible for knowing the contents of this table. It will serve you well, as you work in this lab.*

TIM: (Eyes rolling up, he thinks to himself, "I'm never gonna use this stuff ever again. What a waste. How am I ever gonna memorize all this?")

PHYSICS TEACHER: *Some of you are probably thinking, "When am I ever gonna use this?"*

TIM: (He sits up with a start, waiting for the punch line.)

PHYSICS TEACHER: *Well, for those of you who are plotting a career using the sciences, it's quite clear that the scientific knowledge contained in the chart will be invaluable to you. But what about those of you who already feel that the sciences will not be a life pursuit? Let's talk a little about how learning this table might benefit you in other ways. Let's look at what might transfer for you besides the science content. Any ideas?*

RENEE: *I was thinking that maybe the chart itself might serve as a model for gathering information. Grids and matrices are useful tools to organize data. I use them in social studies a lot.*

PHYSICS TEACHER: *That's pretty insightful. How many of you have used a matrix to sort or depict information?* (Three hands go up.) *What else?*

JOSÉ: *The symbols on the chart remind me of Greek letters and other symbols we use in math. So I guess the idea of decoding symbolic language may be useful in other situations.*

PHYSICS TEACHER: *Quite so! I agree with you. The use of symbols is something we encounter throughout life. Just look at the international road signs. What else?*

ROSA: *Probably because I'm so involved in art, but I think the thing that is most interesting, and maybe most universal in terms of future use of this Periodic Table of Elements, is the pattern in the chart. There are patterns in everything and these patterns help us understand and remember things.*

TIM: (He is now sitting on the edge of his seat.) *Yeah, and I've been thinking, too. Just figuring out how these elements are related to each other might help me see connections in other things. Once I find a way to get this in my head, I'll be able to connect lots of things.*

PHYSICS TEACHER: *I'm amazed at your ingenuity. Great thinking, today. Now, do we agree at least mildly, that this Periodic Table of Elements is worth my teaching and worth your learning?*

Finding the Somethings

Scenario one illustrates that sorting out the somethings worth teaching is a crucial first step for teaching for transfer. In fact, there are three distinct reasons why teachers need to take the time to target the somethings. As never-ending curriculum demands burden already overloaded schedules, teachers find it more and more necessary to sift out the real meat of the curriculum and set curricular priorities. However, in addition to this selection process as a survival tactic, the trend toward more holistic curriculum models of instruction also dictates the need to scrutinize the curriculum for integrating threads. And finally, as illustrated in the scenario, there is a compelling need to emphasize the pieces that have real transfer power, so students can see their relevance.

We can only teach so much. Our time and resources are limited. Yet, we want our students to learn in natural and holistic ways. And of course, we expect them to transfer that learning with ease and frequency. To uncover the sources within our curriculum that provide fertile ground for relevant student transfer, Costa (1991a) says we must "selectively abandon" and "judiciously include" curricular components. It is the work of the skilled teacher to find the somethings worth teaching.

To become good at searching out the somethings, a general framework such as the one illustrated in Figure 2 is used. This framework is a guide to use to look for particular knowledge pieces, skills, concepts, attitudes, principles, and dispositions to emphasize explicitly in the lesson for deliberate transfer later. That is to say that each is examined for possible transfer power. By sifting the content through this framework, the real curricular priorities can be sorted out quite easily as the teacher weighs the results against the district philosophy, academic criteria, and student relevance.

For example, as the teacher examines a unit on the digestive system, a completed frame might look like the one in Figure 3. Note the memos on the right side of the chart, which record the teacher's thoughts about how to approach this unit and get the most transfer power from it.

Figure 2

SOMETHINGS: ____________________

lesson/unit/topic

Knowledge: information, facts, data (e.g., definitions, dates, statistics)

Skill: social, thinking, organization (e.g., cooperation, prediction, ranking)

Concept: domain specific, universal (e.g., photosynthesis, courage)

Attitude: feelings, tone (e.g., inadequacy, optimism)

Principle: rules, laws, theorems (e.g., Second Law of Thermodynamics, Pythagorean Theorem)

Disposition: behaviors, habits, tendencies (e.g., impulsivity, procedural, humorous)

Figure 3
Finging the Somethings: The Digestive System

FIRST PASS	SECOND THOUGHTS
Digestive system search for somethings	*Maybe I should expand the topic to systems in the body or "Your Inner Environment"*
Knowledge: human anatomy, digestive system, vocabulary	*The text is the best resource here, but I will need some library time.*
Skills: diagrams, flow charts, sequencing, use of analogies	*I need to target one major thinking skill—maybe sequencing; can use graphic organizers to illustrate and utilize skill. Using analogies is a possible way to culminate unit.*
Concepts: digestive system, systems, loops, assimiliation, environment	*Systems is the universal concept, but I like the idea of "inner environment." Then I could do health, nutrition, substance abuse prevention, and self-esteem—fertile themes.*
Attitude: value good health, nutritious diet	*This would fit with the expanded concept idea.*
Principles: cause/effect	*Cause and effect could also be the thinking skill focus; more sophisticated than sequencing.*
Dispositions: awareness of bodily functions, whole health and fitness point of view	*Like the idea of connecting this to health/fitness focus.*

SOMETHINGS WITH TRANSFER POTENTIAL

- Inner environment or systems
- Cause/effect
- Self-esteem

NOTE: Use graphic organizers: flow chart, cause/effect circles, decision tree.

This process of searching for the somethings worth teaching can be done quite painlessly after a few practices. Many of us already do this sort of analysis in our heads as we look at upcoming units. However, the point is to make the process of setting curriculum priorities a deliberate and systematic procedure that precedes the instructional activity in the classroom.

Once we begin this conversation of, What's worth teaching? and Where is the transfer power in this content piece? we can use it to examine past units of study as well. Sometimes it is easier to look back at a lesson or unit just completed and sift out the priority pieces for the next time. Or, it may be easier to work through the priorities in professional dialogue with colleagues.

As a pre-planning strategy or as an evaluation tool, setting curricular priorities—finding the somethings worth teaching—must guide the instructional acts in our schools.

THE SOMEHOWS OF TRANSFER

[Scenario Two: Using the history chapter on the causes of World War II as the content target, the history teacher also targets the skill of asking good questions as part of the lesson focus. The specific type of questioning that is targeted is metacognitive reflection questions. This scenario illustrates how a history teacher uses a bridging strategy to facilitate meaningful transfer.]

HISTORY TEACHER: *Your assignment involves two parts. Part one is to review the questions at the back of the chapter and, with a partner, categorize them as either "skinny" questions that can be answered directly from the text reading or as "fat" questions that go beyond the given information.*

MELISSA: *Question? Can you give us examples.*

HISTORY TEACHER: *Better yet, let me pose a question. You value it, fat or skinny. Here's one. What were significant battles of World War II?*

MELISSA: *That seems pretty narrow. I think it's a skinny question.*

HISTORY TEACHER: *How about this? Define one of the following statements: Great men make great events or great events make great men.*

MELISSA: *Definitely a fat question. I would have to give lots of supporting evidence—it would turn into a long answer.*

HISTORY TEACHER: *That's right! You've got the idea. Now, part two of the assignment—I didn't forget!—is to select questions from your list and write your answers to turn in.*

ANDREW: (He waves his hand in the air.)

HISTORY TEACHER: *Will this be a fat or skinny question, Andrew?*

ANDREW: *Skinny!*

HISTORY TEACHER: *OK, what's your question?*

ANDREW: *How many questions should we answer?*

HISTORY TEACHER: *You're right, it is skinny. The answer is four! Write answers to two fat and two skinny questions.*

Identifying the Somehows

While the search for the somethings in our curricular content is of primary concern in the instructional process, the main focus of this essay is to present practical strategies to ensure that those somethings, once found, are taught in such a way that the learning "takes" and that the somethings are internalized, applied, and transferred appropriately. This section, which comprises the bulk of the essay, addresses the somehows of teaching for transfer.

Perkins' and Salomon's good shepherd theory of transfer (1988) proposes that to foster transfer of learning, transfer must be "shepherded," or helped along. The somehows are the shepherding or mediating strategies that promote relevant transfer.

In the theory of mediated transfer, two roads to transfer are posited: the low road of near or simple transfer and the high road of far or complex transfer. We may design lessons that "hug" the expected outcome if we are looking for near or somewhat automatic transfer. For example, if we want students to become better writers, we have them write, rather than circle, answers in a multiple choice worksheet model. Alternatively, we may select "bridging" strategies that call for mindful abstractions to encourage far or more complex transfer. If we want students to connect the problem solving they do in math class with the problem solving they do in science, we orchestrate a discussion that leads students to generalize about problem solving. In the process, we bridge problem solving in math to problem solving in science.

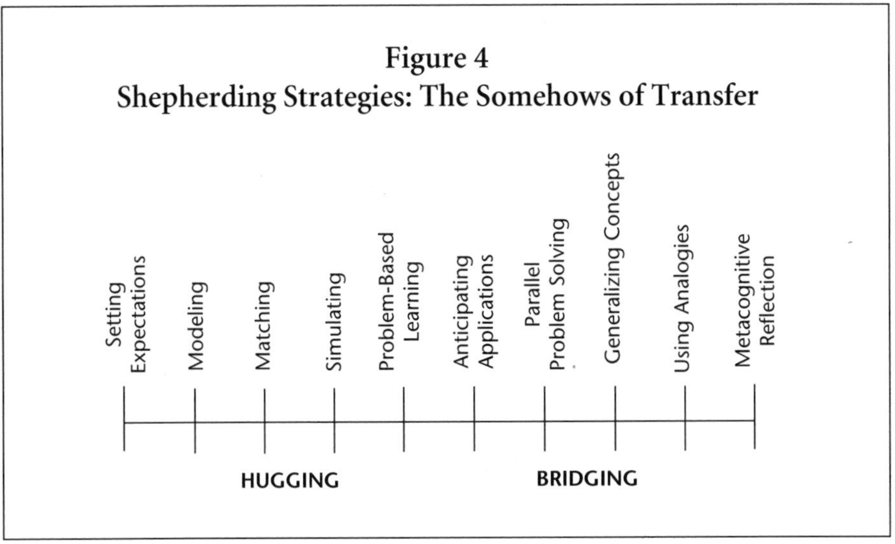

In fact, we may even map out combinations of both hugging and bridging strategies to deliberately induce transfer. A specific example of combining strategies would be the use of simulations in the driver's education lab (to hug for transfer) as well as an exploration of analogies to sports in a discussion of defensive driving techniques (to bridge for transfer).

Figures 4 and 5 illustrate ten somehows—five hugging strategies to facilitate new or simple transfer and five bridging strategies to span wide gaps between original learning and remote situations.

In the discussion of the somehows of transfer, each strategy includes a brief definition and an illustration of its use. In addition, specific examples are cited as practical cues for teacher use.

Setting Expectations—HUGGING

Definition: Talking to students about expectations for transfer to increase the likelihood that transfer occurs; explicitly planning into lessons the questions or tasks that help students connect across content so transfer is more likely to occur.

Example: When studying the skill of detecting bias in social studies, students encourage each other to look for instances of bias in constructing graphs in math class or in point of view pieces in language arts class. Suggest that they look for bias across the curricula and deliberately plant the seed for transfer.

Figure 5
Mediating Transfer

HUGGING STRATEGIES

1. *Setting Expectations:* targeting explicit goals
2. *Modeling:* demonstrating, showing
3. *Matching:* engaging in the very performance being developed, practicing
4. *Simulating:* role playing, acting out
5. *Problem-Based Learning:* experiential learning

BRIDGING STRATEGIES

6. *Anticipating Applications:* developing rationale, scouting for relevant uses
7. *Parallel Problem Solving:* moving learning from one context to another
8. *Generalizing Concepts:* extrapolating generic threads
9. *Using Analogies:* comparing, finding similarities
10. *Metacognitive Reflection:* thinking about thinking, planning, monitoring, evaluating

Verbal Cues:

- "What's the big idea?"
- "How does this connect to what you already know?"
- "Where might you use this?"
- "Do you see how this might fit with what we were working with last week?"
- "How is this relevant?"

Modeling—HUGGING

Definition: Demonstrating the desired behavior with a running monologue about what you're doing to emphasize key elements; modeling the behavior for students to adapt; talking about it; making sense of the demonstration.

Example: When asking students to prioritize their homework, the teacher will first create the list of items on the board while talking about prioritizing. For instance: "Here's how I prioritize. Once I have listed all the things I want to do, I find the most urgent items and rank those numbers one, two, and three.

Then I find the least important items, things I would like to do, but are not due the next day. I rank those toward the bottom. Then I sort out the middle items. Finally, I take the most important items, or the things that need to be done the soonest, and put them at the top. Now I have prioritized my work."

Verbal Cues:

- "Here's an example."
- "Let me illustrate."
- "Give me a specific instance."
- "Show me."
- "Use this as a prototype."

Matching—HUGGING

Definition: Matching the lesson design to the desired outcome; engaging the student in the very performance you're trying to develop; guiding the targeted behavior; using procedural learning.

Example: If the goal is to get students to take a stand, advocate a position, and support an idea with detail, give them many opportunities to practice that behavior. For example, weave agree/disagree questions throughout a lecturette and have students practice taking a stand as they learn the art of public advocacy.

Verbal Cues:

- "Practice the model."
- "Try it."
- "Duplicate this."
- "Repeat the process.
- "Follow the steps."

Simulating—HUGGING

Definition: Role playing, personifying or simulating the real thing to hug the desired outcome; experiencing the actions and feeling of the actual situation by practicing or pretending.

Example: In driver education classes, have students simulate driving before they drive an actual car; or act out the job interview, taking on the role of the job applicant. Stage the trial of the big bad wolf (from *The Three Little Pigs*) to learn about bias and jury selection.

Verbal Cues:
- "Pretend."
- "Put yourself in her place."
- "Imagine."
- "Take his role."
- "How might she think about this?"

Problem-Based Learning—HUGGING

Definition: Placing students in problematic situations; immersing them in the experience in order to pull together relevant information in an inductive teaching method that hugs the target behavior; having students apply their knowledge in the context of the problem, with no "up front" information offered formally.

Example: Construct a situated learning experience from a current newspaper article. For example, in one article a student locker has been searched for drugs. Have students in the class decide if the student's human rights have been violated after gathering and evaluating data.

Verbal Cues:
- "Here's the situation…"
- "What do you need to know?"
- "What can you do?"
- "What is the goal?"
- "How can you accomplish the task?"

Anticipating Applications—BRIDGING

Definition: Thinking about an upcoming opportunity to use the new idea; thinking about an adjustment that will make your application more relevant; targeting future applications or speculating on possible uses.

Example: After working on the division of fractions, guide students to project possible future uses of the skill as you mediate for transfer. Ask students, "How might you use this idea across content or in life?"

Verbal Cues:
- "How might you use this?"
- "What if you adapted it this way?"
- "Do you see any opportunities to try this out?"

- "Can you think of an application?"
- "Have you seen this used somewhere else?"

Parallel Problem Solving—BRIDGING

Definition: Using parallel thinking to ask, Where is this (idea) applicable in my personal life?; taking information and drawing parallels with experiences, with prior information and past knowledge; associating one idea with ideas already known and exploring options and possibilities for the application of an idea.

Example: Have students place a global or historic problem in the context of their personal lives to help them understand the more abstract problem. For example, during the American Revolution the colonists did not want taxes. They were in conflict with the mother country. Ask students, "What do you do when you're in conflict with your mother? She wants you to eat your peas, and you hate peas. What do you do? Boycott? Retreat? Throw a temper tantrum? What strategies do you use? How do these compare to the strategies the colonists used?"

Verbal Cues:

- "Do you see parallels to your own situation?"
- "How is this like your life situation?"
- "Can you relate this to personal issues?"
- "Does this sound familiar?"
- "Do you see any similarities to your own life?"

Generalizing Concepts—BRIDGING

Definition: Asking students to point out elements with general accountability in a given situation; encouraging them to generalize concepts; applying concepts universally.

Example: As students learn geometry, ask them to reflect upon their own problem-solving processes and to generalize about elements of that process that seem to help. For instance, students might say, "Use a diagram." Then ask, "Is that generally useful in other situations? How? Why? Give me some specific examples."

Verbal Cues:

- "What big ideas can you piece together from this?"
- "What truths seem apparent?"
- "What's the real lesson?"

- "Is there a rule, law, principle here?"
- "Can we say that 'Generally speaking…'?"

Using Analogies—BRIDGING

Definition: Finding likenesses to yield useful transfer; finding and analyzing analogies; comparing; using metaphors and making creative connections.

Example: Have students compare courage and rain. For example, courage is like the rain. Both can come upon you unexpectedly. Have students discuss how the unexpectedness of a courageous act is similar to the unexpectedness of a summer shower. Analyze this analogy by engaging students in a discussion about courage that elaborates and extends thinking and explicitly forces transfer through comparison. This seemingly difficult exercise is actually lots of fun. You may be surprised at the connections the students will make!

Verbal Cues:

- "How is a like b?"
- "a is like b because both c."
- "a : b :: c : d."
- "Compare a (abstract) to b (concrete)."
- "Find the similarities in a and b."

Metacognitive Reflection—BRIDGING

Definition: Planning, monitoring, and evaluating one's own thinking; being aware and controlling one's own thinking and behavior; thinking about thinking in tacit, aware, strategic, and reflective ways.

Example: After completing a series of math problems on the associative principle, ask students to think about how they attacked the problems. Ask, "What things were similar problems? What were the stumpers? Were there any elements of this problem that you had encountered before? If so, how did you deal with them?" Have students evaluate their own performance as they think about their thinking strategies and become aware of their own behavior in relation to their learning.

Verbal Cues:

- "What are your aims, goals, and objectives?"
- "Track your steps in this and evaluate your progress."
- "Look back and reflect on your work."

- "Monitor your progress periodically."
- "What would you do the same or differently next time?"

Shepherding the transfer of learning with the selective use of these ten hugging and bridging strategies can easily become an integral part of the instructional design. It is just a matter of consciously targeting transfer as a desired outcome, rather than simply assuming that transfer automatically happens. Once transfer is targeted, the appropriate scaffolding can be provided to carry the transfer.

Although these strategies for mediating transfer comprise only a partial list of the somehows, they represent explicit tools for transfer that we can add to our instructional repertoire. As we become more conscious of teaching for transfer, we will find creative ways to facilitate transfer and continually add these instructional tools to our teacher's tool kit.

THE SOMEWHERES OF TRANSFER

[Scenario Three: By asking students to think back to an experience or to project ahead to a possible application, the teacher targets the somewheres for future transfer.]

LITERATURE TEACHER: *In* The Old Man and the Sea, *Hemingway presents an impressive characterization of a man who perseveres against tremendous odds. Take a moment to think back to a time in your life when you used your will power to stick to something and see it through.* (Allow a minute or two of silence.) *Now, share your stories with a partner.*

DENNIS (turning to Louisa): *Once when I was really little I climbed a tree and when I was trying to get down I slipped and ended up clutching onto this branch. I had to hold on really tight for a long time while my brother went to get the ladder. It seemed like forever.*

LOUISA: *I remember once when I forced myself to finish my social studies project because it was due the next day. I had to paint this salt and flour relief map. It was a lot of fun when I started, but boy did I get sick of it. That was hard to do, just like the old man's struggle with the marlin.*

LITERATURE TEACHER: *Now, go to your logs and think ahead. Write a sentence or two about how this ability to persevere will help you in another class. For example, when will persevering help you in math class or in the science lab? Be specific. Target an upcoming assign-*

ment for another subject area that is going to take lots of will power and "stick-to-itiveness" to get it done. Try to think about how you can use this persevering attitude in other places. See if you can transfer it to another subject.

JOSÉ (writing in his log): *The algebra problems are really hard for me, right now. If I don't give up so easily—if I stick to them longer, like the old man—maybe I can get through them.*

Targeting the Somewheres

The somewheres of transfer are the end targets of the somethings and the somehows. By definition, learning in one situation and using that knowledge in another situation is called transfer. This transfer may occur within the content being taught, across disciplines to other subjects, or into life situations (conversely, of course, life experiences can transfer into school learning, etc.).

When the transfer is shepherded, the likelihood for relevant application and use seems to increase quite dramatically.

To suggest that one would teach something (or learn something) with no expectation for transfer or use is ludicrous. However, in viewing the research, the literature suggests that this transfer of learning, if left alone as in the bo peep and lost sheep theories (Perkins and Salomon, 1988), may not occur as spontaneously or as regularly as we want.

However, when the transfer is shepherded, the likelihood for relevant application and use seems to increase quite dramatically. In order to shepherd or mediate for transfer, we use hugging strategies that engage students in the very behavior desired or we use the bridging strategies of mindful abstractions as delineated previously in this chapter.

However, in addition to hugging and bridging, we can provide further, albeit temporary, scaffolding to the learning process by targeting specific somewheres. This additional targeting of the somewheres for transfer, within the same context, across disciplines, or into life situations, is fairly easy to do.

An example of targeting a somewhere for transfer within a similar context is the science teacher who directs students to relate the concept of the life cycle from the plant unit to the metamorphosis of the butterfly in the insect unit. To target a somewhere for transfer across subject areas, the math teacher may suggest that students check their hand calculations on the computer during their technology lab period. Similarly, to target a somewhere into real life situations, the social studies teacher may cue students to scout the newspapers, magazines, and broadcasts for current illustrations of aggression as an extension of the study of World War II.

Deliberately focusing the learner's attention on possible transfer opportunities is a powerful early-use strategy for promoting the transfer of learning. Over time, of course, less scaffolding is necessary as the learner takes over the task of finding the somewheres for relevant transfer.

CONCLUSION

In summary, by targeting the somewheres for transfer, by facilitating further transfer with leading questions and promoting risk taking with far-reaching applications, the likelihood for meaningful transfer of students' learning is increased significantly.

By looking at previous lessons we've taught or upcoming lessons we are planning to use through the window of transfer, the process for setting curricular priorities becomes pretty clear. In addition, once the priority somethings are sifted out, the specific similarities for transfer within the content, across disciplines, or into life situations can be targeted. To achieve the desired outcomes of taking those important somethings to the specified somewheres, teachers can select the various somehows of hugging and bridging strategies or combinations thereof to ensure transfer of learning.

In closing, there are somethings that we want somehow to transfer somewhere. Hopefully, this discussion will provide the catalyst to begin the work of teaching not for a test, but for a lifetime.

REFERENCES

Bellanca, J., & Fogarty, R. (1990). *Blueprints for thinking in the cooperative classroom.* Palatine, IL: IRI/Skylight Publishing.

Beyer, B. (1987). *Practical strategies for the teaching of thinking.* Boston: Allyn & Bacon.

Brandt, R. (1988, April). On teaching thinking: A conversation with Arthur Costa. *Educational Leadership,* p. 11.

Costa, A. (1991a, Winter). Orchestrating the second wave. *Cogitare,* p. 1.

Costa, A. (1991b). The search for intelligent life. In *The school as a home for the mind.* (pp. 19–31). Palatine, IL: IRI/Skylight Publishing.

Costa, A., & Garmston, R. (1985, March). *The art of cognitive coaching: Supervision for intelligent teaching.* Paper presented at the Annual Conference of the Association for Supervision and Curriculum Development, Chicago.

Cousins, N. (1981). *Human options.* New York: Norton.

Feuerstein, R. (1980). *Instrumental enrichment.* Baltimore: University Park Press.

Fogarty, R. (1991). *The mindful school: How to integrate the curricula.* Palatine, IL: IRI/Skylight Publishing.

Fogarty, R. (1989). *From training to transfer: The role of creativity in the adult learner.* Doctoral dissertation, Loyola University of Chicago.

Fogarty, R., & Bellanca, J. (1989). *Patterns for thinking: Patterns for transfer.* Palatine, IL: IRI/Skylight Publishing.

Fogarty, R., Perkins, D., & Barell, J. (1991). *The mindful school: How to teach for transfer.* Palatine, IL: IRI/Skylight Publishing.

Fullan, M. (1982). *The meaning of educational change.* New York: Teachers College Press.

Hord, S., & Loucks, S. *A concerns-based model for delivery of inservice.* CBFM Project - Research and Development Center for Teacher Education, The University of Texas at Austin.

Hunter, M. (1982). *Teach for transfer.* El Segundo, CA: TIP Publications.

Joyce, B. (1986). *Improving America's schools.* New York: Longman.

Joyce, B., & Showers, B. (1983). *Power in staff development through research and training.* Alexandria, VA: Association for Supervision and Curriculum Development.

Joyce, B., & Showers, B. (1980, February). Improving inservice training: The message of research. *Educational Leadership,* p. 380.

Marzano, R., & Arredondo, D. (1986, May). Restructuring schools through the teaching of thinking skills. *Educational Leadership,* p. 23.

Parnes, S. (1975). *Aha! Insights into creative behavior.* Buffalo, NY: D.O.K.

Perkins, D. (1988, August 6). *Thinking frames.* Paper delivered at ASCD Conference on Approaches to Teaching Thinking, Alexandria, VA.

Perkins, D. (1986). *Knowledge as design.* Hillsdale, NJ: Lawrence Erlbaum.

Perkins, D., & Salomon, G. (1989, January/February). Are cognitive skills context bound? *Educational Researcher,* pp. 16–25.

Perkins, D., & Salomon, G. (1988, September). Teaching for transfer. *Educational Leadership,* pp. 22–32.

Polya, G. (1957). *How to solve it.* Princeton, NJ: Doubleday.

Posner, M., & Keele, S. (1973). Skill learning. In R. Travers, (Ed.), *Second handbook of research on teaching.* (pp. 805–831). Chicago: Rand McNally.

Sergiovanni, T. (1987, May). Will we ever have a true profession? *Educational Leadership,* pp. 44–49.

Sternberg, R. (1986). *Intelligence applied: Understanding and increasing your intellectual skills.* New York: Harcourt Brace Jovanovich.

Sternberg, R. (1984, September). How can we teach intelligence? *Educational Leadership,* pp. 38–48.

Tyler, R. (1987, January). The first most significant curriculum events in the twentieth century. *Educational Leadership,* pp. 36–37.

Wittrock, M. (1967). Replacement and nonreplacement strategies in children's problem solving. *Journal of Educational Psychology, 58*(2), 69–74.

The Most Significant Outcome

by Robin Fogarty

Our mission as educators is to help every child become a more active, engaged, committed, and skillful learner, not just for a test, but for a lifetime.—James Bellanca

WHY TEACH FOR TRANSFER?

Transfer of learning simply means using something in a new context that was learned in an earlier context. All teaching is for transfer. All learning is for transfer. It's that simple. Yet considerable research shows that a startling amount of the knowledge that people acquire in subject matter instruction is inert. This means that the knowledge is there in memory for the multiple-choice quiz, but the knowledge is passive. It is not retrieved in the context of active problem solving or creativity, such as in writing an essay. Inert knowledge does not contribute much to the cognitive ability of the learner except for performance on school quizzes. One of the goals of teaching for transfer is teaching for active rather than inert knowledge.

Considerable research shows that a startling amount of the knowledge that people acquire in subject matter instruction is inert.

The mission of the thinking classroom is to extend learning, to bridge the old to the new, and to lead students toward relevant transfer and use of knowledge across academic content and into life situations. Once we accept this mission, we explicitly target skills, concepts, and attitudes for transfer. Once targeted, we mediate or shepherd the transfer of learning within the content we teach, across to other disciplines, and into life situations.

WHAT ARE THE LEVELS OF TRANSFER?

Once transfer of learning becomes the targeted outcome, the search for ways to assess that outcome follows. Transfer of learning can be assessed by comparison with a continuum of transfer behavior. This continuum has been developed as a tracking or assessment tool. With it the teacher can begin to track students' transfer, and learners can begin to reflect—using skills of metacognition—on their own levels of transfer.

The continuum in Figure 1 represents levels of transfer that range from simple or near transfer to more complex or far-reaching transfer. Six distinctions are made depicting learner dispositions that overlook, duplicate, replicate, integrate, map, and innovate with transfer. The model is framed, however, by the philosophical stance that these various levels of transfer offer evidence that is extremely situational. That is to say, transfer of learning—using what is learned in one context in an entirely new context—seems to depend on a number of significant variables.

Figure 1
Situational Dispositions Toward Transfer

		Does the learner:	
SIMPLE	OVERLOOK:	Miss appropriate opportunities; persist in former ways?	NEAR
SIMPLE	DUPLICATE:	Perform the drill exactly as practiced; duplicate with no change; copy?	NEAR
SIMPLE	REPLICATE:	Tailor, but apply knowledge only in similar situations; produce work that all looks alike?	NEAR
COMPLEX	INTEGRATE:	Subtly combine knowledge with other ideas and situations; use information with raised consciousness?	FAR
COMPLEX	MAP:	Carry a strategy to another content and into life situations; associate?	FAR
COMPLEX	INNOVATE:	Invent; take ideas beyond the initial conception; take risks; diverge?	FAR

For example, learner dispositions to internalize and apply ideas, concepts, skills, and attitudes may depend on past knowledge and prior experience (How much background does the learner have?); the physical learning environment (Is the climate conducive to learning?); the match between teaching and learning styles (Is the learner enabled by the ways the material is being presented?); the feelings, mood, and emotional state of the learner and teacher (Does the learner [or teacher] have affective variables that are enhancing or blocking learning?); and innumerable other external and internal influences. Thus, the continuum is presented simply as a loose framework of situational dispositions toward transfer. In no way is the model intended for judgmental, summative evaluation. The examples are offered as guides to provide insight into student transfer both for the teacher or observer and the student or learner.

In Figure 2, each of the six situational dispositions for transfer are represented both figuratively and graphically. Each disposition toward transfer is defined and elaborated with classroom examples of what one might see and hear from students at each level. To know what the disposition looks like and sounds like provides concrete clues to the level of transfer occurring.

We *see* in student work, in essence, collected artifacts that provide graphic evidence of transfer. Similarly, what we *hear* students say gives verbal clues to the personal connections that are made in their thought processes. Both the graphic representation of students' thinking and the oral articulation of how they are internalizing ideas are helpful (see Figure 3). One provides evidence of the external product of transfer, while the other provides evidence of the internal process of making the transfer. Both are powerful cues that suggest where students are in the transfer process, what they have learned, and how they're using it.

Overlooking Transfer

Ollie the Head-in-the-Sand Ostrich overlooks transfer. This learner misses appropriate opportunities, persists in former ways, and may be intentionally or unintentionally overlooking the opportunities for transfer. Sometimes learners choose not to use something new. Whatever the stated reasons—"The com-

Figure 2
Looking and Listening for Transfer

Model	Illustration	*Transfer Disposition*	Looks Like	Sounds Like
Ollie the Head-in-the-Sand Ostrich		***Overlooks***	Persists in writing in manuscript form rather than cursive. (New skill overlooked or avoided.)	*"I get it right on the dittos, but I forget to use punctuation when I write an essay."* (Not applying mechanical learning.)
Dan the Drilling Woodpecker		***Duplicates***	Plagiarism is the most obvious student artifact of duplication. (Unable to synthesize in own words.)	*"Mine is not to question why—just invert and multiply."* [When dividing fractions.] (No understanding of what she or he is doing.)
Laura the Look-Alike Penguin		***Replicates***	"Bed to Bed" or narrative style. "He got up. He did this. He went to bed." or "He was born. He did this. He died." (Student portfolio of work never varies.)	*"Paragraphing means I must have three 'indents' per page."* (Tailors into own story or essay, but paragraphs inappropriately.)
Jonathan Livingston Seagull		***Integrates***	Student writing essay incorporates newly learned French words. (Applies by weaving old and new.)	*"I always try to guess (predict) what's gonna happen next on T.V. shows."* (Connects to prior knowledge and experience; relates what's learned to personal experience.)
Cathy the Carrier Pigeon		***Maps***	Graphs information for a social studies report with the help of the math teacher to actually design the graphs. (Connecting to another subject.)	From a parent: *"Tina suggested we brainstorm our vacation ideas and rank them to help us decide."* (Carries new skills into life situations.)
Samantha the Soaring Eagle		***Innovates***	After studying flow charts for computer class, student constructs a Rube Goldberg-type invention. (Innovates; diverges; goes beyond what's expected and creates something novel.)	*"I took the idea of the Mr. Potato Head and created a mix-and-match grid of ideas for our Earth Day project."* (Generalizes ideas from experience and transfers creatively.)

puter takes too long"—these learners sometimes unintentionally overlook an opportunity to apply something in a new context, because they just don't get it; they miss the connection. If asked, "Why don't you just multiply the number of words in a

Figure 3
Assessing Transfer

WHAT WE SEE (External Product)	WHAT WE HEAR (Internal Process)
• student work	• student conversations
• collected artifacts	• verbal clues
• concrete evidence	• personal connections
• graphic representation	• oral articulation

line by the number of lines instead of counting every word?", one of these learners might reply, "Oh, I never thought of that."

Transfer that Duplicates

Dan the Drilling Woodpecker duplicates in transfer. This learner performs the drill or reproduces the product exactly as practiced. There is no deviation or personalization. The transfer appears quite rehearsed, mechanical, directed, and procedural. ("Divide, multiply, subtract. Bring down. Divide, multiply, subtract. Bring down.")

Plagiarism is the ultimate example of duplication. "Where can I get a copy of that?"; "I used the definition verbatim"; or "I need a pattern in order to make this" are all verbal clues to duplicated transfer.

Transfer that Replicates

Laura the Look-Alike Penguin replicates. This learner duplicates, but tailors the learning for personal relevance. Using a given model, the learner structures the variables to meet personal needs. ("I used the idea of note cards, but I didn't actually use cards. I just divided the paper into sections so I could do it on my computer.") However, every application in this example (although modified for relevant use) is used in a similar contextual framework. The learner who replicates exemplifies simple transfer and does not break out of the model she or he establishes.

Transfer that Integrates

Jonathan Livingston Seagull integrates with a raised consciousness. This learner, acutely aware of an idea, combines the new learning with prior knowledge and past experiences. The transfer is subtle and may not always be easy to track because the learning is assimilated so smoothly into the learner's existing framework. In fact, sometimes the learner says, "I already knew how to outline" or "I've always done my essays from an outline." It's not new, but the prior learning is refined and enhanced. In this integrated level of complex transfer, the learner folds the new learning in with the old, blending the two together.

Transfer that Maps

Cathy the Carrier Pigeon deliberately moves learning in one context to a different context. The learner makes explicit bridges by strategically planning future applications. The transfer seems crystal clear and application is made with ease. The learner at this level of transfer might comment, "I'm going to use the science report on pollution in my communications class. We have to develop a public service commercial message."

What distinguishes this transfer from the previous model of integrated use is the explicitness with which the learner applies the ideas. There is obvious intent to move ideas from one context to another in this learner transfer model and the risk taking required is greater than in the previous levels.

Transfer that Innovates

Samantha (or Sam) the Soaring Eagle innovates. This learner creatively transforms learning by grasping the seeds of an idea and researching, reshaping, reforming, and renaming to such an extent that the original learning may be almost indistinguishable or at least vastly modified in unique ways. This learner might say, "Rather than write about my summer vacation from my point of view, I wrote about it from the point of view of my dog, Rags. I bet you wondered why I called it 'Dog Days of Summer.'" This level of transfer is noted for its novel ideas and the risk taking that accompanies such creative thinking. Sams are wonderful connection makers—anything goes!

CONCLUSION

The six dispositions of transfer do not necessarily occur in sequence, but there seems to be an inherent hierarchy. The first three are considered simple transfer with minimal risk taking involved, while the last three models seem more complex and require considerable mindfulness and risk taking.

However, teacher and learner knowledge about and awareness of the levels of transfer by themselves increase the likelihood of moving learning along. In other words, once you know about the levels and cues to transfer, you can't *not* know! The awareness is there. The level of transfer starts to be consciously monitored with even this relatively minor attention to it. Interestingly, this self awareness also seems to be accompanied by a sense of responsibility. Once aware of transfer, learners seem to feel accountable to attempt transfer and to use new ideas. In addition, once teachers and learners put their radar out for evidence of transfer, transfer gets more attention.

REFERENCES

Bellanca, J., & Fogarty, R. (1990). *Blueprints for thinking in the cooperative classroom.* Palatine, IL: IRI/Skylight Publishing.

Beyer, B. (1987). *Practical strategies for the teaching of thinking.* Boston: Allyn & Bacon.

Brandt, R. (1988, April). On teaching thinking: A conversation with Arthur Costa. *Educational Leadership,* p. 11.

Costa, A. (1991). The search for intelligent life. In *The school as a home for the mind.* Palatine, IL: IRI/Skylight Publishing.

Cousins, N. (1981). *Human options.* New York: Norton.

Fogarty, R. (1989). *From training to transfer: The role of creativity in the adult learner.* Doctoral dissertation, Loyola University of Chicago.

Fogarty, R., & Bellanca, J. (1989). *Patterns for thinking: Patterns for transfer.* Palatine, IL: IRI/Skylight Publishing.

Fogarty, R., Perkins, D., & Barell, J. (1991). *The mindful school: How to teach for transfer.* Palatine, IL: IRI/Skylight Publishing.

Hunter, M. (1982). *Teach for transfer.* El Segundo, CA: TIP Publications.

Joyce, B. (1986). *Improving America's schools.* New York: Longman.

Perkins, D. (1988, August 6). *Thinking frames.* Paper delivered at ASCD Conference on Approaches to Teaching Thinking, Alexandria, VA.

Perkins, D. (1986). *Knowledge as design.* Hillsdale, NJ: Lawrence Erlbaum.

Perkins, D., Barell, J., & Fogarty, R. (1989). *Teaching for transfer* (Course Notebook). Palatine, IL: IRI/Skylight Publishing.

Perkins, D., & Salomon, G. (1989, January/February). Are cognitive skills context bound? *Educational Researcher,* pp. 16–25.

Posner, M., & Keele, S. (1973). Skill learning. In R. Travers, (Ed.), *Second handbook of research on teaching.* Chicago: Rand McNally.

Tyler, R. (1986–87, December/January). The five most significant curriculum events in the twentieth century. *Educational Leadership,* pp. 36–37.

Wittrock, M. (1967). Replacement and nonreplacement strategies in children's problem solving. *Journal of Educational Psychology, 58*(2), 69–74.

Vignettes: Levels of Transfer

by Robin Fogarty

As teachers begin to incorporate the ideas for thinking into the classroom, students move from tacit use, to aware, strategic, and reflective use of metacognition as they plan, monitor, and evaluate their work. In essence, they think about their thinking and learn about their learning.

Self-awareness propels one along the learning journey—once we know, we can't *not* know.

However, to close this section on reflective transfer, there is one overriding idea still to address. And that is the idea of the power of self-awareness in changing ourselves. Self-awareness propels one along the learning journey—once we know, we can't *not* know. In the knowing, we can then take action. An illustration of the potential of self-awareness is captured in this simple vignette:

> A young woman is a guest participant in her friend's yoga class on Saturday morning. Following a wonderful workout of stretching and meditation, the yogi invites the friend to breakfast at a local vegetarian café. As the guest proceeds to order, she says, "A cheese omelet with a side of Canadian bacon." Of course, the waitress admonishes her with, "I'm sorry, we do not serve any meat."
>
> At this point the guest is a bit embarrassed, laughs nervously at herself and revises her order. Then she turns to her friend and makes a statement reflecting her self-awareness. "I never realized how engrained my habits are . . . and how unaware I am about

From *The Mindful School: How to Teach for Metacognitive Reflection,* pp. 291–302. © 1994 by IRI/Skylight Publishing, Inc.

things like the vegetarian movement. I need to be more sensitive."

By commenting on herself, the young woman crystallizes not only her awareness of the mistake, but her self-awareness of her own shortcomings. That metacognitive comment, once expressed, provides an indelible insight into one's self and provides fertile ground for improvement, development, and real learning.

It is through self-awareness of the level of transfer that the learner can then deliberately proceed to a level of more depth.

While this story serves only as a simple illustration of self-awareness as a tool for change, the birds of transfer, as described in the previous chapter, provide a similar kind of personal insight. This metacognitive model delineates six levels of self-awareness that are associated with the depth of learning or the transfer level of that learning. These six levels of transfer are overlooking, duplicating, replicating, integrating, mapping, and innovating. The metaphor of the birds simply provides visual images to accompany the levels. For example, Ollie the Ostrich has his head in the sand and overlooks the possibility of using an idea, while Samantha the Soaring Eagle creatively adapts an idea to the extent that it becomes an innovation in itself.

While the birds of transfer provide mental models of the levels of learning and the depth of transfer, it is in the personal application of the models that startling insights occur. It is through self-awareness of the level of transfer that the learner can then deliberately proceed to a level of more depth.

Again, let's look at personal situations that exemplify each bird and how, just in the awareness of each level, the learner gains invaluable insight into his or her own development. Since the author assumes that most of the readers are teachers themselves, the illustrations focus on personal teaching episodes or teacher training situations. Each is expressed as a separate vignette.

OLLIE THE HEAD-IN-THE-SAND OSTRICH
(Overlooks opportunities for transfer)
Volcanoes and Earthquakes
During an inservice workshop on the structured overview, a reading strategy to help students understand the science text, the leader passes out a one-page article on volcanoes for participants to use as they practice the strategy.

As the teachers eagerly work with the strategy, they become excited about the information on volcanoes. In fact, they become so immersed in the content, that the strategy inadvertently takes second place in their focus. Just listen to two teachers as they *overlook* the possibilities of using the structured overview and focus, instead, on the topic of volcanoes.

> Fifth Grade Teacher: *You're really lucky, Carol. You're studying Hawaii this semester. You can use this great lesson on volcanoes.*
>
> Sixth Grade Teacher: *Yeah, you're right* (laughing). *Too bad you're doing earthquakes. It won't work for you.*

The teachers are so enamored with the idea of volcanoes that they have just experienced, they have forgotten or *overlooked* the strategy of structuring an overview or making a concept map as a pre-reading strategy. However, if the instructor reminds them, "Remember, this is about structured overviews. How can you use it?" transfer could be quite different.

DAN THE DRILLING WOODPECKER
(Duplicates exactly or copies an idea)
Music to My Ear
Invariably, at some point during every workshop, a participant will stop by the podium and say, "May I have a copy of that? I know just where I can use it." Now, this annoys some presenters because they're feeling a bit protective about sharing their workshop material (their bread and butter—so to speak). However, I, on the other hand, am pleased when I hear this request. It signals me that someone has made a critical connection to my content and, in fact, has already targeted a personal application for the material. "May I have a copy of that?" is music to my ears. I welcome the Ditto Dans in my audience because I know they are transferring the learning to a relevant application.

LAURA THE LOOK-ALIKE PENGUIN

(Replicates an idea with new uses, but in a similar way)

Teacher!

My story of replicated learning is rooted in the work of Sylvia Ashton Warner, as described in *Teacher*. As a primary school teacher, I knew in my heart that the lock-step, basal approach to reading was not working. Then I came upon this book in which a dynamic model of teaching was not only described in beautiful detail, but filled with animated photographs of children drawing, writing, reading, and dancing. I knew I had happened upon a treasure in Sylvia Ashton Warner's work, *Teacher*.

In my effort to duplicate this rich experience in my own first grade, I scrupulously underlined every key idea in the book, wrote in the column, reread the passages, and even cross-referenced it to her first book—a fictional work called *Spinster*. However, in my enthusiasm to copy her methodology, I found gaps in my understanding of what she actually did and subsequently charted my own course—sometimes slightly adrift from her original path and at other times, totally off the beaten path.

In the final analysis, I had not duplicated this New Zealand classroom because I had some that was hers and some that was mine. On the surface, it was a definite look-alike, but I had really *replicated* the original idea by tailoring the model in my own fashion.

JONATHAN LIVINGSTON SEAGULL

(Subtly integrates the new with the old; sometimes not consciously aware of the transfer)

The Weaver

The story I like to tell about the subtle integration of an idea into the classroom involves a high school biology teacher who attended my training in thinking skills. I call him The Weaver because he is a master at taking an idea and threading it into his existing format. Let me illustrate.

I had spent the better part of one day demonstrating higher-order questions as a thought-provoking strategy for the classroom. Later that week, I visited The Weaver's biology class and heard this exchange:

"José, do you agree or disagree with Watson on this?" (Watson is the author of the biology text.)

"I think I agree with him because his theory matches my experience."

"Good! Now, class, Watson and José say . . . . Does anyone want to disagree? Can someone give us another view?" and the teacher continues proceeds to weave the higher-order questions and the personal references to his students into his mini-lecture.

I think this is a rich example of integrated transfer—transfer of high-order questions from the workshop in the staff room to subject matter instruction in the classroom. He did not duplicate the workshop activity, but wove the idea into his usual format.

CATHY THE CARRIER PIGEON

(Strategically plots to use the idea in multiple situations)

Real Estate and Gifted Education

A foreign language teacher maps out deliberate applications of newly learned ideas. First, she has her students web the word *France* to see what they know. After this practice of the attribute web with her French I class, she decides to try the same webbing strategy with her adult evening class in which she teaches real estate. She selects *Home Buyer* as her focus words.

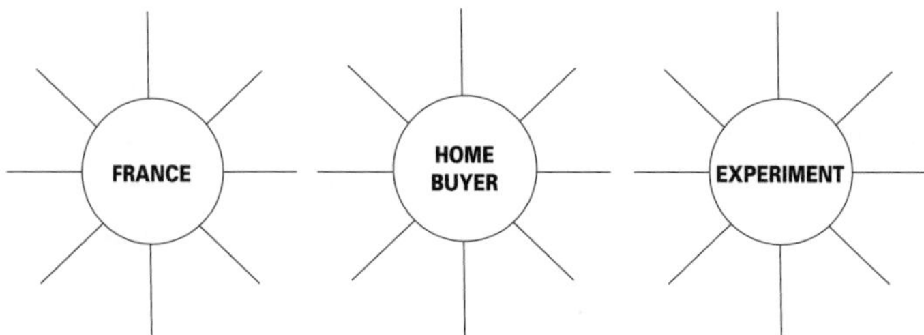

On her drive home that night, her mind is searching and scanning for other uses of this interesting strategy, when she suddenly remembers her upcoming summer school job in which she'll be teaching science to primary-aged children. She makes a mental note to web the word *Experiment* on opening day. And the strategic, planned applications go on as the mapper thinks ahead to other uses.

SAMANTHA THE SOARING EAGLE

(Creative, inventive, divergent transfer of an idea)

The Lucy Jacobs Story

My favorite story of creative transfer involves several other trainers who also conduct workshops on thinking in the classroom. Early in my career I attended a session in which Lucy Jacobs demonstrated a technique called The Human Graph.

> "Group around me and when I say 'Move,' choose the side you prefer and take your place on that side. Be ready to tell why you're there.
>
> "Okay? Now, would you rather be a mountain climber or a deep-sea diver? Mountain climbers to the right. Deep-sea divers to the left."

The activity was such fun, I immediately incorporated it into my classes, but I changed the idea a bit:

> "When I say 'Move,' pick a designated spot, A, B, C, or D, and form a human bar graph. A means slightly agree, B - believe it for myself, C - convince others, and D - die for it. Degrees of disagreement are also A, B, C, or D but on the opposite side.
>
> "The statement for you to agree or disagree with is 'Student rights are infringed upon when there are drug checks of lockers.' Now, move."

Years later, Lucy called me and asked for permission to use my human graph strategy. I laughed and said, "Don't you recognize it? I stole this idea from you."

Of course, the idea had been modified to such an extent that Lucy had never connected the two. Now, that's an innovative idea!

LEVELS OF TRANSFER

Hopefully, these personal anecdotes serve to illustrate the potential of metacognitive insight and self-awareness as self-imposed change agents. But, the true power is only captured by the learners as they examine their own levels of transfer. As they reflect on situations in their own lives in which they exhibit "Ollie" behavior or innovate like a "Sam," learners become privy to insightful thoughts about their own development.

It is this self-awareness and the thoughtful articulation about the personal insight that actually create the conditions necessary for change.

To illustrate in a different way the power of self-awareness and thoughtful insight, it is never more obvious than when it is *lacking* in someone. And we all know that individual who captures everyone's attention in an obnoxious display of temper and is totally, profoundly unaware of the impression he or she leaves.

It is this self-awareness and the thoughtful articulation about the personal insight that actually create the conditions necessary for change.

In this example, the learner is oblivious to the impact of his or her actions—in essence, non-reflective and not metacognitive in any way. Of course, it follows that this individual is not likely to change that behavior either because awareness must precede action. If one is not even aware, then change is not an issue.

However, knowing what we do know about the possibilities for personal growth based on self-awareness and self-knowledge, it behooves the teacher to conduct a personal inventory of the levels of transfer. Take a few minutes to recapture personal learning situations that illustrate the various birds of transfer.

These anecdotes are invaluable resources as teachers begin their work on metacognitive reflection with students. Once teachers can identify the levels of transfer in themselves, they more readily recognize these levels in their students. Naturally, this is yet another step in the process of mediating skillful metacognitive reflection in the students.

And, once there is an awareness and understanding of one's level of transfer, specific cueing questions can easily guide that transfer to a next level. For example, for each of the six transfers, a thought-provoking question cues further movement (see Figure 1).

Figure 1
Making Connections with Questions

OVERLOOKING
Think of an instance when the skill or strategy would be inappropriate.
"I would not use ________ when__________."

DUPLICATING
Think of an opportunity when you could have used the skill or strategy.
"I wish I'd known about ________ when __________."

REPLICATING
Think of an adjustment that will make your application of __________ more relevant.
"Next time I'm going to __________."

INTEGRATING
Think of an analogy for the skill or strategy.
"__________ *is like* ________ *because both* __________."

MAPPING
Think of an opportunity to use the new idea.
"A strategy to carry across is ____________."

INNOVATING
Think of an application for a real-life setting.
"What if________."

While the birds of transfer represent a highly sophisticated metacognitive strategy, as soon as they're introduced, people often sense an "Aha" experience. They gain instant insight into themselves, their peers and colleagues, and their students.

These levels of transfer, once in our consciousness, seem to provide a magical window for reflection on ourselves and on others. As mentioned earlier, once we know, we can't not know.

Section 5

Authentic Assessment . . . The Measure of Man

I'd rather learn from one bird how to sing than teach ten thousand stars how not to dance. —E. E. Cummings

Assessment is about measuring what one knows and can do and what one doesn't know and cannot do. Yet, if the true mission of teaching is to help kids learn, the measurement must foster growth and development; it must not close the gates to opportunity, but, rather, open the gateways of potential.

If this premise is accepted, assessment must be authentic, dynamic, fluid, and formative. That is not to say that normative, standardized evaluations have no place in the overall assessment scheme.

Yet, as Dewey so aptly put it, "Perhaps the greatest of all pedagogical fallacies is the notion that a person learns only the particular thing he is studying at the time" (Dewey in Eisner, 1979, p. 87). How do teachers assess the totality of human potential, the development of the growth of the learner in all the interrelated realms? How do students reflectively acknowledge the changes and the development within themselves as they learn and grow and progress? How do we authentically, yet practically, measure and assess?

To answer the queries proposed in the preceding paragraphs, several articles in this section target student self-reflection. Specifically, a comprehensive article on the benefits of using learning logs, "The Thinking Log," opens the assessment section. Examples abound as stem statements and varied purposes are outlined for immediate teacher use.

In the second essay, focusing on student self-assessment and reflective evaluation, "'The Portfolio Connection': Real World Examples," ten steps to portfolio development are listed: project, collect, select, interject, reflect, inspect, perfect, connect, inject/eject, and respect. Each of the phases is introduced with a real-world example. A brief description of each step follows the illustrations to arm readers with a number of practical, ready-to-use strategies as they develop portfolios with their students.

Moving from assessment as product only, the third article in the section develops the concept of "Multiple Intelligences as Assessment Tools." In this timely piece, Gardner's seven intelligences become natural tools for assessing both *product* and *performance.* Using the verbal, visual, logical, bodily, musical, interpersonal, and intrapersonal intelligences, the student is afforded many avenues to demonstrate what he or she knows and can do.

To emphasize the point that assessment must measure all aspects of human potential, "The Tri-Assessment Model" advocates traditional, portfolio, and performance assessment. Using all three measures ensures both formative assessment of growth and development and normative evaluation of grades and rankings.

As in the other sections, the final curtain falls with "Vignettes: Jagged Profiles," illustrating the best practices highlighted in the chapter. In this case, seven learners are profiled to emphasize assessment in each of the seven intelligences.

The Thinking Log: The Inking of Our Thinking

by Robin Fogarty

JOURNAL + NOTEBOOK = THINKING LOG

A thinking log is much like a footprint. Both are uniquely personal impressions that mark one moment in time. Yet, whereas the footprint may disappear with the wind, the thinking log cements the thought-filled page for all of time.

The log is a hybrid created from the personal journal and the traditional class notebook. A journal is usually a daily barometer of events and feelings that are evoked by day-to-day happenings, while a notebook typically is a collection of classroom notes and doodles, permanently recorded on paper in a personalized shorthand that is all too soon indecipherable. Neither the journal nor the notebook offers the scope of the thinking log, for between the pages of the log are spontaneous, gut reactions to learning that just occurred (see Figure 1).

Neither the journal nor the notebook offers the scope of the thinking log, for between the pages of the log are spontaneous, gut reactions to learning that just occurred.

TEACHABLE MOMENTS: INKING OUR THINKING

By planning for youngsters to process their thinking in written form, teachers ultimately have at their disposal a versatile and valuable teaching tool.

Taking advantage of the teachable moment, students process reflectively by logging their thinking. They catch the

---

Adapted from the pamphlet *Inking Our Thinking: How to Use Journals to Stimulate Reflective Thinking in Your Students No Matter What the Subject Area.* © 1990 by IRI/Skylight Publishing, Inc.

Figure 1
Entries on Various Concepts

LOGGING

NOTHING IN LIFE IS TO BE FEARED. IT IS ONLY TO BE UNDERSTOOD.

MARIE CURIE

Nov. 17, 1989: A theory I have about this thing called fear is that only I can control my fears. And the first step is to face them.

Feb 3, 1990: My own thinking on this idea of freedom is that the more we have, the more responsibility we have also. I think this is good. It forces us to become our own keepers.

May 23, 1990: My hypothesis on conflict is simple. If we reach out, look at the other person's point of view (which isn't easy), we can usually find a middle ground.

freshness of first impressions; jot down the milieu of ideas swarming about their heads; explore for understanding; analyze for clarity; synthesize into personal meaning; apply functionally; judge worth; and make the critical connections between new data and past experience (see Figure 2).

THE LOOK OF THE LOG

The writing in the thinking log may take many forms. It may be a narrative, a quote, an essay, jottings, a drawing, a cartoon, a diagram, webs or clusters, a soliloquy, a riddle, a joke, doodles,

Figure 2
A Series of Entries on a Single Concept: Bias

an opinion, a rebuttal, a dialogue, a letter, a flow chart, or just an assortment of phrases and ideas (see Figures 3 and 4).

The entries may be reflective, evaluative, questioning, personal, abstract, introspective, cynical, incomplete, revealing, humorous, communicative, thoughtful, poetic, rambling, formative, philosophical, or none of the above. There are no right or wrong ways to do the log. It's just a log of one's thinking—whatever that thinking may be. It's a personal record of the connections being made within the framework of students' cognitive capacities and experiences (see Figure 5).

Figure 3
Sketches of Thinking Log Entries

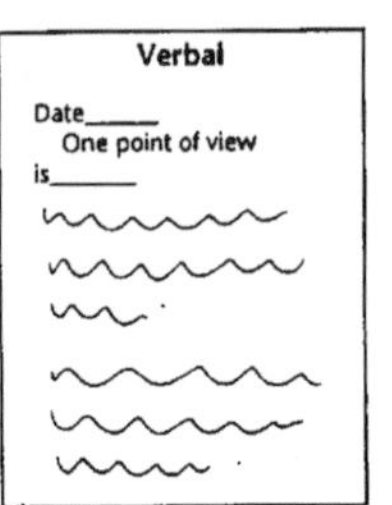

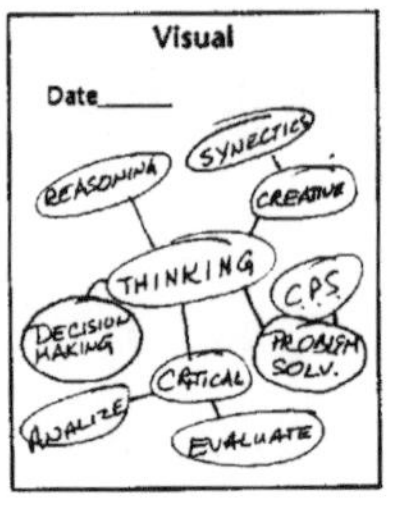

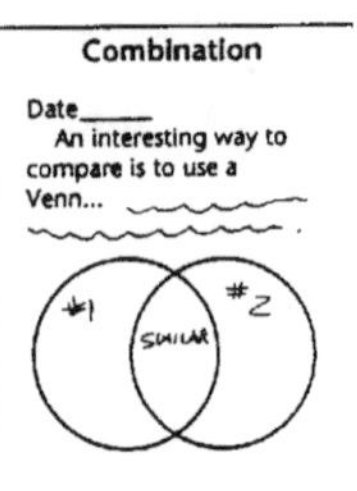

Figure 4
Visual and Verbal Thinking Log Entries

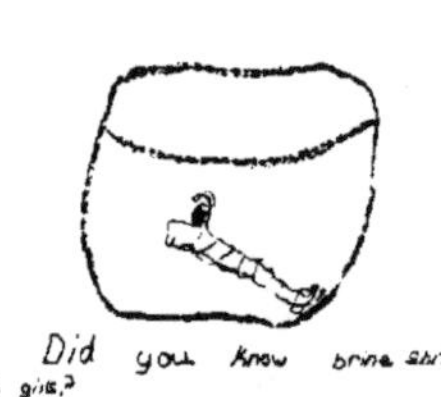

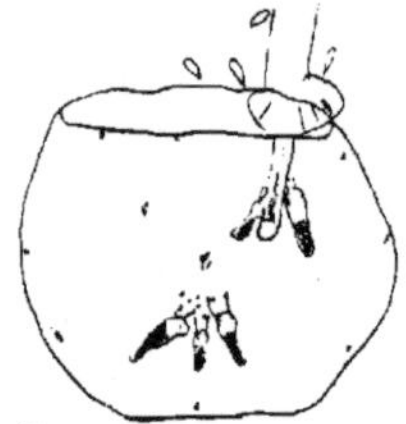

Figure 5
Entries Sampled from Several Students

RECORDING

WHAT A MAN IS IS THE BASIS OF WHAT HE DREAMS AND THINKS, ACCEPTS AND REJECTS, FEELS AND PERCEIVES.

JOHN MASON BROWN

Drug pushers are like Hallmark Cards. They will tell you anything to make a sale.

Taking drugs is like living under a dictator. You never feel like you are in control of your life.

A TIME TO THINK

The few minutes immediately following a lesson are ideal for using the thinking log. This transitional time allows flexibility for the fast finishers and for the students who need a minute or two more.

The log may be used solely in one subject area or as a focused follow-up at randomly selected spots on the lessons presented throughout the day. It can be structured formally with designated sections for information or it can be informally structured through student preference and use (see Figure 6).

Figure 6
Log Entries in One Subject Area

(We put some soil in a cup and watered it. I think it will grow in 10 days.)

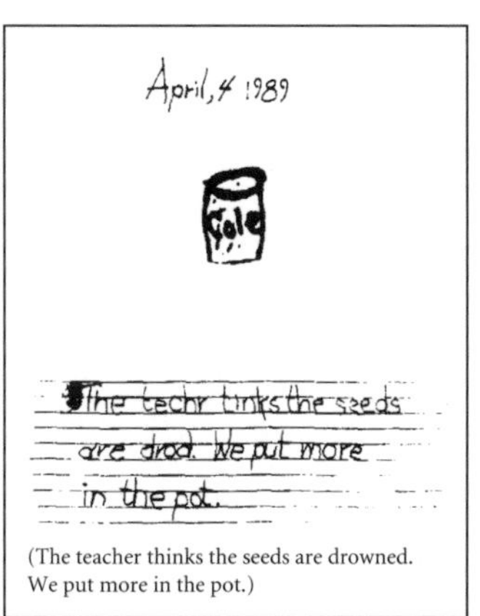

(The teacher thinks the seeds are drowned. We put more in the pot.)

(My plant is not growing. All I see is dirt in the pot.)

(No plants today.)

LEAD-INS FOR LOGGING

Thinking log lead-ins can draw students into higher-level thinking processes and provide the versatility needed to develop alternative patterns for thinking. The lead-in dictates to some degree the mode of thought. For example lead-ins can encourage responses that are analytic, synthetic, or evaluative. They can also be used to promote problem solving and decision making or to foster a particular style of learning. Figures 7, 8, and 9 suggest some possibilities to illustrate the focus flexibility of lead-ins.

Figure 7
Lead-Ins That Promote Thinking at Higher Levels

Analysis

- Compared to . . .
- The best part . . .
- On the positive side . . .
- An interesting part is . . .
- Take a small part like . . .
- A logical sequence seems to be . . .
- On the negative side . . .
- Similarly . . .
- By contrast . . .

Synthesis

- Suppose . . .
- Combine . . .
- Possibly . . .
- Imagine . . .
- Reversed . . .
- What if . . .
- I predict . . .
- How about . . .
- I wonder . . .

Evaluation

- How . . .
- Why . . .
- It seems important to note . . .
- The best . . .
- The worst . . .
- If ___ then . . .

Application

- Backtracking for a minute . . .
- A way to . . .
- I want to . . .
- A connecting idea is . . .
- A movie this reminds me of is ___ because . . .
- If this were a book, I'd title it . . .
- I think this applies to . . .
- Does this mean . . .

Problem solving

- I'm stuck on . . .
- The best way to think about this . . .
- I conclude . . .
- I'm lost with . . .
- I understand, but . . .
- I'm concerned about . . .
- My problem is . . .
- A question I have is . . .

Decision making

- I disagree with ___ because . . .
- I prefer ___ because . . .
- If I had to choose . . .
- I believe . . .
- My goal is . . .
- I hate . . .
- One criticism is . . .
- I can't decide if . . .

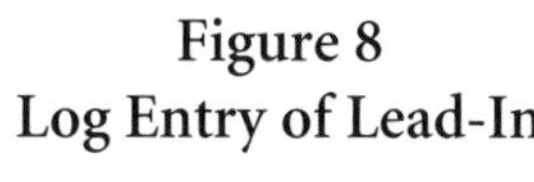

Figure 8
Log Entry of Lead-In

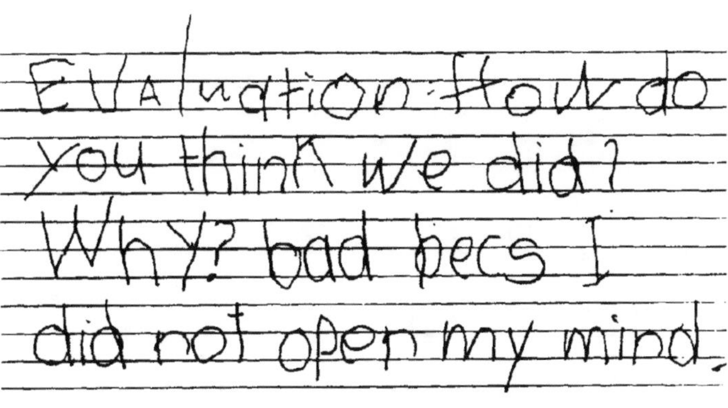

Figure 9
Lead-Ins That Promote Different Styles of Thinking

Visual Representations

- Try to visualize . . .
- My picture of this . . .
- A diagram of this idea looks like . . .
- I feel like . . .
- A chart . . .
- I'm ___ like ___ because . . .
- A map of my perception of this is . . .
- This cartoon . . .

Verbal Representations

- Another way of saying this is . . .
- I learned . . .
- I discovered . . .
- A quote that seems to fit is . . .
- I want to read ___ because . . .
- I want to talk to ___ because . . .
- I want to ask ___ about . . .
- Synonyms to describe . . .

As students grapple with new material and struggle with fleeting, disconnected thoughts, the thinking log helps students in yet another way. Students begin to become aware of the thought process itself. Again, the sensitive teacher captures the moment by prodding students to think about their thinking in deliberate and intentional metacognitive discussions. Kids start to see that they do have patterns for thinking as they find the words to articulate their thought processes. They assign labels to these processes, labels that identify strategies like reasoning by analogy, classification, logical thought, and intuitive leaps.

Figure 10
Log Entries That Promote Problem Solving

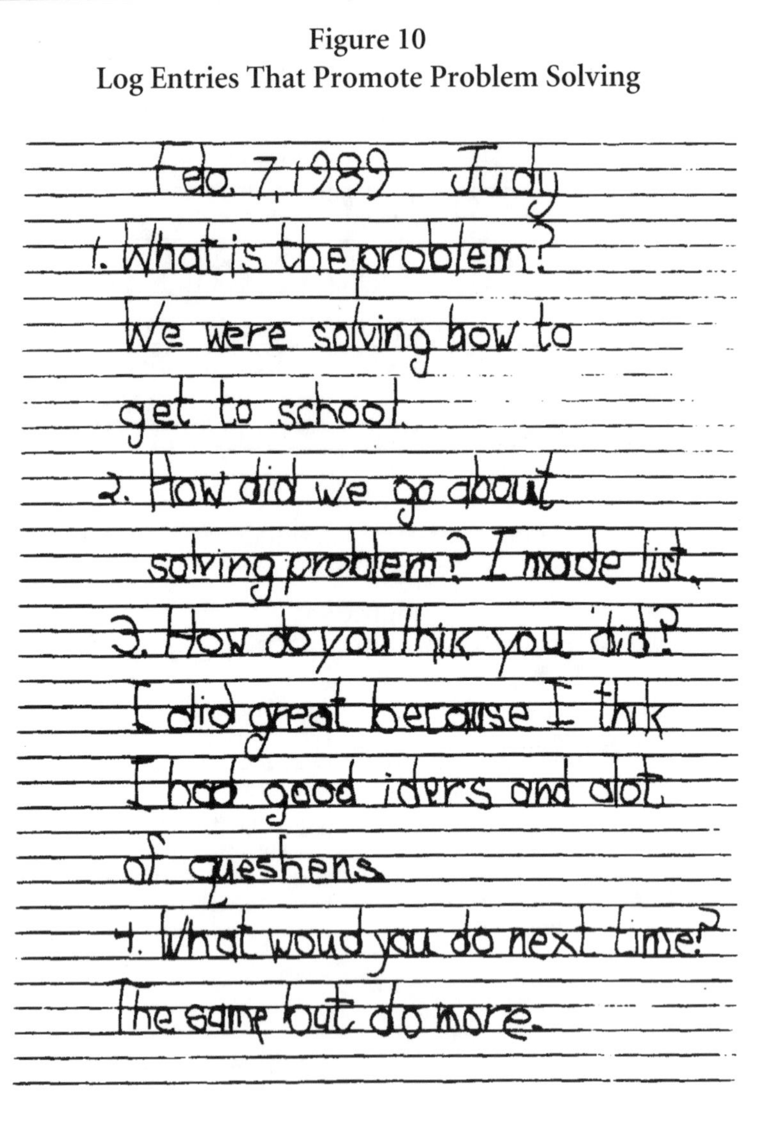

Feb. 7, 1989 Judy

1. What is the problem?
We were solving how to get to school.
2. How did we go about solving problem? I made list.
3. How do you thik you did?
I did great because I thik I had good iders and alot of queshens
4. What woud you do next time?
The same but do more.

They begin to choose HOW they want to process new ideas. They begin to build a repertoire of thinking patterns as they express their ideas in writing. In short, they begin inking their thinking.

The log also becomes an indicator for instructional assessment, as teachers note the inner language of the thinking mind, for the students have deliberately and consciously been given modern society's most precious commodity—time: time to think; time to wrestle, even if but momentarily, with new ideas; time to grasp threads of information and begin to weave them into the tapestry of personal experiences.

TRACKING THE INKING OF OUR THINKING

Initially, students log their thinking and record an immediate reaction to an experience. In a later reading, they have a chance to ponder the first interpretation and to modify or enhance it with a seasoned second look. In the final analysis, they have logged evidence to learn about *how they think*. Their favored patterns for thinking are revealed as they leaf through their logs. And that, perhaps, is the most significant outcome of all: kids that can articulate not only *what* they are thinking, but *how* they arrive at that thinking . . . for they have a log of their thinking (see Figure 10).

Figure 11
Reflective Log Entries

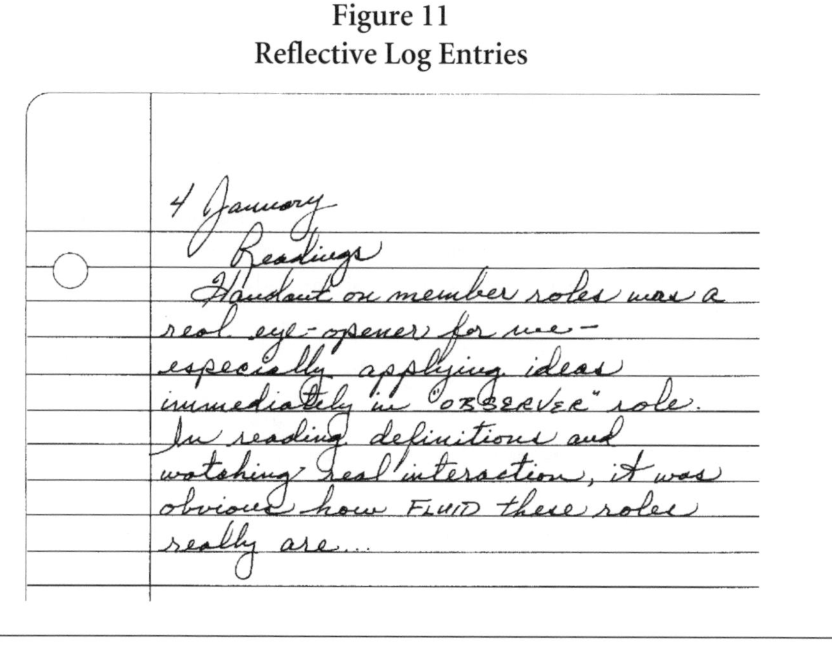

4 January
Readings
Handout on member roles was a real eye-opener for me— especially applying ideas immediately in "OBSERVER" role. In reading definitions and watching real interaction, it was obvious how FLUID these roles really are...

Figure 12
Log Entry Dialogue

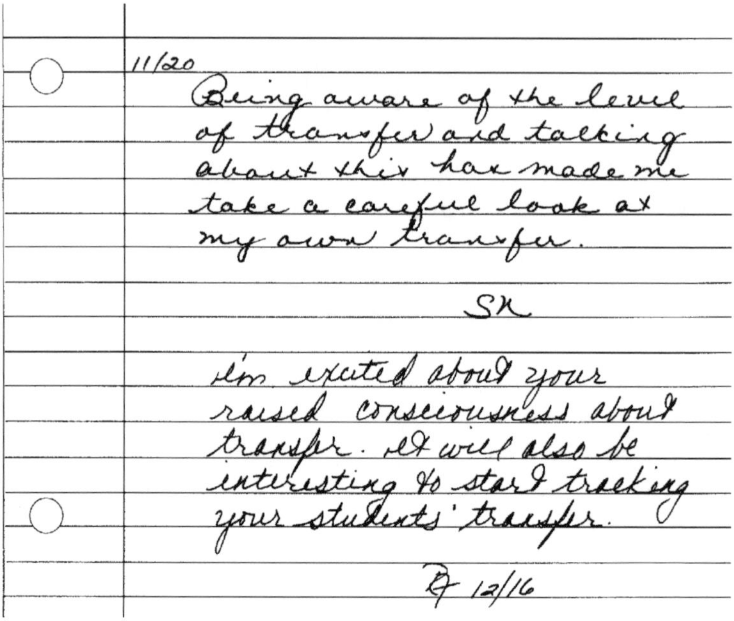

11/20

Being aware of the level of transfer and talking about this has made me take a careful look at my own transfer.

SK

I'm excited about your raised consciousness about transfer. It will also be interesting to start tracking your students' transfer.

RF 12/16

LOGS FOR ADULT LEARNING

One last note about thinking logs concerns the value of this reflective tool for both youngsters and adults. Using the thinking log concept as a means of processing ideas is becoming a common practice in staff development. Both individual reflection and peer-partner dialogues are viable models (see Figures 11 and 12).

REFERENCES

Applebee, A. (1984, Winter). Writing and reasoning. *Review of Educational Research,* pp. 577–596.

Bellanca, J., and Fogarty, R. (1989). *Patterns For Thinking: Patterns For Transfer.* Palatine, IL: IRI/Skylight Publishing.

Costa, A. L. (1984, November). Mediating the metacognitive. *Educational Leadership,* pp. 57–62.

Crowhurst, M. (1979, October). The writing workshop: An experiment in peer response writing. *Language Arts,* pp. 757–762.

Elbow, P. (1973). *Writing with power.* New York: University Press.

Elbow, P. (1973). *Writing without teachers.* New York: Oxford University Press.

Fulweiler, T., & Young, A. (Eds.). (1982). *Language connection: Writing and reading across the curriculum.* Urbana, IL: National Council of Teachers of English.

Healy, M. K. (1984). *Writing in a science class: A case study of the connection between writing and learning.* Doctoral dissertation, New York University Press.

Killian, J. P., & Todnem, G. R. (1989, Summer). Mentorship through journal writing as a means of professional development for staff developers. *Journal of Staff Development,* pp. 22–26.

Mayher, J. S., Lester, N. B., & Pradl, G. M. (1983). *Learning to write/Writing to learn.* Upper Montclair, NJ: Boynton-Cook.

Moffett, J., & Wagner, B. J. (1976). *Student-centered language arts & reading, K–13.* 2nd ed. Boston: Houghton-Mifflin.

Rico, G. L. (1983). *Writing the natural way.* Boston: J. P. Tarcher.

Sanders, A. (1985, February). Learning logs: A communication strategy for all subject areas. *Educational Leadership,* p. 7.

Wotring, A. M., & Tierney, R. (1982). *Using writing to learn science.* Berkeley, CA: Bay Area Writing Project, University of California.

The Portfolio Connection: Real World Examples

by Robin Fogarty, Kay Burke, and Susan Belgrad

The object of education is to prepare the young to educate themselves throughout their lives.—Robert Maynard Hutchins

The quest for more authentic assessments to complement the more traditional measures of evaluation is manifested in the concept of learner portfolios. While the portfolio itself focuses on the *products* of the learner's efforts, in current practice, the emphasis is also on the *process* of portfolio development (Wolf, 1989).

In fact, it is the process, in its simplest form, that becomes the focus. This process encompasses three macrophases: collection, selection, and reflection (Hamm, 1991). For the teacher who is beginning the adventure with portfolio assessment, these three stages are the basic steps needed for portfolio development. As the process becomes more clearly defined, however, a number of secondary phases come into play.

The complete list of options for portfolio development include ten considerations (see Figure 1).

In this discussion, each phase of the process opens with a real-world example and ends with a listing of ideas for immediate use. While some of the scenarios present examples of portfolio development in the *classroom*, others illustrate similar uses in the *staff room*. However, whether used with the student learners or as a professional development tool, "the portfolio connection" is an important intersection between instruction and assessment in today's schools (Paulson, Paulson, & Meyers, 1991).

Figure 1
Portfolio Development Options

1. PROJECT purposes and uses
2. COLLECT and organize
3. SELECT valued artifacts
4. INTERJECT personality
5. REFLECT metacognitively
6. INSPECT and self-assess goals
7. PERFECT, evaluate, and grade (if you must)
8. CONNECT and conference
9. INJECT AND EJECT to update
10. RESPECT accomplishments and show with pride

PROJECT PURPOSES AND USES

In Whitby, Ontario, an instructional facilitator for the Durham Board of Education, immerses teachers in portfolio use by having them keep portfolios of their own. They gather items from their teaching over a predetermined period of time and meet periodically for discussion. By experiencing the process, teachers are able to "walk the talk" about the essential elements of portfolios as assessment tools. As a result, they are better able to share their expertise with both the students and the parents.

To ensure effective use of the portfolio, it is critical that teachers look at the "big picture" to determine the many uses of portfolios. They need to ask hard questions: Why involve the students in the ongoing process of gathering artifacts? How are the portfolios going to be used? What is the real purpose? What are the potential uses, overuses, and abuses of portfolios for assessment purposes and beyond?

The purposes of portfolios tend to fall into three distinct categories: personal, academic, and professional (Burke, Fogarty, & Belgrad, 1994). Of course, within each of these broad categories, a range of models exist (see Figure 2).

Figure 2
Portfolio Models

Personal	Academic	Professional
Hobbies	Graded	College Admission
Collections	Integrated	Employability
Scrapbooks	Cooperative	Performance Review
Journals	Multi-year	

COLLECT AND ORGANIZE

At a conference in Battle Creek, Michigan, one teacher shared how her primary students are proud of the personally tailored, family-size cereal box portfolios they bring into the classroom, decorate, and use to store artifacts of their work. Easily obtained, just the right size, handy, and accessible for the students, these cereal box portfolios are marvelously versatile starter kits. Both the children and the teacher regularly add items to the portfolio, which are akin to student mailboxes. Periodically, artifacts are sorted and weeded out as the boxes become too full.

Students start the ongoing process of gathering and collecting their work for possible inclusion in their final portfolios. Deciding how to put things together for easy reference and logical continuity requires a number of considerations including the *type of container* (notebook, box, envelope, file folder, or photo album); the *labeling technique* (tabs, table of contents, or registry); the *order of things* (sequential, prioritized, thematic, or random); and, of course, the *overall look* of the collection (academic, aesthetic, personal, or eclectic). Order reigns over chaos when the number and assortment of things can easily be managed using these ideas (see Figure 3).

SELECT VALUED ARTIFACTS

Jane Franklin, an instructional facilitator for the Durham Board of Education in Ontario, leads a study group comprised of primary teachers who are interested in learning about portfolios. To help them understand the selection process, as applied to portfolio

Figure 3
Portfolio Organization Options

Storage	**Flow**	**Tools**
Hanging file	Collecting	Tabs
Colored folder	Selecting	Colored dots
Accordion folder	Reflecting	Table of contents
Cereal boxes	Perfecting	Registry
Computer disks	Connecting	Labels
Notebooks		Index

management, she uses the "book shelf" activity. Each teacher is asked to select a representational sampling of books from her personal collection to share with the group. Interestingly, as the teachers mull over their selections, they invariably begin to selectively abandon some of their favorites in order to give a true representation. Teachers simulate this activity with students, asking them to select from their collections of shells, stamps, or coins as they prepare for portfolio selection.

Selection is to abandonment as *collection* is to abundance. Decisions must be made about the context and contents of the portfolio based on the intent and purposes that the portfolio serves. Alignment to the goals and standards must be considered. Periodically, candidate artifacts must face the election process. Decisions must be made and the final vote taken as nominated items are included and excluded.

General guidelines may state the number of items, the type, stages and phases, variety and/or personal choices. Key words that guide that selection process are "Who?" "When?" and "What?" (see Figure 4).

INTERJECT PERSONALITY

In the Richmond Schools in British Columbia, an art teacher requires students to create a portfolio of work for the cartooning class. Throughout the semester, students keep a journal of ideas for cartoon characters. Students also collect finished products and artifacts in an art portfolio (much like designers, architects, illustrators,

Figure 4
Guiding Questions for Selection

Who?	**When?**	**What?**
Self-select	Parent conference	Representative work
Teacher selects	Quarters	Best work
Student and teacher select	Semesters	Significant work
Peers	End of year	Work in progress
Juried	Cumulative	Biography of work

photographers, fashion designers, and political cartoonists keep). Students in the cartooning class review and preview their work over time and interject their personal touches to the collection for the semester end submittal.

Each portfolio is as unique as one's fingerprint. No two look exactly alike, even if they contain similar elements, because the student tailors the look of the portfolio to reflect an up-close-and-personal view that allows a more intimate look at the total person.

Some say that the portfolio, in fact, is a window into the personality, skills, and talents of its owner. Typically, one interjects personality and pizzazz into the portfolio through several critical elements, including the cover, the organizational scheme, the page layout, and the mood or tone reflected in the content and design (see Figure 5).

Figure 5
Interjecting Personality in Portfolios

Cover	**Organization**	**Page Layout**	**Mood/Tone**
Color	Shape	Straight	Humorous
Design	Size	Geometric	Serious
Texture	Type	Cluster	Aesthetic
Style	File or pile	Threads	Technical

Figure 6
Stages of Metacognitive Reflection

Planning	**Monitoring**	**Evaluating**
Imagery	Labeling	Registering
Strategic Plan	Self-Questioning	Anecdotal Stories

REFLECT METACOGNITIVELY

As part of the district's partnership project, one teacher took a three-day visit to schools in Vermont. She returned to her school in Pickering, Ontario, with a wealth of knowledge, information, and practical strategies for implementing portfolios in her math classes. In fact, she put together a handbook to guide the development of the portfolios and to promote genuine understanding of math concepts and problem-solving models for her grade 9 "transition years" students. Often, throughout the portfolio development, students are required to comment on their metacognitive thinking by responding to thought-provoking statements about their best work and how math portfolios might be improved (Bower, 1994).

The true essence of the student portfolio is revealed as the students highlight the subtleties of the selected work. Each piece needs several metacognitive moments: moments when the student surveys her portfolio plan, monitors and adjusts her collection to date, and evaluates the value of each artifact, both as an individual piece and in the grand scheme of things. One relatively easy way to do this is to label each piece and provide the needed rationale. These labels provide the running monologue that brings the portfolio alive at various stages of metacognitive reflection (see Figure 6).

INSPECT AND SELF-ASSESS GOALS

On Chicago's West Side, a neighborhood school (K–8) has embraced the visual and performing arts as its focus for integrating the curricula. One innovative technique teachers employ is videotaped assessment. Each student is given a videotape that is donated by a local firm. Each student is taped participating in significant

Figure 7
Portfolio Inspection Steps

Getting Started	Goal Setting	Final Decisions
Use stem statements	Logs	Standards
Build checklist	Journals	Criteria
Set criteria	Learning lists	Rubric
Develop scoring rubrics	Double-entry journal	Best work
Give feedback	Reflective journal	Significant work
Review standards		Representative work

schoolwide and classroom events. The tape travels back and forth to the home and school as the student shares highlights of her school day with her family.

The student inspects her entire collection of work for insights. This time is designated for the student to review both long-term and short-term goals and to note strengths and weaknesses.

This stage is aptly labeled "inspect" because the student self-evaluates her overall direction and focus. It's the moment of truth that signals the learner whether or not she is on track and what measures might be needed to align with her aims and goals. There seem to be three distinct steps that help students to inspect: getting started, goal setting, and final decisions (see Figure 7).

PERFECT, EVALUATE, AND GRADE (IF YOU MUST)

A portfolio scoring rubric solves the ever-present problem of grading in a sixth grade class at a school in upstate New York. Using the rubric as a guide to evaluate the entire portfolio, students are clear on the criteria and indicators needed to obtain the grade they want (1=Not ready, 2=Acceptable, 3=Out of sight). Interestingly, the rubric is scored separately by both the teacher and the students. The students may improve each item and resubmit them for the final grade.

Figure 8
Portfolio Grading Options

Each Artifact	Selected	Entire Portfolio	Weighted Scores
Previously graded	Student selects	Rubric scoring	Predetermined
Item by item	Teacher selects	Holistic grade	Student decides
	Randomly chosen	Averaged grade	Teacher decides

In preparation for the portfolio conference with parents, students perfect their portfolios by adding finishing touches. At this stage, both the teacher and the student take a final look.

Students examine the entire portfolio with a special eye for inconsistencies, such as missing labels or torn or tattered artifacts, as well as for accuracy in the registry.

Teachers, on the other hand, often use this stage to evaluate the portfolio formally. They apply scoring rubrics and assign grades (or a grade) to the portfolio. In fact, the options for grading are surprisingly varied (see Figure 8).

CONNECT AND CONFERENCE

Students in a seventh grade class in Richmond, B.C., use their portfolios to help them prepare for three-way, student-led parent conferences. First, they survey the myriad artifacts in their collections to aid in their sketches of Venn diagrams that show how the subject-related items integrate with one another (see Figure 9). Then, using the portfolio itself and their Venn diagrams as notes, they actually lead the parent/teacher/student conference and share reflections of their work.

Student portfolios are assembled, arranged, rearranged, and refined in preparation for the portfolio conference. This is a crucial step in portfolio use as an assessment tool because, as students know, what is inspected is respected. If portfolios are to be valued as viable complements to more traditional assessments, they must be critiqued by others. The conference format offers a number of options (see Figure 10).

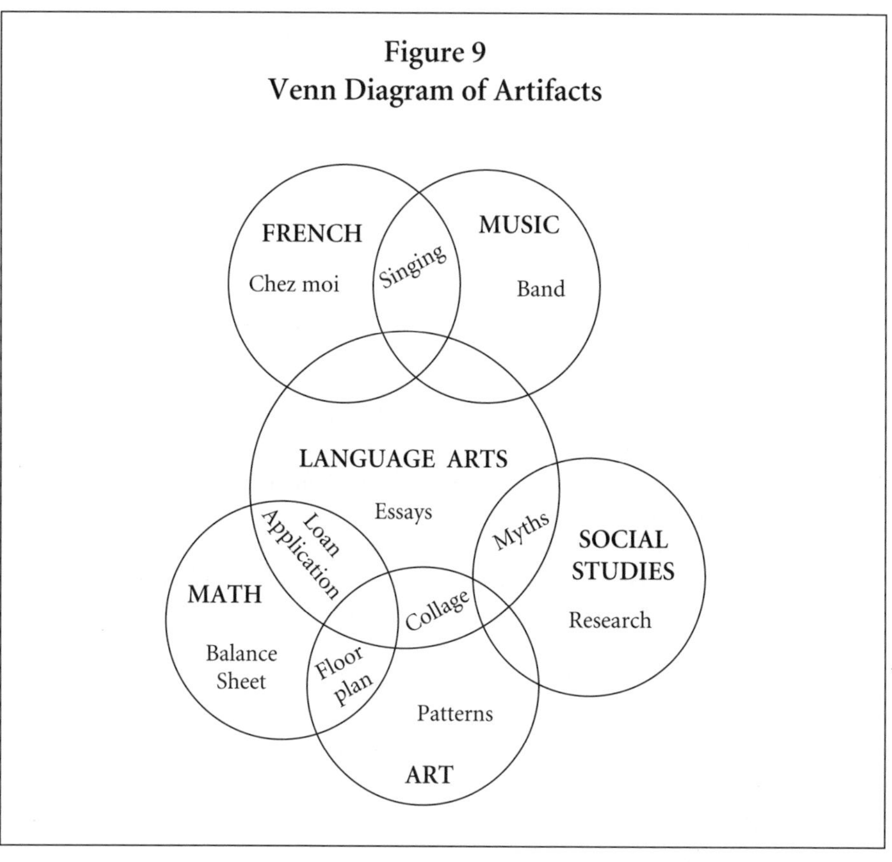

Figure 9
Venn Diagram of Artifacts

Figure 10
Portfolio Conference Options

Traditional	Student Conducted	Three-Way	Home
Teacher-led	Student prepares	Student/ Parent/ Teacher	Student/ Parent
Teacher-parent present	Student presents		

INJECT AND EJECT TO UPDATE

A manager at the southern consortium in San Diego, California, uses the Professional Development Portfolio *to evaluate the impact of staff development services and to assist planning teams in making strategic decisions.* The Teacher's Briefcase, *developed by*

Figure 11
Inject/Eject Options

Periodic	**Momentary**	**Shift in Focus**	**Spontaneous**
Routine	Make-over	Radical	Refresher
Predetermined	Purposeful	Change in direction	Spring cleaning
Intervals	Quick	Different effect	Unplanned

Mary Dietz, consists of three separate items: a journal with structured entry activities; a mini-guide that describes what to do; and a canvas bag to hold videotapes, student artifacts, and the journal. A critical element that gives teachers insight into managing portfolios is the artifact registry. This is a running record of artifacts logged in and logged out of the portfolio in order to keep the sheer number of items somewhat manageable. It also provides an at-a-glance inventory of items, which is a keen management technique (Dietz, 1991).

While the focus of the portfolio is often the parent conference, ideally the portfolio process extends beyond that immediate use and becomes a true collection of work over time that the student continues throughout her school career and beyond. People who use portfolios as part of the college entrance and career interview processes take great pains to continually inject and eject artifacts to update their portfolio and to reflect not only past, but also current work. There are several options for updating the portfolio (see Figure 11).

RESPECT ACCOMPLISHMENTS AND SHOW WITH PRIDE

Teachers in a field-based master's program in Wheeling, Illinois, use portfolio exhibitions to display "biographies of work" (Wolf, 1989), that depict the processes and products of their action research project. A site facilitator orchestrates the exhibition in the spring prior to the graduation ceremonies. The exhibition serves as a culminating activity in which teachers in the two-year program share their work with other professionals. First-year students in the program are invited to view the exhibits to prepare for their next year's work on their own master's projects.

Figure 12
Elements in a Portfolio Exhibition

Goal	**Audience**	**Time/Type**	**Media Options**
Summative	Parents	Browsing	Video
Formative	Peers	Presenting	Audio
Admission	Public	Responding	Computer disk
Employment	Mentors	Traveling	Slides
Commission	Apprentices	Group/ Individual	Multimedia

The primary purpose for portfolios in schools today is to enhance the assessment process. The actual artifacts of work are evidence of student development beyond the test score or arbitrary grade point average. Myriad uses for portfolios are beginning to surface, however, as their actual use becomes more prevalent. In fact, the student may find a portfolio exhibition to be a viable tool to use in certain circumstances.

The exhibition brings the work alive. As the student represents her pieces to others, the viewers gain valuable insight into the person behind the work. There are many points to consider in presenting one's portfolio at an exhibition (see Figure 12).

In the words of George Bernard Shaw, "what we want is to see the child in pursuit of knowledge, not knowledge in pursuit of the child." The portfolio connection and these real world examples illustrate that very concept.

REFERENCES

Belanoff, P., & Dickson, M. (1991). *Portfolios: Process and product.* Portsmouth, NH: Boyton & Cook Publishers.

Burke, K. (1994). *The mindful school: How to assess authentic learning.* Palatine, IL: IRI/Skylight Publishing.

Burke, K. (1992). *Authentic assessment: A collection.* Palatine, IL: IRI/Skylight Publishing.

Burke, K., Fogarty, R., & Belgrad, S. (1994). *The mindful school: The portfolio connection.* Palatine, IL: IRI/Skylight Publishing.

Costa, A., Bellanca, J., & Fogarty, R. (1992). *If minds matter: A foreword to the future*, vol. II. Palatine, IL: IRI/Skylight Publishing.

Dietz, M. E. (1991). *Professional Development Portfolio: Facilitator's Guide and Journal.* San Ramon, CA: Frameworks.

Gardner, H. (1993). *Multiple intelligences: The theory in practice.* New York: Basic Books.

Hamm, M., & Adams, D. (1991, May). Portfolio: It's not just for artists anymore. *The Science Teacher*, p. 18–21.

Hansen, J. (1992, May). Literacy portfolios: Helping students know themselves. *Educational Leadership*, pp. 66–68.

Kallick, B. (1992). Evaluation: A collaborative process. In A. L. Costa, J. A. Bellanca, & R. Fogarty (Eds.) *If minds matter: A foreword to the future, Vol. 2* (pp. 313–319). Palatine, IL: IRI/Skylight Publishing.

Stiggins, R. J. (1991, March). Assessment literacy. *Phi Delta Kappan*, pp. 534–539.

Paulson, F. L., Paulson, P. R., & Meyer, C. A. (1991, February). What makes a portfolio a portfolio? *Educational Leadership*, pp. 60–63.

Stiggins, R. J. (1985, October). Improving assessment where it means the most: In the classroom. *Educational Leadership*, pp. 69–74.

Wiggins, G. (1990, August). Put portfolios to the test. *Instructor*, p. 51.

Wolf, D. P. (1989, April). Portfolio assessment: Sampling student work. *Educational Leadership*, pp. 116, 35–38.

The Multiple Intelligences as Assessment Tools

by Robin Fogarty

How do we know what students know and can do if it doesn't show up on a pencil-and-paper task? How do students express themselves in other realms? How is the skill of the athlete appreciated within the walls of the classroom? How is musical talent displayed in traditional academic settings? What value do we give to the doodles, sketches, and designs that represent intricate intellectual interpretation? How does the comic or the actor express his knowledge?

To tap into the full range of human potential, Gardner's seven intelligences seem not only appropriate, but, in fact, perfectly tailored as *expressive tools* for today's classroom. Usually regarded as ways of knowing and learning, Gardner's intelligences are more than just *receptive tools.* Not only do students learn through the verbal, logical, visual, bodily, musical, interpersonal, and intrapersonal channels, but teachers can easily use the seven intelligences as tools of assessment and evaluation.

> **To tap into the full range of human potential, Gardner's seven intelligences seem . . . perfectly tailored as *expressive tools* for today's classroom.**

Using Ferrara and McTighe's "Framework for Assessment" (Costa et al, 1992, p. 340) and the multiple intelligences grid of activities and assessments (Burke et al, 1994, p. 36) to complete the Tri-Assessment Chart of Multiple Intelligences (see Figure 1), teachers have a ready reference to guide their assessment plans. By selecting a tool from each of the three major assessment categories, a trio of traditional, portfolio, and performance assessments are targeted to give balance and breadth to the evaluation process.

Figure 1
Tri-Assessment Chart of Multiple Intelligences

Assessment Category / Multiple Intelligences	Traditional	Portfolio (product/process)	Performance
Verbal	label a diagram; script; oral questions; biography; novel; short story	written essay, story, poem; bibliography; diary, journal	interview; monologue; dialogue; presentation
Logical	true/false test; symposiums; multiple choice test; outline; notecards	computer printout; research report; Venn diagram; matrices; time line; artifact registry	debate; argument; presentation; rubric; computer program
Visual	fill in the blank; figural representation; symbol; show your work; diagram; matching	storyboard; scrapbook; props; comics; art exhibit; pictures; concept map; photographs	videotape; slides; film
Bodily	model building; outdoor education; field trip	science fair project; models; lab results	science lab demo; dance, dramatic performance; typing demo; athletic competition; sport; game
Musical	mnemonics; rote memory; song; rhyming poem; choral reading	written rap, jingle, song, cheer	musical; instrumental demo; voice demo; audiotape; cheer; rap; jingle
Interpersonal	teacher comments; peer editing; pen pal; invitation	dialogue journal; cooperative learning product	wraparound; think aloud; e-mail; telephone conversation; student-led conference; round robin
Intrapersonal	open-ended essay; visualization; self-discovery; inquiry	goals statement; homework; rough drafts; self-assessment	monologue; portfolio presentation; student-planned conference

For example, a classroom unit on Invention adapts easily to the tri-assessment system and, at the same time, taps into a combination of intelligences. Students may sketch and label their invention in a traditional task and, at the same time, build on the invention as a semester-long project for the spring science fair. Pictures of the display become a viable part of a portfolio collection. To complete the trio of assessments, students demonstrate their invention and are graded on their performance with a scoring rubric.

Most will prefer to use the Tri-Assessment Chart of Multiple Intelligences by selecting three tools for each intelligence, moving horizontally across the columns. However, a look at the vertical columns is useful to reveal the categorical assortment of tools (see Figures 2, 3, and 4).

Figure 2
Traditional Tools
(pencil-and-paper tasks, tests)

Verbal	label a diagram; script; oral questions; biography; novel; short story
Logical	true/false test; symposiums; multiple choice test; outline; notecards
Visual	fill in the blank; figural representation; symbol; show your work; diagram; matching
Bodily	model building; outdoor education; field trip
Musical	mnemonics; rote memory; song; rhyming poem; choral reading
Interpersonal	teacher comments; peer editing; pen pal; invitation
Intrapersonal	open-ended essay; visualization; self-discovery; inquiry

Figure 3
Portfolio Tools
(visual artifacts, representational and real)

Verbal	written essay, story, poem; bibliography; diary, journal
Logical	computer printout; research report; Venn diagram; matrices; time line; artifact registry
Visual	storyboard; scrapbook; props; comics; art exhibit; pictures; concept map; photographs
Bodily	science fair project; models; lab results
Musical	written rap, jingle, song, cheer
Interpersonal	dialogue journal; cooperative learning product
Intrapersonal	goals statement; homework; rough drafts; self-assessment

Teachers who use the repertoire of assessment tools consistently target various combinations of the multiple intelligences. By including different intelligences as a component of the tri-assessment model, teachers inspect the full range of human potential.

The completed Tri-Assessment Chart of Multiple Intelligences is a handy reference, ready for immediate use. Yet, teachers may want to either add their own tools to the lists or create an entirely new chart, personally tailored to the tools they favor or tools that fit more appropriately with their curricular content.

In addition, using the Tri-Assessment Chart of Multiple Intelligences for its intended purpose—as a repertoire of assessment tools—teachers are reminded that many of these assessments are activities, too. Thus, the chart acts as an instructional

Figure 4
Performance Tools
(actions, demonstrations, presentations, performances)

Verbal	interview; monologue; dialogue; presentation
Logical	debate; argument; presentation; rubric; computer program
Visual	videotape; slides; film
Bodily	science lab demo; dance, dramatic performance; typing demo; athletic competition; sport; game
Musical	musical; instrumental demo; voice demo; audiotape; cheer; rap; jingle
Interpersonal	wraparound; think aloud; e-mail; telephone conversation; student-led conference; round robin
Intrapersonal	monologue; portfolio presentation; student-planned conference

focus as well as an assessment guide. In fact, that is exactly what authentic assessment is all about—real, hands-on application and use of ideas. Through authentic use, one easily assesses growth, development, and acquisition of knowledge as well as strengths and weaknesses in the seven intelligences areas.

REFERENCES

Bellanca, J., Chapman, C., & Swartz, B. (1994). *Multiple assessments for multiple intelligences.* Palatine, IL: IRI/Skylight Publishing.

Burke, K. (1994). *The mindful school: How to assess authentic learning.* Palatine, IL: IRI/Skylight Publishing.

Burke, K., Fogarty, R., & Belgrad, S. (1994). *The mindful school: The portfolio connection.* Palatine, IL: IRI/Skylight Publishing.

Costa, A., Bellanca, J., & Fogarty, R. (Eds.). (1992). *If minds matter: A foreword to the future, Vol. 2.* Palatine, IL: IRI/Skylight Publishing.

Gardner, H. (1993). *Multiple intelligences: The theory in practice.* New York: Harper Collins.

Gardner, H. (1983). *Frames of mind: The theory of multiple intelligences.* New York: Basic Books.

The Tri-Assessment Model

by Robin Fogarty and Judy Stoehr

In the process of integrating content by developing significant themes and by threading life skills through subject matter, the lines begin to blur between disciplines. While some blurring of disciplines is desirable in order to create holistic, project-oriented learning, too much blurring causes concern about valid assessments, grades, and traditional discipline-based evaluations. In many cases, schools that use authentic learning and the multiple intelligences to move toward an integrated curriculum continue to use traditional assessment measures to determine grades, grade-point averages, and rankings. However, these measures don't always match active, holistic learning models.

The tri-assessment model provides a reasonable compromise for teachers who are moving toward more authentic assessments, but are reluctant to totally abandon more traditional measures (see Figure 1). By *combining* portfolio and performance assessments with traditional assessments, a truer, more holistic look at students is permitted. Each assessment targets a focus as well as specific features that are practical and relevant to the total picture. Each assessment also utilizes multiple intelligences to assess a wider range of human potential.

Traditional assessment often focuses on grades, grade-point averages, and rankings. Included in traditional assessments are classwork, homework, criterion-referenced and standardized measures. Typically, traditional assessments tap

---

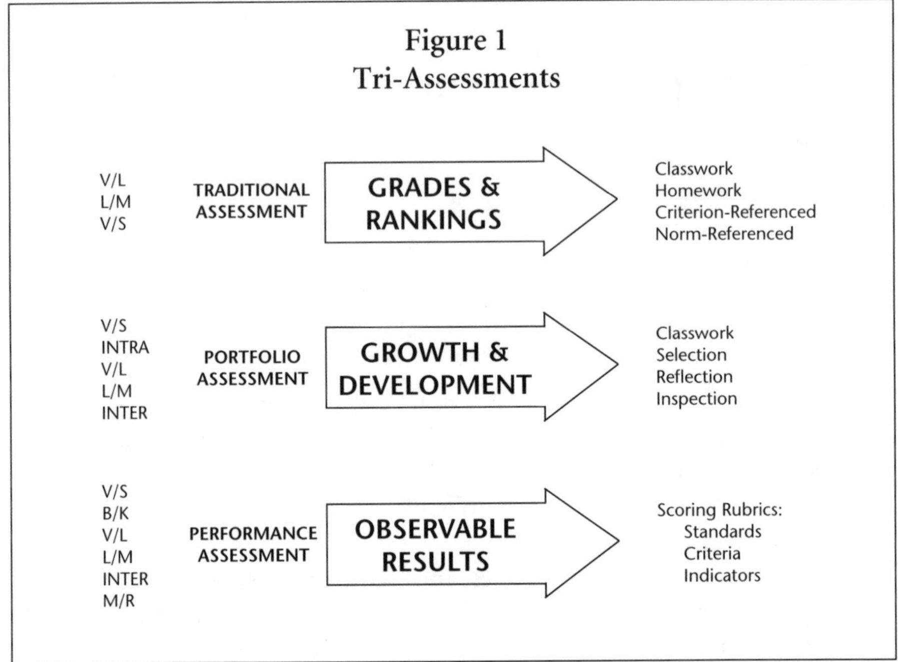

Figure 1
Tri-Assessments

Figure 2
Traditional Assessment

You Teach Me and Test Me

primarily the verbal/linguistic and the logical/mathematical intelligences, although the visual/spatial might also be included (see Figures 2 and 3).

Portfolio assessment, on the other hand, tends to focus on the growth and development of student potential. Phases of the portfolio development process include collecting and selecting items, reflecting on the significance of the items as indicators of growth, and inspecting the portfolio for signs of progress. Often, portfolio development calls into play the intrapersonal and interpersonal intelligences as well as the verbal, logical, and visual intelligences used in the traditional measures (see Figures 4 and 5).

Figure 3
Traditional Assessment: A Checklist

Multiple Intelligence	Classwork?
Interpersonal Verbal/Linguistic	❑ Participation? ______ ❑ Quality? ______ ❑ Frequency? ______ ❑ Written assignments? ______
	Homework?
Verbal/Linguistic Logical/Mathematical Visual/Spatial	❑ Is it done? On time? ______ ❑ Is it correct? Accurate? ______ ❑ Quality? ______
	Criterion-Referenced Tests and Quizzes?
Verbal/Linguistic Logical/Mathematical Visual/Spatial	❑ Type? ______ ❑ Weight? ______ ❑ Accuracy? ______ ❑ Completed? ______ ❑ Quality? ______
	Norm-Referenced Tests?
Verbal/Linguistic Logical/Mathematical Visual/Spatial	❑ Class rank ______ ❑ School rank ______ ❑ District rank ______ ❑ State/national/international rank ______

Figure 4
Portfolio Assessment

Let Me Show You

Figure 5
Portfolio Assessment: A Checklist

Multiple Intelligence	Collection:
Visual/Spatial	❑ Over time? ______
Logical/Mathematical	❑ Number? ______
Verbal/Linguistic	❑ Types? ______
	❑ Quality? ______
	❑ Other? ______
	Selection:
Logical/Mathematical	❑ Required pieces ______
Visual/Spatial	❑ Self-selected ______
	❑ Number ______
	❑ Type ______
	❑ Quality ______
	Reflection:
Logical/Mathematical	❑ Rationale? (Why?) ______
Intrapersonal	❑ Context? (Fit?) ______
Visual/Spatial	❑ Elaboration? ______
Verbal/Linguistic	❑ Completed? ______
	❑ Quality? ______
	Inspection:
Interpersonal	❑ Long-term goals ______
Intrapersonal	❑ Short-term goals ______
	❑ Overall ______

Performance assessment focuses on the direct observance of a student's performance. Procedures for using performance assessment effectively include developing scoring rubrics and using predetermined standards, criteria, and indicators. With this assessment, the bodily intelligence becomes a vehicle for showing what a student knows and can do. The visual, verbal, logical, musical, and interpersonal intelligences are also critical components (see Figures 6 and 7).

Figure 6
Performance Assessment

Let Me Do It

Figure 7
Performance Assessment: A Checklist

Multiple Intelligence	**Standards:**
Bodily/Kinesthetic	❑ Goals? ____________
Visual/Spatial	❑ Aims? ____________
Verbal/Linguistic	❑ Objectives? ____________
Logical/Mathematical	
Musical/Rhythmic	**Criteria:**
Interpersonal	
Intrapersonal	❑ Quality? (Completeness) ____________
	❑ Quantity? (Time lines) ____________
	Indicators:
	❑ Range ____________
	❑ High ____________
	❑ Medium ____________
	❑ Low ____________

A WORD ABOUT RUBRICS

Traditional measures as well as portfolio and performance assessments rely on preestablished standards and criteria; therefore, it follows that these criteria dictate how progress is shown. A scoring rubric is a typical tool used to fairly evaluate student growth (see Figure 8). This rubric suggests criteria and indicators to judge the themes and threads established by teacher teams. Using this model, other scoring rubrics can easily be constructed to fit appropriate student contexts.

Figure 8
Scoring Rubric Example

Criteria for Theme/Thread ________________			
Relevancy (Real)	Inert Knowledge	Relates to Student	Real-World Application
Rigor (Hot)	"Pour and Store"	Challenge	Struggle
Richness (Multi-dimensional)	Superficial	Contrived	Breadth and Depth

Extrapolated from Doll, 1993, and ASCD/IMSA Consortium for Interdiscipline, Atlanta, 1994.

REFERENCES

Bellanca, J., Chapman, C., & Swartz, B. (1994). *Multiple assessments for multiple intelligences.* Palatine, IL: IRI/Skylight Publishing.

Burke, K. (1994). *The mindful school: How to assess authentic learning.* Palatine, IL: IRI/Skylight Publishing.

Burke, K., Fogarty, R., & Belgrad, S. (1994). *The mindful school: The portfolio connection.* Palatine, IL: IRI/Skylight Publishing.

Doll, W. (1993). Curriculum possibilities in a "post-future." *Journal of Curriculum and Supervision, 8*(4), 270–292.

Gardner, H. (1983). *Frames of mind: The theory of multiple intelligences.* New York: Basic Books.

Vignettes: Jagged Profiles

by Robin Fogarty and Judy Stoehr

Using Gardner's seven intelligences, the following seven vignettes profile human potential, including a six-year-old entering first grade, a college student majoring in education, and an adult learner changing careers. These vignettes clearly show that humans each have a jagged profile as unique as their fingerprints. Notice that there is not *one* intelligence that is highlighted, but a number of different intelligences that interact with one another.

These vignettes clearly show that humans each have a jagged profile as unique as their fingerprints.

JUANITA (SIX YEARS OLD)

Juanita is labeled "gifted" in the first grade. Not only can she read at the age of six, she has also completed the trilogy of *The Hobbit.* Her vast vocabulary is evident in her speech and writing, and she can spell spaghetti as easily as cat. She loves both nonfiction and the classic literature her father introduced her to. Juanita's verbal skills are extraordinary and her teachers are challenged to keep her moving forward in this area.

Accompanying Juanita's forte for verbalization is her naturally developed musical intelligence, an intelligence Gardner classifies as language-related. Schooled in the Suzuki method from the age of three, Juanita is an accomplished pianist. Her repertoire of classical pieces is impressive, and one senses Juanita's immersion in her performances. In fact, when she plays the piano, she's happier all day. This musical intelligence

---

Adapted from *Integrating Curricula with Multiple Intelligences: Teams, Themes, and Threads*, pp. 43–48.

spills over into her written work. She writes about the piano and illustrates many of her ideas with musical notes.

Paints, crayons, chalk, and pastels are the favorite tools of this image-conscious youngster. Illustrations fill her written works, regardless of their content. Her science paper is filled with progressive sketches of her beans growing in the window, and her morning sentences and stories are accented with detailed drawings that enhance her words. Even Juanita's printing and lettering are elaborated with scrolls, swirls, and squiggles, and decorative engravings border her daily work. Juanita's images are so strong that she converses with an imaginary friend and playmate, Bunny. Yet, when someone else acknowledges the existence of Bunny, Juanita giggles and says, "Oh, he's only pretend."

Lupe's amazing sense of logic is complemented by his keenness for visualizing. By picturing possible moves of game pieces, he can "see" the outcomes.

LUPE (EIGHT YEARS OLD)

Lupe, a third grader, is proficient at the highly complex game of Dungeons and Dragons. Beginning with the strategic logic of chess, Lupe quickly moved into the voluminous paraphernalia and many layers of the Dungeons and Dragons episodes. Also indicative of his logical reasoning is his fascination with nonfiction. Lupe often plows through encyclopedia entries, moving from the top of a page right on through to the last entry on the page. His ability with numbers is phenomenal. He makes computations in his head and calls out answers that are usually verified by his calculator.

Lupe's amazing sense of logic is complemented by his keenness for visualizing. Even at a young age, he took an unusual interest in his clothes and often selected colorful sweaters to wear with matching socks and coordinated shirts to assemble a look that was pleasing. Connected closely to his skillful and strategic logic in gamesmanship is this ability to visualize. By picturing possible moves of game pieces, he can "see" the outcomes. His mind's eye, in effect, directs his play.

Lupe prefers to be alone with his books, games, and creative toys. He likes to invent electronic devices and gadgets such as burglar alarms, and he likes to experiment with chemistry sets and the like. Lupe is well aware of his own inquisitiveness as well as his likes and dislikes. He appears comfortable with himself and often explains his motivations to his parents. Knowing himself at such a young age, Lupe shows that he has an unusual propensity for self-reflection.

ALICIA (TEN YEARS OLD)

If there isn't music or rhythm where Alicia is, she creates her own! At the age of ten, she is taking keyboard lessons and willingly practices an hour every day after school. She loves music in school and has already starred in two musical performances. Alicia and her family live several miles from the nearest large city, which suits her just fine because her family sings and harmonizes all the way there and back.

Alicia's teachers know how much she loves music. When they see her tapping her toe or pencil, they often ask what song she's singing in her head. She is very proud of the perfect score she recently received on a name-the-states test. She gives credit to the song "Fifty Nifty United States," which lists every state alphabetically. Her teacher agrees that the song must have helped, because he noticed that during the test Alicia's head nodded in a steady beat before she wrote each answer.

When she is not creating or practicing her music, Alicia is off and running. Her parents enrolled her in dance at the age of four. She wants to learn to twirl the baton so that she can become the majorette for the band when she is older. Her favorite day at school is "Track and Field Day," where she enters almost every event. She especially enjoys jumping the hurdles. Settling down seems to take longer for Alicia than some of her classmates and sitting for long periods of time is sheer torture! She loves being teacher's helper and volunteers to help set up centers, perform science experiments, play classroom instruments, and anything else that involves active learning.

When Alicia's pencil isn't tapping out a beat, it is usually drawing or doodling. She loves making collages and mobiles and understands best when her teacher uses graphics such as semantic maps and Venn diagrams. Alicia has found that "making pictures in her head," as she calls it, helps her to understand and remember what she is learning. She first discovered the powerful effect of visualizing when she had to a memorize a piano solo for recital. She had practiced and practiced, but when she sat down on the piano bench, her mind went blank. She couldn't even remember the name of her solo! Alicia looked straight ahead, wishing there were some music in front of her. Suddenly, she could "see" it, every page of it, in her head, and by the time she finished playing her solo flawlessly, she even remembered its title!

TREVOR (TWELVE YEARS OLD)

Trevor is a seventh grader who is just as proud of his collection of doodles and pictures as he is of his good grades. Many of his drawings are done during school in classes that are lecture-based or "just plain boring," as Trevor puts it. Others are a result of long hours of detailed work on sketches and designs. While his classmates make simple book covers, Trevor creates covers with intricate and complex geometrical designs or cartoon characters.

Trevor is drawn to classrooms that are picture rich. Slides, mobiles, photos, overhead transparencies, and other visuals that reinforce the lesson make all the difference in his motivation and understanding. He is easily frustrated by an overdose of words, whether he's reading, writing, or listening to them. His frustration about long writing assignments quickly changes to excitement, however, when he is encouraged to include visuals. He doesn't seem to mind doing required research or writing if he can express himself through his drawings and pictures. Trevor's teacher can identify Trevor's reports without his name because they always have one picture on the front, one on the back, and several throughout.

Trevor spends most of his free time putting together and painting models. Watching him work is truly a "moving" experience, because he begins at a table, then lies on the floor, then stands. He loves math class this year because, as he says, the teacher "keeps us really busy when we learn. We move around to different centers and use manipulatives."

Trevor is definitely not a social butterfly. He couldn't care less about having a wide circle of friends. Instead, he has a small group of close friends and is happy to spend time alone. His mental and physical well-being are very important to him, as is his academic achievement. Trevor tried out several groups and organizations in school before he settled on OM (Odyssey of the Mind). He seems to have found his niche: the sponsor says that when the group is working on a problem, Trevor seems to be able to visualize what is needed to solve it. Then he goes off by himself and makes a prototype, which the group refines and develops.

TRACY (SIXTEEN YEARS OLD)

Tracy, a high school junior, is on the pompon squad and in the swing choir. She takes dance lessons and also helps teach dance to young children. Tracy operates video equipment for her parents and sets the VCR when anyone in the family wants to record something. She loves to go on errands, whether for teachers or her parents, especially if it means driving the car.

Tracy seems to have an endless supply of energy when she is interested and motivated. She is always ready to pitch in on special school and classroom projects.

Tracy seems to have an endless supply of energy when she is interested and motivated. She is always ready to pitch in on special school and classroom projects. At other times, when she has been sitting too long or when the entire class is engaged in quiet reading, she gets fidgety. Only the teachers who understand Tracy know to suggest that she stand up or move.

Music is a large part of Tracy's world. In addition to being on the pompon squad and singing in the swing choir, Tracy plays the piano, sings in the concert choir, and knows every song from the musical her school put on last year. Her current kick in preferred style is country, but that changes fairly regularly. She begs to see every musical production that comes to town, and she can sing or rap to every commercial. If it were up to Tracy, music would be piped into every classroom as a background to learning. It's never off in her bedroom!

Tracy loves people. Almost everything she is a part of involves others. Interacting with people is second nature to Tracy. Not long ago, a boy in one of her classes asked her, "Who are you, anyway? You talk to everybody!" She spends hours on the phone and doesn't feel that a weekend is a success unless she is invited to at least one party. She likes to study with friends and worries when there is conflict. She is the unofficial peacekeeper within each of her groups. Cooperative learning activities and all-group discussions are definitely her cup of tea.

HEATHER (TWENTY YEARS OLD)

If ever there were a perfect coed, Heather would be it. A twenty-year-old college student at a large university, she never even seemed to be homesick when she left for her first year of school. Now a sophomore, she has many friends, both male and female, and every one of her teachers knows and likes her. She was recently in charge of a community service event for her sorority. The event needed a high percentage of participation in order for it to be successful, and Heather pulled it off. Speaking of sororities, Heather shares her room with three other girls and loves it. She says the only problem they have is in divvying up phone time. Because of her high grades, Heather qualified for several honors classes. She particularly likes English because it involves a lot of group discussion and problem solving. She plans to major in elementary education and special education.

In high school, Heather was on the soccer team and the cheerleading squad. Now, in college, she jogs and walks every day and is actively involved in campus activities. Last year she was a dancer in a charity production on campus. She likes to sit on her bed to study, with her books and papers spread around her; however, she must get up and move regularly. Her class schedule suits her because she has time to move about during the day.

Heather's strengths in reading, writing, and speaking have helped her fit into both educational and social settings easily. She loves to read and comprehends what she is reading without really trying. When speaking, she uses metaphors, humor, and wit, which isn't usually so well developed in a person her age. She is sensitive to language and responds in tears when she interprets someone's remarks as critical, sarcastic, or belittling. People like being around her because she is careful of other's feelings in her own conversations.

IRA (THIRTY-SEVEN YEARS OLD)

Ira is grounded by an unusual insightfulness, which is partially a result of his self-exploration into his own spirituality. This exploration has lead Ira to understand what motivates him. He is clear on what he values and where those values are rooted. This introspective nature spills over into others also, and Ira's intuitive and knowing ways are sought out by trusting family members and friends alike. His advice is valued because it seems to echo an inner voice.

Ira is grounded by an unusual insightfulness, which is partially a result of his self-exploration into his own spirituality.

Linked to his introspective nature is his acuity for language. He is a voracious reader and loves to create fictional works of his own. Readers invariably remark about the striking and memorable quality of his written words.

Related to Ira's inward nature is his natural ability to run long distances. In contrast to his love of running marathons is his fondness and skill for team sports. Ira displays above-average athletic abilities from years of playing basketball, baseball, and football. His propensity for athletics is so keen that even now in his adult years he is able to attack new sports such as swimming, skiing, rollerblading, and tennis with the same grace and ease that punctuated his youth.

Interestingly, Ira's gentle way with people is often noted by others. Although he is somewhat shy upon meeting people, he somehow manages to put others at ease. They seem to sense his sincere nature, which brings about loyalty and friendship from many people he encounters.

Ira has had some musical training in playing the baritone. In addition, he formed a lyrical opera club in college. He also has a fondness for the rhythm of rap music. Interestingly, both opera and rap music are closely entwined with the language of lyrics.

Ira's writings are frequently punctuated with images and extended metaphors: "You're like a bicycle, as soon as you stop moving, you fall down." This visualization skill surfaces in another realm. Trained as a chef, Ira has an uncanny sense of presentation. He serves the simplest foods in ways that are pleasing to the eye.

Another intelligence is manifested in Ira's exceptional ability to recall facts such as sports statistics, historical sequences, and film trivia. In addition, the logic he brings to an argument or point of view is, more often than not, right on target.

Epilogue

As implied in the introduction, *Best Practices for the Learner-Centered Classroom* is a work-in-progress and, just as in any ongoing project, late developments are sometimes so compelling that they must somehow be incorporated into the greater work.

As we were about to go to press, the Learner-Centered Psychological Principles, developed by the American Psychological Association (APA) and Mid-continent Regional Educational Laboratory (McREL), surfaced as a comprehensive set of guidelines for school reform. Interestingly, these research-based principles parallel many best practices that teachers have ferreted out on their own. The principles are listed in an abbreviated form in Figure 1.

Figure 1
Learner-Centered Psychological Principles

Principle 1: Learning is a natural process of pursuing personally meaningful goals, and it is active, volitional, and internally mediated. It is a process of discovering and constructing meaning from information and experience, filtered through the learner's unique perceptions, thoughts, and feelings.

Principle 2: The learner seeks to create meaningful, coherent representations of knowledge regardless of the quantity and quality of data available.

Principle 3: The learner links new information with existing and future-oriented knowledge in uniquely meaningful ways.

Principle 4: Higher-order strategies for "thinking about thinking"—for overseeing and monitoring mental operations—facilitate creative and critical thinking and the development of expertise.

Principle 5: The depth and breadth of information processes, and what and how much is learned and remembered, are influenced by (a) self-awareness and beliefs about personal control, competence, and ability; (b) clarity and saliency of personal values, interests, and goals; (c) personal expectations for success or failure; (d) affect, emotion, and general states of mind; and (e) the resulting motivation to learn.

Principle 6: Individuals are naturally curious and enjoy learning, but intense negative cognitions and emotions (e.g., feeling insecure, worrying about failure, being self-conscious or shy, and fearing corporal punishment, ridicule, or stigmatizing labels) thwarts this enthusiasm.

Principle 7: Curiosity, creativity, and higher-order thinking are stimulated by relevant, authentic learning tasks of optimal difficulty and novelty for each student.

Principle 8: Individuals progress through stages of physical, intellectual, emotional, and social development that are a function of unique genetic and environmental factors.

Principle 9: Learning is facilitated by social interactions and communication with others in flexible, diverse (in age, culture, family background, etc.), and adaptive instructional settings.

Principle 10: Learning and self-esteem are heightened when individuals are in respectful and caring relationships with others who see their potential, genuinely appreciate their unique talents, and accept them as individuals.

Principle 11: Although basic principles of learning, motivation, and effective instruction apply to all learners (regardless of ethnicity, race, gender, physical ability, religion, or socioeconomic status), learners have different capabilities and preferences for learning modes and strategies. These differences are a function of environment (what is learned and communicated in different cultures or other social groups) and heredity (what occurs naturally as a function of genes).

Principle 12: Personal beliefs, thoughts, and understandings resulting from prior learning and interpretations become the individual's basis for constructing reality and interpreting life experience.

Adapted from *Learner-Centered Psychological Principles: Guidelines for School Redesign and Reform* by the APA Presidential Task Force on Psychology in Education. © 1993 by the American Psychological Assocation and the Mid-continent Regional Educational Laboratory. Adapted with permission.

Subsequently, the twelve principles have been distilled into five more general statements. According to Alexander and Murphy (in press), the reframed principles (see Figure 2) pertain to broad dimensions of learning that have been systematically investigated and are well-represented in any comprehensive review of the literature on learner-centered schooling.

An interesting match is made in comparing the five general statements related to the learner-centered principles to the five main topics in this book of best practices. In fact, upon closer scrutiny, the "principles" and "practices" convincingly support each other (see Figure 3). Based on the comparison, not only are the principles psychologically sound and prevalent in the research literature, they have also evolved as commonsense practices from the grassroots up.

Figure 2
Five General Statements Related to the Learner-Centered Principles

The Knowledge Base:

One's existing knowledge serves as the foundation of future learning by guiding organization and representations, by serving as a basis of association with new information, and by coloring and filtering all new experiences.

Development and Individual Differences:

Learning, while ultimately a unique adventure for all, progresses through various common stages of development influenced by both inherited and experiential/environmental factors.

Situation or Context:

Learning is as much a socially-shared undertaking, as it is an individually-constructed enterprise.

Strategic Processing or Executive Control:

The ability to reflect upon and regulate one's thoughts and behaviors is essential to learning and development.

Motivation and Affect:

Motivational or affective factors, such as intrinsic motivation, attributions for learning, and personal goals, along with the motivational characteristics of learning tasks, play a significant role in the learning process.

From The Research Base for the Learner-Centered Psychological Principles by P. A. Alexander and P.K. Murphy, in N. Lambert and B. L. McCombs (Eds.), *Issues in School Reform: A Sampler of Psychological Perspectives on Learner-Centered Schools.* © (in press) by APA Books. Reprinted with permission.

Figure 3
Principles and Practices: A Comparison

Learner-Centered Principles	Common Focus	Best Practices
1. The Knowledge Base	Conceptually-based learning and life skills	Integrated Curricula: Commonsense Connections
2. Development and Individual Differences	Use of the multiple intelligences theory to reach and teach all kids with HOT	Thoughtful Instruction: Teaching with Rigor and Vigor
3. Situation or Context	Cooperative interactions for intense learner involvement	Active Learning: I Teach, but You Must Learn
4. Strategic Processing and Executive Control	Metacognitive reflection for meaningful application and use	Reflective Transfer: Teach Them to Fish
5. Motivation and Affect	Self-initiating, self-evaluating lifelong learners	Authentic Assessment: The Measure of Man

As suggested in Figure 3, skillful and knowledgeable teachers (1) know that nothing can substitute for a solid knowledge base of conceptual learning and life skills; (2) understand the delicate balance between challenge and frustration and the tools that tap into the special talents of each child; (3) know how and when to subtly shift the responsibility to the student and how to foster intense involvement as students assume the role of active learners; (4) embrace the concept of lifelong learning and deliberately frame discussions and reflections that foster future applications; and (5) understand the motivational aspects of self-initiating learners and the empowerment of setting and meeting personal goals. These teachers inherently put these principles to work in their repertoire of best practices.

REFERENCES

APA Presidential Task Force on Psychology in Education. (1993, January). *Learner-centered psychological principles: Guidelines for school redesign and reform.* Washington, DC: American Psychological Association and the Mid-continent Regional Educational Laboratory.

Alexander, P. A., & Murphy, P. K. (in press). The research base for the learner-centered psychological principles. In N. Lambert & B. L. McCombs (Eds.), *Issues in school reform: A sampler of psychological perspectives on learner-centered schools.* Washington, DC: APA Books.

Index

There are
one-story intellects,
two-story intellects, and three-story
intellects with skylights. All fact collectors, who
have no aim beyond their facts, are one-story men. Two-story men
compare, reason, generalize, using the labors of the fact collectors as
well as their own. Three-story men idealize, imagine,
predict—their best illumination comes from
above, through the skylight.

—Oliver Wendell
Holmes